Patient-Centred Health Care

Organizational Behaviour in Health Care

Titles include:

Annabelle Mark and Sue Dopson; 1999
ORGANISATIONAL BEHAVIOUR IN HEALTH CARE

Lynn Ashburner; 2001
ORGANISATIONAL BEHAVIOUR AND ORGANISATION STUDIES
IN HEALTH CARE

Sue Dopson and Annabelle Mark; 2003
LEADING HEALTH CARE ORGANIZATIONS

Ann L. Casebeer, Alexandra Harrison and Annabelle Mark; 2006
INNOVATIONS IN HEALTH CARE

Lorna McKee, Ewan Ferlie and Paula Hyde; 2008
ORGANIZING AND REORGANIZING

Jeffrey Braithwaite, Paula Hyde and Catherine Pope; 2009
CULTURE AND CLIMATE IN HEALTH CARE ORGANIZATIONS

Helen Dickinson and Russell Mannion; 2011
THE REFORM OF HEALTH CARE

Mary A. Keating, Aoife M. McDermott and Kathleen Montgomery; 2013
PATIENT-CENTRED HEALTH CARE

Patient-Centred Health Care

Achieving Coordination, Communication and Innovation

Edited by

Mary A. Keating
School of Business, Trinity College, Dublin, Ireland

Aoife M. McDermott
Cardiff Business School, Cardiff University, Cardiff, UK

and

Kathleen Montgomery
School of Business Administration, University of California, Riverside, USA

First published 2013 by
PALGRAVE MACMILLAN

Palgrave Macmillan in the UK is an imprint of Macmillan Publishers Limited,
registered in England, company number 785998, of Houndmills, Basingstoke,
Hampshire RG21 6XS.

Palgrave Macmillan in the US is a division of St Martin's Press LLC,
175 Fifth Avenue, New York, NY 10010.

Palgrave Macmillan is the global academic imprint of the above companies
and has companies and representatives throughout the world.

Palgrave® and Macmillan® are registered trademarks in the United States,
the United Kingdom, Europe and other countries.

ISBN 978–1–137–30892–4

This book is printed on paper suitable for recycling and made from fully
managed and sustained forest sources. Logging, pulping and manufacturing
processes are expected to conform to the environmental regulations of the
country of origin.

A catalogue record for this book is available from the British Library.

A catalog record for this book is available from the Library of Congress.

Contents

Tables and Figures

Tables

Figures

Foreword

The Eighth Biennial Conference in the Organizational Behaviour in Healthcare Conference (OBHC) series held in Dublin took as its theme two fundamental parts of the healthcare environment: patients and teams. The scope of the subject is ambitious and contested, but of all the OBHC conferences held so far the subject of this conference should continue to remain at the forefront of healthcare systems the world over.

The rise in the focus on patients has, in part, become an issue not only because of the consumer-centred society in which we now live but also because the organizations providing health care have become so large that they, and those who work within them, have sometimes lost sight of their reason for being there, that is the patients themselves. This was demonstrated most recently in the Francis Report of the Public Inquiry into the Mid Staffordshire NHS Foundation Trust published in February 2013.

Meanwhile, teamwork, in spite of professional and organizational silos, is also now integral to the multidisciplinary delivery of care, if for no other reason than that no individual has all the answers or can represent all the issues and opinions; furthermore, teams can also provide a sense of belonging, a source of help and support and a shared sense of purpose in the effective delivery of health care.

Part I of this book sets out the origins of the approach of patient-centredness, allowing the reader to recognize what this means and looks like, institutionally and educationally, as well as recognizing the implications of its absence. Part II concentrates on the process of teamwork itself which may be patient-centred but is also involved with cooperation and coordination across professional and organizational boundaries. Part III takes as its focus communication within, between and across patients and teams, and Part IV seeks to highlight the innovations in patient-centred care that will enable further progress in the field.

The contributions provide the reader with a comparative view across systems and countries and allow them to reiterate elements drawn out in the 2006 review of the agenda set for research at the first OBHC Conference in 1998 by showing 'the degree of difference revealed, rather than because ideas and processes are necessarily transferable; the gaps between throw the real shape of things into sharper relief than would otherwise have been the case' (Mark 2006).

At a more personal level, I would like to thank the conference organizers who demonstrated to me, in a very personal way, the care and support for my presence in Dublin after a daunting but successful encounter as a patient, with what was a very effective UK healthcare team. Reinforcing for academics, particularly those working in health care, the need to remain mindful of the impact of their relationships with each other, as well as their research subjects. This has subsequently been highlighted in the outcomes of the UK Academy of Social Sciences Symposia 'Generic Ethics Principles in Social Science Research' in which SHOC our Learned Society for Studies in Organizing Healthcare participated. The symposia also discussed at length the crossovers and intersections between interested groups and their separate ways of contributing to research and practice, and it is such an intersection that will be at the heart of the 9th OBHC conference in Copenhagen entitled 'When Health Policy Meets Everyday Practices'.

Annabelle Mark
Prof. Emerita
London 2013

Reference

Mark, AL. (2006) Notes from a small island: Researching organizational behaviour in healthcare from a UK perspective. *Journal of Organisational Behaviour* 27(7): 1–17.

Contributors

Juergen Bengel is Professor and Director of the Department of Rehabilitation Psychology and Psychotherapy, Department of Rehabilitation Psychology and Psychotherapy, University of Freiburg, Freiburg, Germany.

Annette Boaz is Reader in Health Care Research at St. George's University of London & Kingston University, London, UK.

Jeffrey Braithwaite is Foundation Director of the Australian Institute of Health Innovation, Director of the Centre for Clinical Governance Research and Professor in the Faculty of Medicine, University of New South Wales, Sydney, Australia.

Jackie Bridges is Senior Lecturer in Nursing at the University of Southampton, Southampton, UK.

Diane Burns is Lecturer in Human Resource Management and Organisational Behaviour at the University of Sheffield Management School, University of Sheffield, Sheffield, UK.

Nicholas G. Castle is Professor at the Graduate School of Public Health, University of Pittsburgh, Pittsburgh, PA, USA.

David Coghlan is Professor at the School of Business, Trinity College, Dublin, Ireland.

Douglas A. Conrad is Professor at the Department of Health Services, School of Public Health, University of Washington and Director, Center for Health Management Research, University of Washington, Seattle, WA, USA.

Jan Maree Davis is Director of Palliative Care Service, St George Hospital, Kogarah, Sydney, Australia.

Adrian Edwards is Professor in General Practice at the Institute of Primary Care and Public Health, Cardiff University, Cardiff, Wales, UK.

Heike Ehrhardt is Scientific Assistant at the Department for Counseling, Clinical and Health Psychology, University of Education, Freiburg, Germany.

Jamie C. Ferguson-Rome is Project Director at the Graduate School of Public Health, University of Pittsburgh, Pittsburgh, PA, USA.

Jonathan Fielden is Medical Director at University College London Hospitals' NHS Foundation Trust, London, UK.

Mary Flatley is Lead Nurse at St Joseph's Hospital, London, UK.

Jill Gordon is Honorary Associate Professor, Centre for Values, Ethics and the Law in Medicine, University of Sydney, Sydney, Australia.

David Greenfield is Senior Research Fellow at the Centre for Clinical Governance Research, Australian Institute of Health Innovation, UNSW Medicine, University of New South Wales, Sydney, Australia.

Paula Hyde is Senior Lecturer in Organisation Studies in Manchester Business School, University of Manchester, Manchester, UK.

Geralyn Hynes is the Ussher Associate Professor in Palliative Care, School of Nursing and Midwifery, Trinity College, Dublin, Ireland.

Mary A. Keating is Associate Professor in Human Resource Management at the School of Business, Trinity College Dublin, Dublin, Ireland.

Ian Kerridge is Director of Centre for Values, Ethics and the Law in Medicine, University of Sydney, Sydney, Australia.

Anne Killett is Lecturer in Occupational Therapy in the Faculty of Medicine and Health Sciences, University of East Anglia, Norwich, UK.

Roman Kislov is Research Associate at Manchester Business School, University of Manchester, Manchester, UK.

Mirjam Koerner is Assistant Professor at the Department of Medical Psychology and Medical Sociology, Faculty of Medicine, Albert-Ludwigs-Universitat, Freiburg, Germany.

Wendy Lipworth is NH and MRC Post-doctoral Research Fellow at the Australian Institute of Health Innovation, University of New South Wales, Australia and Centre for Values, Ethics and the Law in Medicine, University of Sydney, Sydney, Australia.

Miles Little is Emeritus Professor, Centre for Values, Ethics and the Law in Medicine, University of Sydney, Sydney, Australia.

Louise Locock is Deputy Research Director Health Experiences Research Group, Department of Primary Care Health Sciences, University of Oxford, Oxford, UK and Health Experiences Fellow, Oxford NIHR Biomedical Research Centre, Oxford, UK.

Jill Maben is Director of National Nursing Research Unit at King's College London, London, UK.

Linda Magann is Clinical Nurse Consultant, Palliative Care Service, St George Hospital, Kogarah, Sydney, Australia.

Pippa Markham is Research Assistant, Centre for Values, Ethics and the Law in Medicine, University of Sydney, Sydney, Australia.

Gillian S. Martin is Associate Professor at the School of Germanic Studies, Trinity College, Dublin, Ireland.

Mary McCarron is Professor of Nursing at the School of Nursing and Midwifery and Dean of Faculty of Health Sciences, Trinity College, Dublin, Ireland.

Julienne Meyer is Professor of Nursing, City University London, London, UK.

Kathleen Montgomery is Professor of the Graduate Division; Professor of Organizations and Management, Emerita University of California, Riverside, USA and Honorary Associate, Centre for Values, Ethics, and the Law in Medicine, University of Sydney, Sydney, Australia.

Caroline Nicholson is the NIHR Post -Doctoral Fellow at the National Nursing Research Unit, King's College London, London, UK.

Mike Nolan is Professor of Gerontological Nursing, School of Nursing and Midwifery, University of Sheffield, Sheffield, UK.

Peter Nugus is Assistant Professor at the Center for Medical Education, Faculty of Medicine, McGill University, Montreal, Canada.

Glenn Paull is Clinical Nurse Consultant, Cardiology, St George Hospital, Kogarah, Sydney, Australia.

Catherine Pope is Professor of Medical Sociology at the University of Southampton, Southampton, UK.

Anne D. Renz is Research Project Manager at Group Health Research Institute, Group Health Cooperative, Seattle, WA, USA.

Glenn Robert is Professor of Healthcare Quality & Innovation at the National Nursing Research Unit, Florence Nightingale School of Nursing & Midwifery, King's College London, London, UK.

Anne Schoenmakers is an alumnus of Utrecht University and a medical doctor at Westfriesgashuis, Hoorn, The Netherlands.

Andrea C. Schöpf is Research Assistant at the Department of Quality Management and Social Medicine, University Medical Centre, Freiburg, Germany.

Caroline Shuldham is Director of Nursing and Clinical Governance at the Royal Brompton and Harefield NHS Foundation Trust, London, UK.

Ros Sorensen is Professor and Head, School of Public Health, Griffith Health Institute, Griffith University, Gold Coast, Queensland, Australia.

Anne-Kathrin Steger is Scientific Assistant, Deanery of Student Affairs, Faculty of Medicine, Competence Centre for Evaluation, University of Freiburg, Freiburg, Germany.

Marianne Storm is Associate Professor at the Department of Health Studies, University of Stavanger, Stavanger, Norway.

Joanne Travaglia is Director of the Health Management Program and Senior Lecturer in the School of Public Health and Community Medicine, University of New South Wales and Senior Research Fellow, Centre for Clinical Governance Research, Australian Institute of Health Innovation, University of New South Wales, Sydney, Australia.

Maria Tziggili is Senior Assistant Psychologist at Barts Health NHS Trust in London and DPsych., Health Psychology Trainee, City University, London, UK.

Carolyn A. Watts is Professor and Chair, Department of Health Administration, School of Allied Health Professions Virginia Commonwealth University, Richmond, VA, USA.

Charlotte Wilkinson is Senior Lecturer in Nursing, City University, London, UK.

Sue Ziebland is Research Director in the Health Experiences Research Group, Department of Primary Care Health Sciences, University of Oxford, UK and Reader in Qualitative Health Research, University of Oxford, Oxford, UK.

Introduction

Mary A. Keating, Aoife M. McDermott and Kathleen Montgomery

This edited volume presents selected research papers from the 8th International Organisational Behaviour in Healthcare Conference (OBHC) hosted by Mary A. Keating of Trinity College Dublin, Ireland, in April 2012. Reflecting the global reach of the OBHC community and the international composition of Society for Studies in Organizing Healthcare (SHOC) membership, more than 130 delegates from 17 countries converged on Dublin for the interdisciplinary conference – the flagship event for members of SHOC. SHOC aims to promote advancement in the organization of healthcare through research, education and service to the community. Previous conferences have been held in Birmingham, Sydney, Aberdeen, Alberta, Banff, Oxford and Keele. The inaugural conference was hosted at Middlesex University in the United Kingdom by Professor Annabelle Mark, founding Chair of SHOC. Professor Mark is Professor Emerita at Middlesex University and a Fellow of the Royal Society of Medicine. She was honoured at the Dublin conference for her role in founding and developing SHOC and for her broader contributions to the Organizational Behaviour (OB) in healthcare community. Professor Mark is series editor for the edited volumes produced from each conference.

The theme of the Dublin conference considered: 'Patient-centred healthcare teams: Achieving collaboration, communication and care'. Full paper review was a new departure for the conference. A record number of full paper submissions led to approximately 150 papers being peer reviewed by the Scientific Organizing Committee and more than 40 international reviewers. Its success is both a great tribute to the collegiality and commitment of the SHOC community and evidence of the international interest in OB in healthcare. Submissions came from authors representing schools of healthcare management,

1

nursing, medicine, business and social sciences. This led to international and interdisciplinary comparison, discussion and debate regarding how patient-centred care (PCC) can be conceptualized, delivered and enhanced.

There was no debate regarding the quality of the plenary keynote sessions. During the course of the conference, Kathleen Montgomery, Professor of Organizations and Management at the University of California, Riverside and Honorary Associate at the University of Sydney spoke on the 'paradoxes of delivering patient-centred care to the seriously ill'. Alexis Donnelly, Assistant Professor at the School of Computer Science and Statistics at Trinity College Dublin, responded to Kathleen's talk. Alexis has lived with a progressive condition for 21 years and gave a redoubtable voice to a patient perspective. In the second keynote address, Mike Nolan, Professor of Gerontological Nursing at the University of Sheffield, spoke on 'creating an enriched care environment for older people, staff and family carers: relational practice and organisational culture change'. We are pleased that their work is represented in this volume.

This book serves as a historical record of a selection of the best papers at the conference and presents an opportunity to advance the conceptualization and practice of PCC. PCC represents an increasingly widespread, global movement in the delivery of healthcare. While the general concept of PCC is not new, it is receiving elevated emphasis in how healthcare is delivered today. At the core of PCC is the recognition that patients' values and preferences should take centre stage in the delivery of care, at both the organizational and the professional level. This recognition has led to an emphasis on the importance of communication, leading many healthcare organizations to redesign their processes to incorporate the tenets of PCC and to healthcare professionals receiving specific training in this model of care delivery. Despite these well-intentioned efforts, its implementation can be fraught with challenges.

The chapters in this book address conceptions of PCC as well as some of the implementation challenges involving the coordination, communication and innovation aspects of PCC. Specifically, our book comprises four parts. Each presents four chapters focusing on a specific theme central to the concept of PCC. Part I focuses on conceptions and cultures of PCC; Part II looks at coordinating for care; Part III is organized around communication in PCC; Part IV presents innovations in research, theory and practice in PCC.

Part I: Conceptions and Cultures of Patient-Centred Care

The first three chapters in this part (Chapters 1–3 by Montgomery; Castle and Ferguson-Rome; Burns et al.) provide background to the concept of PCC and illustrate its implementation in different contexts. Each chapter offers a perspective of PCC that can be viewed as an indication of the culture of the organization. Chapter 4, by Lipworth et al., asks the question of culture from the perspective of the medical profession and medical education.

Montgomery's chapter (Chapter 1) introduces the reader to an overview of the historical origins of PCC over the past century, identifying early forerunners to the concept of PCC, followed by more recent themes prevailing today. Despite the widespread appeal of tenets of PCC, Montgomery argues that its implementation is not straightforward across all healthcare contexts. She illustrates the particular challenges, both practical and ethical, that medical professionals encounter when seeking informed consent and providing high-risk therapy for patients with serious acute illnesses. Data from two qualitative studies of cancer patients in Australia inform the analysis, yielding insights about the PCC-related culture in highly specialized academic health centres.

The next two chapters (Chapters 2 and 3) shift the context to residential care facilities for older individuals and address the challenges of changing the institutional culture in this context. Both chapters recognize societal pressures to develop a culture of care that respects the dignity and preferences of the residents and suggest that resident-centred care (RCC) in these institutions is analogous to PCC in acute or primary care settings. Castle and Ferguson-Rome draw on quantitative data from a large survey of nursing home administrators ($n = 2,680$) in the United States to assess the extent to which a culture of resident-centred practices has become embedded in the nursing home industry (Chapter 2). They find that about one-fifth of nursing homes may be using RCC practices to the extent that a culture change to RCC may be taking place, while 16% do not report using any RCC practices. The authors identify some of the factors that facilitate the adoption of such practices, as well as potential barriers to implementation.

Burns et al. also study residential treatment in elder care homes, using case studies of eight facilities in England providing residential and nursing care (Chapter 3). Their qualitative approach allows a deeper look at the nature of everyday problems for residents (such as those related to mealtime and toileting) and the challenges of devising resident-centred solutions that maintain respect for residents' dignity. The authors illustrate that well-meaning, but short-sighted solutions to some of these problems have the potential to rise, inadvertently, to the level of institutional abuse by staff.

In Chapter 4, Lipworth et al. pursue the question of a culture of PCC among the medical profession, regardless of the context of care. The authors acknowledge that the widespread support for PCC (and RCC), and recognition of the many challenges to implementing such practices, may raise questions about the extent to which the education and experience of healthcare providers can adequately equip them to function within this model of care. Analysing interviews with Australian doctors, the authors report that doctors both understand and value the principles underpinning PCC, suggesting that augmenting medical education to explicitly incorporate a culture of PCC may not be necessary; instead, they argue for a focus on institutional and organizational structures and processes that can help to support PCC.

Part II: Coordinating for Patient-Centred Care

Part II profiles a variety of types of coordination for PCC. The chapters in this part deal with coordination challenges that occur within and across stakeholder groups and organizations in healthcare delivery and improvement. The first two chapters (Chapters 5 and 6) firmly place the patient at the centre of coordination processes, considering the organizational conditions affecting coordination in the nurse–patient relationship (Bridges et al.) and the need for coordination between patient, staff and family carers to enrich the care environment (Nolan). The next two chapters (Chapters 7 and 8) consider how inter-professional collaboration (Greenfield et al.) and within- and cross-group collaboration (Kislov) can be used to enhance patient care.

Chapter 5, by Bridges et al., is based on a meta-ethnographic study. It integrates findings from a number of qualitative studies to consider nurses' experiences and concerns regarding their relationships with patients. Despite a range of claims that nurses lack compassion and humanity, this chapter illustrates that nurses aspire to develop individualized, strong personal relationships with patients, to involve patients and their families in decision-making and to support the therapeutic process. However, unit-level work conditions can undermine their capacity to do so, leading to negative emotional implications for the nurses themselves and potential disengagement from the nurse–patient relationship as a coping strategy. From a managerial perspective, the importance of the unit-level conditions in shaping nursing work raises questions regarding appropriate interventions including how nurses can be afforded control to coordinate their work and to engage with patients and peers in a manner that will enhance therapeutic relationships.

Nolan develops this theme in Chapter 6, presenting a relational approach to creating an enriched environment of care for older people. He argues that the needs of patients, staff and family carers have to be considered for high-quality care to be attained. He outlines how elderly patients and their carers each have to experience six senses, including: security, belonging, continuity, purpose, achievement and feeling significant in order to experience a truly enriched care environment. Like Bridges et al., Nolan argues that for this to occur the relational work of staff has to be valued in their organizations' culture. They need to be supported and afforded time to spend with patients and their families. This relationship-centred approach is argued to be particularly valuable in the care of people with long-term conditions. The six 'Senses Framework' is presented as potential tool for culture change, and the leadership behaviours supporting this approach are detailed.

The next two chapters (Chapters 7 and 8) shift attention towards coordination between professionals. Greenfield et al. present their empirically derived organizational model of inter-professional collaboration. Inter-professional collaboration has been advocated as a driver to promote and improve patient-centred healthcare, by reducing inter-professional rivalries and enhancing teamwork. Supporting factors include: (1) interpersonal capacity, influencing ability to communicate positively with colleagues and patients; (2) clinical skills, including awareness of conditions from a range of disciplinary and patient perspectives; (3) an inter-professional orientation, premised on collaborative practice and (4) an organizational orientation, enhancing culture and the care environment. These factors need to be displayed by a majority of staff to impact PCC. Their impact is affected by (5) the broader organizational context and policies. Together, these five factors comprise the 'organizational model of inter-professional collaboration'. These factors depend on interpersonal competence and work individually and in configuration to promote PCC.

Last, Kislov moves to consider the cross-professional and cross-organizational coordination challenges characteristic of multi-agency service delivery (Chapter 8). His analysis considers: (1) how groups can make the transition from teams to less formal but often highly engaged communities of practice, characterized by mutual enterprise and knowledge exchange and (2) factors influencing the permeability of knowledge at the boundaries between a multi-professional community of practice and other external and internal organizational groups. Practical implications include the identification of factors that may help cultivate communities of practice to enhance PCC and the identification of tensions undermining cross-team learning within organizations.

Part III: Communication in Patient-Centred Care

All four chapters in this part (Chapters 9–12) are based on the premise that effective instrumental and relational communication between clinicians and patients and within healthcare teams is fundamental to PCC. These chapters focus on how the preferences, expectations and fears of patients with chronic illnesses can be accommodated. This is variously achieved through shared decision-making (SDM) (Koerner et al.); through the use of humour in medical consultations (Schopf et al.); by integrating palliative care into end-of-life care (Hynes et al.) and in how clinicians communicate about patient care at the end-of-life stage (Sorensen et al.). Two of the research studies led to the development of practice outcomes. Specifically, Koerner et al. developed the first SDM/communication training programme in Germany and nurse practice was developed on the basis of the work of Hynes et al. in Ireland (Chapters 10 and 12).

Sorensen et al. note that, regardless of the type of disease, end of life care is often suboptimal, with poor communication between clinicians recognized as a major contributor (Chapter 9). They report on part of a large-scale Australian study ($n = 109$ clinicians, including doctors, nurses and allied health professionals). The authors examine communication methods used by multi-disciplinary treating clinicians to establish the medical care required by patients dying of chronic illness. Their findings evidence widely differing methods of eliciting information about medical care for patients and a variety of forms through which the information is presented and accessed by different clinical cohorts. Sorensen et al. emphasize the lack of a cohesive, patient-centred team approach to determine required medical care, with a deficit of effective communication methods.

Turning to Ireland, Hynes et al. suggest that palliative care should not be left exclusively to palliative care specialists. Instead, they argue, it should be integrated into the care provided for patients with advanced chronic illnesses at the end-of-life stage. The authors use the concept of heteroglossia, which is the stratification of language/voices, to reflect and focus attention on the competition for dominance between chronic versus acute narratives in the hospital context. The authors used an action research study to establish the palliative care needs of advanced chronic obstructive pulmonary disease (COPD) patients in an acute general hospital context. A second phase of he study then utilized a cooperative inquiry process, whereby respiratory nurses came together to develop nursing practice to address the identified needs.

Schopf et al. explore the use of humour in patient–clinician communication in a chronic illness setting, namely diabetes (Chapter 11). This chapter presents part of a larger interactional sociolinguistic study comprising 50 consultations and 32 interviews conducted in Ireland. Schopf et al. report on how patients initiate and use humour as a resistance strategy against treatment recommendations, and she explores clinician reactions. Humour is presented as a patient strategy to engage and to mitigate the face-threat of a disliked reaction. The rejection of treatment recommendations provides clinicians with an opportunity to discuss treatment options with the patient and to follow a more patient-centred approach. However, in the main clinicians missed or chose to miss the opportunity to explore the patient perspective and involve them in decision-making regarding their treatment.

In Chapter 12, Koerner et al. expand upon a model of SDM to investigate the key factors influencing internal (inter-professional clinician teamwork) and external (clinician–patient) communication and participation in SDM about patient care. The authors posit that SDM at both the internal and external level allows for a more patient-centred approach in the medical decision-making and communication process. Focus groups of patients considering their communication needs and a survey of expert clinicians ($n = 31$) confirmed the importance of participation in SDM and more time for communication. The findings have been used to develop the first inter-professional SDM training in Germany.

Part IV: Innovations in Patient-Centred Care

The chapters in this part (Chapters 13–16) present innovations in the area of PCC. To begin, Locock et al. examine understandings of patient experience and report on their study of accelerated experience-based co-design (EBCD), undertaken in the United Kingdom (Chapter 13). Second, Renz et al. report on their demonstration study regarding the use of SDM in the United States (Chapter 14). This aims to allow patients and health providers to make the most appropriate decision based on the best scientific evidence. Third, Nugus et al. use an innovative methodology to conduct a cross-country, comparative study of emergency departments (EDs) (Chapter 15). Finally, Storm and Edwards focus on the challenges associated with the implementation of PCC, SDM and the recovery model in the mental health context (Chapter 16).

Locock et al. start from the premise that improving patient experience is important to PCC and to healthcare systems worldwide. Improvement requires an understanding of how patients experience care, but there remains uncertainty about the best way to collect and use patients' experiences to inform improvement. To address this deficit, this chapter showcases an innovative improvement method – Experience-Based Co-Design. EBCD uses in-depth video interviews with local patients. However, this is a time-consuming and costly method of data collection. The current study replaced the local discovery phase of EBCD with the use of an existing collection of narrative patient interviews. This approach was acceptable to both staff and patients. It resulted in similar co-design activities and delivered a comparable set of tangible patient-centred service improvements at reduced cost.

One of the ethical imperatives of PCC is that healthcare providers make patients aware of the evidence-based risks and benefits of treatment options through SDM. Patient decision aids are often used to facilitate patient-centred communication with the provider about treatment. Renz et al. report on a two-year exploratory demonstration project in the United States considering SDM. This arose in response to 2007 legislation in the State of Washington. In the course of the study 200 decision aids for six preference-sensitive conditions and four chronic conditions were distributed to facilitate SDM. Interviews were conducted with five key stakeholder groups whose commitment would be necessary to implement an SDM approach, including health system leaders, project managers, providers, health plan leaders, and malpractice insurers. A grounded theory approach was adopted in analysing the qualitative data. Interviewees expressed a positive view of SDM, tempered by concerns over the costs of implementation, required time commitments, and competing organizational priorities.

Nugus et al. adopt an innovative comparative ethnographic methodology in studying ED in The Netherlands, Australia and the United States. The authors point out that ethnographic studies remain relatively scarce in OB research – in healthcare and more generally – as they are often assumed to apply only to local settings and are deemed to be very labour intensive. Yet, ethnographies can help explain the presence of macro structures arising from local interaction. Nugus et al. find differences in political, economic, social and organizational structures evident in five ED sites across the three countries. Their 'comparative international ethnography' is shown to be valuable in understanding social action and in describing similarities and differences in social structures across local, national and international settings. This methodology enabled the authors to identify international differences and complexities that would not have been made apparent by other research methods such as questionnaire surveys or statistical comparisons.

Finally, Storm and Edwards examine challenges in the implementation of concepts and practices that incorporate patients' perspectives on their treatment and care in the mental health context. In considering the implementation of PCC, shared decision-making, patient participation and the recovery model, they identify tensions between patients' and providers' perspectives on treatment and care. They also raise issues relating to the person's capacity for user involvement and lack of competence among providers. They note the need for further work on implementing, evaluating and training, to ensure that mental health services can adapt user-oriented care models.

Taken together these brief chapter summaries evidence the wide-ranging issues researched and presented at the OBHC conference in Dublin. The contributions in this volume demonstrate a wide variety of perspectives on how we think about and practice patient-centred healthcare. The contributors from Europe, Australia and North America utilize a wide diversity of theoretical and methodological approaches. Findings are included from research studies utilizing surveys, case studies, interviews, meta-ethnography, action research and collaborative inquiry, sociolinguistics, grounded theory and comparative international ethnography. These research studies question and inform conceptualizations of PCC, provide suggestions for enhancing coordination and communication processes and present innovations in how PCC can be delivered. We hope you are inspired.

·

Part I

Conceptions and Cultures
of Patient-Centred Care

1
Developments in Conceptions of Patient-Centred Care: Implementation Challenges in the Context of High-Risk Therapy

Kathleen Montgomery

Background

The term 'patient-centred care' (P-CC) is relatively recent, but concepts at its core have been part of health care for over a century. Early hints of P-CC were evident in the words of Dr William Mayo, founder of the renowned Mayo Clinic in Rochester, Minnesota, in 1910: 'the best interest of the patient is the only interest to be considered' (Berry, 2004). Nevertheless, this well-intended goal still placed the doctor as the central voice in the doctor–patient relationship, in a somewhat paternalistic 'doctor-knows-best' approach. That is, doctors were the experts, and – while Mayo insisted that the patient's interest should prevail – it was the doctor's judgement about what would be in the best interest of the patient.

Not until the 1970s was greater attention devoted to the patient as an active participant in the doctor–patient interaction, rather than being a passive recipient of the doctor's best judgement. However, this new approach was not without some controversy. Practitioners and scholars alike expressed concern that inviting greater patient involvement in medical decision-making would demystify medicine (Freidson, 1970; Haug, 1973), opening the door for challenges to medical judgement from a lay public who did not have appropriate education or expertise to weigh in.

Other observers saw advantages to a more involved, informed and educated patient population, and this latter perspective became dominant, reinforced by several strands of empirical research investigating how to improve healthcare quality. One strand emphasized the importance of better communication between doctors and their patients, including listening to patients and crediting patients' own attributions of their symptoms as a salient source of diagnostic information (Waitzkin and Stoeckle, 1972).

Also part of this strand was a growing awareness of the role of patient education, including the need for doctors to make a greater effort to assure that information was conveyed to patients in an understandable way (Korsch, 1989; Roter and Hall, 2006). Initially, this movement was thought to be a valuable way to improve patient compliance with and adherence to medical recommendations (DiMatteo et al., 2002). Greater patient education also has been viewed as important to facilitate patient involvement in shared healthcare decisions that affect them (Barry et al., 1995; Hibbard, 2007).

A second strand called for attention to patient satisfaction (Ware et al., 1983), with a particular focus on defining the concept and measuring its determinants and outcomes. Initial patient-satisfaction dimensions were concerned with issues of access, availability, cost and the technical quality of health care. Paralleling work on doctor–patient communication, the concept of patient satisfaction was subsequently widened to include dimensions assessing the character of the doctor–patient relationship and the extent to which patients perceived that they were cared about, not just cared for.

These areas of attention coalesced and paved the way for acceptance of what is now known as P-CC.

Landmark articulations of patient-centred care

The P-CC movement began in earnest with concerted efforts to be more concrete and draw together these threads into a formal model of care. Two landmark studies have served as the foundation for the current extensive literature on P-CC.

The first of these studies is attributed to the Picker Institute, founded by Henry Picker in 1986. Picker, who many consider to be the pioneer of P-CC, proclaimed that understanding and respecting patients' values, preferences and expressed needs constitute the core principles of P-CC. In a classic report from the Picker Institute, *Through the Patient's Eyes: Understanding and Promoting Patient-Centered Care* (Gerteis et al., 1993), several dimensions of P-CC were articulated. These included (1) respect for patients' values, preferences and expressed needs, (2) coordination and integration of care, (3) information, communication and education, (4) physical comfort, (5) emotional support and alleviation of fear and anxiety, (6) involvement of family and friends and (7) transition and continuity of care.

In essence, these dimensions capture the focus on the patient's interests as potentially distinct from the doctor's, as well as the need for healthcare professionals to engage in greater education and communication.

The second landmark articulation emerged from the 2001 report from the Institute of Medicine, *Crossing the Quality Chasm*, which was the result of an extensive study aimed at improving the quality of health care in the United States. The report articulated six dimensions of quality: that health care should be (1) safe, (2) effective, (3) timely, (4) efficient, (5) equitable and (6) patient-centred. The last dimension, patient-centredness, was further articulated to mean 'providing care that is respectful of and responsive to individual patient preferences, needs, and values and ensuring that patient values guide all clinical decisions' (Institute of Medicine, 2001, p. 3). The report further clarifies that patient-centredness should consider 'the patient [as] the source of control' in decisions about his or her care (Institute of Medicine, 2001, p. 304). This has been succinctly captured in the rallying call: 'Nothing about me without me' (Delbanco et al., 2001).

The tenets of P-CC have been enthusiastically endorsed by healthcare professionals, policy makers and patient advocates across the globe. There is a growing literature about implementing P-CC in various contexts, including primary care, acute care, disability and mental health care, and chronic illness (Lynn et al., 2007). However, there is scant literature about the challenges of applying P-CC in the specialized context of high-risk therapy for serious illness. Challenging aspects of care in this context occur both at the informed-consent process and in delivery of the therapy itself. The following discussion draws on two empirical studies to elaborate on these challenges.

Patient-centred care and the informed-consent process

As noted above, a central principle of P-CC is to ensure that patient values and preferences guide all clinical decisions and that patients are given the necessary information about proposed treatments they are being asked to consent to. Consistent with P-CC tenets are bioethical principles of informed consent, whereby a patient's consent must be fully informed, including the disclosure of the risks and benefits of any proposed procedure. While the Institute of Medicine's P-CC principle adds the qualifier that patients should be invited to participate in healthcare decisions to the extent they choose, the bioethical principles do not allow for the possibility that patients might not choose to become informed, yet may still agree to proceed with treatment. Furthermore, legal precedent requires that 'choice is meaningless unless it is made on the basis of relevant information and advice' (Canterbury v Spence, 1972).

The reality of this dilemma has been seen in a study of healthcare professionals engaged in the care of patients undergoing allogeneic bone marrow [stem cell] transplantation, offered only to patients with advanced cancer when previous treatments have been unsuccessful (for additional details of the study, see Jordens et al., 2013).[1] The therapy is aggressive, involving prolonged hospitalization, recurrent invasive medical procedures, with many potential severe and toxic side effects. Thus, healthcare professionals are deeply committed to assuring that patients fully understand the nature of the therapy and its attendant risks before undertaking any associated procedures for the therapy. These professionals report concerted and dedicated efforts to educate patients about the therapy, including multiple physician consultations with patients and families, written materials and opportunities to meet with former patients and with the healthcare team.

Nevertheless, the study found a widespread lack of engagement on the part of patients to respond to and interact with healthcare professionals' efforts inform them, including occasional outright refusal to engage in the informed-consent process. Typical observations were the 'wake-me-when-it's-over' mentality, as reported by healthcare professionals working with these patients:

One girl pulled the blankets up over her head when you tried to talk to her.

Some patients will say, 'Don't tell me about it, I don't want to know.'

Another oncology nurse involved in the patient-education process lamented,

He obviously wasn't hearing it.

In frustration, professionals further reported that some patients gave their consent but later complained that they hadn't been fully informed, with a recurring comment from patients that

If I had known what it would be like, I wouldn't have done it.

Yet, these professionals could readily document their systematic efforts to inform patients and the patients' agreement to proceed, which was frequently followed by a somewhat defensive aside to the researchers:

Yes, they were told … they just didn't want to hear it.

Other comments from members of the healthcare team revealed the potential for conflict and blame among team members for failing to convince the patients to become involved in the informed-consent process.

As shown in this research, the P-CC tenet of respecting patients' values and preferences (including a preference not to become informed before undergoing treatment) can be in direct conflict with legal and bioethics principles that require a treatment decision to be fully informed in order to be valid. P-CC proponents may argue that patients and their families may feel too burdened by disease to engage in the informed-consent process and should be allowed not to engage, while healthcare professionals may argue that the high degree of risk from the treatment itself makes it even more important that patients understand the treatment regimen they are consenting to undergo.

This study reveals a little-recognized paradox, and it is clear that simply reiterating the basic P-CC tenets will not provide sufficient guidance to healthcare professionals about how to deal with this dilemma.

Patient-centred care and the delivery of high-risk therapy

A second study within a similar context reveals additional difficulties applying the central tenet of P-CC that the patient is the source of control and that all efforts should be made to ensure the patient's emotional and physical comfort. In this study, interviews were conducted with patients undergoing autologous stem cell reinfusion for advanced cancer; family members were also interviewed. The study included only patients who had given their consent for the procedure (for additional details of the study, see Montgomery and Little, 2011).[2]

As discussed above in the section on informed consent, considering the patient as the source of control is assumed to mean that it is the patient's choice about whether to proceed with treatment or not. However, P-CC tenets are silent about the reverse situation: when a patient may wish to proceed with further treatment, but the medical team decides that further treatment would be futile. As the following comments reveal, such a predicament caused intense emotional distress for patients and their families, who were desperate for successful treatment for the cancer:

> [Family member]: *The oncology [team] announced that they can't do anything about it, she will die. I thought, this is a big hospital, is supposed to have a more, like machine and those kinds of things... and do something about it. They can't do anything to save her. I looked at him and [said] 'I know there's another machine there.'*

> [Family member]: *It wasn't long after the stem cell [reinfusion] that they said, 'Sorry, we can't do anything more for you.' We felt like the doctors had just given up.*

Although patients could exercise their preferences to insist that treatment be stopped or never started in the first place, it was the judgement of the medical professionals that determined when treatment would no longer be administered. This clearly illustrates the limitations in interpreting the P-CC tenet that the patient is the source of control.

Another telling finding from this study is that, not only was the patient not the source of control, but, to a large extent, neither were the healthcare professionals. Rather, the disease itself was in control. Doctors were able to administer the treatment and to decide when to conclude treatment, but they were not able to control whether or not the treatment was effective, nor the body's response to the treatment. Patients and family members expressed this realization, often talking of the disease as a distinct and dominant actor. Below are two examples:

> [Family member]: *The lymphoma was just too aggressive, just too quick growing for the stem cells to mature enough to work.*

> [Patient]: *At the moment my cells are friendly cells and they're accepting the cancer... they're not fighting it.*

Another tenet of P-CC that is extraordinarily difficult to adhere to in some contexts is that of providing patients with physical comfort, emotional support and alleviating fear and anxiety. This is due in part to the frightening nature of cancer, coupled with the uncertainty of the treatment side effects and outcome. While healthcare professionals routinely embrace opportunities to care for such patients with tenderness and kindness, the interventions for patients undergoing ASCT nevertheless can be severe and upsetting. Indeed, this was recognized by an oncology nurse in a recent *New York Times* editorial reflecting on the challenges of harsh chemotherapy. She noted that, for some patients, 'in order to heal [them], we must first hurt' (Brown, 2012).

While patients in this study seemed to accept that there was no alternative to the demands of therapy, they nevertheless experienced substantial discomfort and emotional distress, as one patient explained,

> [Patient]: *Once you get a cancer like I've got, your body's not your own anymore. You've got to give over... you are pushed and needles and every-thing... you're on the tables, you're on the x-rays, you're this, you're that. What went on there this morning wasn't even easy, thing put in there and 'put your arms back up' and then they inject this dye into you, and you burn up all over, and it feels terrible.*

Finally, the patient's experience described here demonstrates a particular challenge for the healthcare provider. That is, despite recognizing that the therapeutic procedures would be likely to cause physical and emotional discomfort for patients (as noted above by the oncology nurse's editorial), there is little attention in the P-CC guidelines to the extra burden this reality places on the healthcare professionals.

Realities of serious illness, high-risk therapy and patient-centred care

The two studies described in this chapter highlight the contextual limitations of the P-CC approach. Most important, it is not realistic to expect formulations of P-CC at the level of primary care, acute care or even chronic care, to be readily applicable to the context of serious illness and aggressive, high-risk therapy. In these circumstances, it is unrealistic to maintain the P-CC tenets that the patient is the source of control, that patient values guide all healthcare treatment decisions and that physical discomfort and emotional distress can be alleviated.

First, all too often, the disease is the most dominant actor, overtaking both the patient's and the doctor's sense of control. Moreover, patients, who may feel overwhelmed by the disease itself, may find themselves simply unable to participate in meaningful informed-consent discussions.

Second, a patient's own values may dictate that treatment should be continued at all costs, but those values cannot override a decision of the healthcare team to cease further treatment if, in their professional judgement, further intervention would be futile.

Third, it is impossible to protect patients undergoing aggressive therapy from physical discomfort and the concomitant emotional distress that typically arises during the periods of such harsh treatment and its aftermath.

As many hospitals and healthcare systems intensify their reliance on an approach to patient care that is grounded in P-CC models, it is important to reflect on the downsides of such an approach. In particular, healthcare professionals working in this context may feel increased stress and frustration if their performance is being assessed, at least in part, by how closely it aligns with the P-CC tenets listed earlier. In some cases, healthcare organizations and systems have begun to incorporate results from patient-satisfaction surveys into their financial incentives and reimbursement schemes for healthcare providers. While this may be considered a useful approach for primary care providers, we have shown that its application in other contexts would be wholly inappropriate.

Ethical dilemmas and patient-centred care

We note also some ethical dilemmas that arise when attempting to apply P-CC tenets in certain contexts. The first relates to the challenge of obtaining informed consent for high-risk treatment. The importance of informed consent prior to treatment applies in any healthcare context, of course, but here we highlight the particular difficulties when the proposed treatment is extraordinarily complex, with the potential for severe but unpredictable side effects.

As seen in the first study, the informed-consent process can be fraught with uncertainty and dissatisfaction on the part of the healthcare team when patients agreed to go forward with the therapy but do so without fully engaging in the education process. This can create a high degree of uneasiness among the healthcare team, knowing how arduous the proposed treatment will be for the patient. This uneasiness can be compounded if patients later complain, after having had the treatment, that they would not have agreed to go forward had they known how harsh the treatment would be. To deflect their uneasiness (and potential legal liability), some members of the healthcare team can become defensive, knowing how intensive and determined their efforts had been to educate the patients. Not surprisingly, we found evidence of blame from the healthcare team towards the patients (along the lines of, 'you didn't try hard enough to become informed'), as well as blame of other members of the healthcare team (such as, 'some doctors have never learned how to communicate'). Healthcare providers have received little guidance about how to navigate this kind of situation ethically.

Two related ethical challenges can arise during the course of treatment, in decisions about whether or not to continue. As noted, a central tenet of P-CC states that the patient is the source of control, which is understood to mean that the patient decides whether or not to undertake treatment. We have just discussed the challenges of the informed-consent process in this context. Once treatment has begun, however, that decision becomes murkier. In particular, aggressive chemotherapy followed by stem cell transplantation or reinfusion involves rigorous protocols that, if not completed, could lead to almost certain death because the patients would be left with no functioning immune system. Some patients, who do not fully understand the 'rescue' role of the stem cell stage of the therapy, place the healthcare team in an untenable ethical situation if they insist on stopping all treatment after the chemotherapy but before the stem cell reinfusion.

At the other extreme, another ethical dilemma arises when the course of treatment has concluded and the healthcare team has determined that another round of treatment would be futile, given the patient's response to the initial stem cell therapy. If such patients try to insist that further therapy be undertaken, the healthcare professionals are placed in another challenging situation, having to go against the patient's wishes and values.

Reconciliation: Respect and dignity

The foregoing discussion is not intended to minimize the importance of the fundamental principles of P-CC, as articulated at the beginning of this chapter. Rather, its aim is to urge a more nuanced approach, recognizing that modifications in the application of P-CC are essential in some healthcare contexts. Nevertheless, there are some common threads that can be emphasized, regardless of the context. Most central among these is respect and dignity.

Berwick (2009), a physician and health policy maker, and one of the early proponents of P-CC, has recently argued for distilling P-CC to its essence of maintaining respect for a patient's dignity, noting from his recent experience as a patient that 'what chills my bones is indignity' (2009, p. 564). Respect has featured prominently in discussions of P-CC, from the early landmark articulations of P-CC (Gerteis et al., 1993; Institute of Medicine, 2001). However, in those reports, respect was framed as providing care that is respectful of patients' expressed needs, values, preferences and choices. A more generalized reframing would shift the object of respect from the patients' needs, values, preferences and choices, to respect for the individual patient as a person, deserving of dignity, regardless of the circumstances and context. In other words, the object of respect becomes the fundamental essence of the patient, not just elements of the patient's attitudes and beliefs.

Some thoughtful writing about the centrality of respect for the patient as a person has been referred to as humane medicine (Little, 1995) and, more recently, person-centred medicine (Miles and Mezzich, 2011). For example, Miles and Mezzich argue for respecting the 'autonomy, responsibility, and dignity of every person involved' in the healthcare encounter (2011, p. 216). To briefly summarize this argument, person-centred medicine is '(1) of the person – of the totality of the person's health, including its ill and positive aspects; (2) for the person – promoting fulfillment of the person's life project; (3) by the person – with clinicians extending themselves as full human beings, well grounded in science and with high ethical aspirations; and (4) with the person – working respectfully in collaboration and in an empowering manner through a partnership of patient, family, and clinician' (Mezzich et al., 2011, p. 331).

Of particular note, this formulation appropriately brings the healthcare clinicians back into the picture (*'by the person*...well grounded in science and with high ethical aspirations'), in recognition of the serious challenges and ethical dilemmas they may increasingly confront, in the context of delivering more sophisticated and technologically advanced healthcare treatments such as those described above. Interestingly, this balanced model is somewhat reminiscent of the biopsychosocial model first proposed by Engel (1977), which calls for personalized medicine, while maintaining a strong respect for the science side of medicine.

In conclusion, the P-CC movement may have begun as a response to concerns that the interests, preferences and wishes of patients were being overlooked in a wave that gave priority to needs, interests and goals of the healthcare providers and organizations. The ideals of the P-CC movement are highly appealing and rightfully so. In this chapter, I have sought to add a note of caution in the midst of the enthusiasm for an across-the-board implementation of guidelines and policies based on P-CC tenets, by drawing attention to the limitations of P-CC and calling for more nuanced thought about P-CC in certain healthcare contexts.

Notes

1. The procedure for allogeneic stem cell transplantation involves locating a matched donor for bone marrow cells; harvesting them from the donor; storing the cells for infusion into the patient following chemotherapy and administering an intensive chemotherapy treatment, which kills the patient's immune system, leaving the patient highly vulnerable to infection. Following the chemotherapy, the patient is infused with the donor's harvested stem cells in order to restore the patient's immune system. Of key importance is that the chemotherapy is highly toxic and can cause extreme illness, during which time the patient must remain hospitalized until the stem cell reinfusion. Thus, the treatment cannot be stopped until the full cycle has been completed.

2. The procedure for autologous stem cell reinfusion is similar to that for using donor stem cells [see above note], except in this case, rather than relying on cells from a donor, the patient's own stem cells are harvested and stored. Following an aggressive chemotherapy treatment, which will have killed the patient's immune system, the stored cells are reinfused into the patient. Until the reinfused cells have begun to generate new immune cells, the patient is highly vulnerable to infection.

References

Barry, M.J., Fowler, F.J., Mulley, A.G., and Henderson, J.V. (1995) 'Patient Reactions to a Program Designed to Facilitate Patient Participation in Treatment Decisions for Benign Prostatic Hyperplasia', *Medical Care*, 33, 771–782.

Berry, L.L. (2004) 'The Collaborative Organization: Leadership Lessons from Mayo Clinic', *Organizational Dynamics*, 33, 228–242.

Berwick, D. (2009) 'What "Patient-Centered" Should Mean: Confessions of an Extremist', *Health Affairs*, 28, 555–565.

Brown, T. (2012) 'Hospitals Aren't Hotels', *The New York Times*, March 15, 2012, A35.

Canterbury v. Spence (1972) 464 F.2d 772 (Washington DC: Circuit Court).

Delbanco, T., Berwick, D., Boufford, J., Edgman-Levitan, S., Ollenschlager, G., Plamping, D., and Rockefeller, R. (2001) 'Healthcare in a Land Called PeoplePower: Nothing About Me Without Me', *Health Expectations* 4, 144–150.

DiMatteo, M.R., Giordani, P., Lepper, H., and Croghan, T. (2002) 'Patient Adherence and Medical Treatment Outcomes: A Meta-Analysis', *Medical Care*, 40, 794–811.

Engel, G.L. (1977) 'The Need for a New Medical Model: A Challenge for Biomedicine', *Science*, 196, 129–136.

Freidson, E. (1970) *Profession of Medicine: A Study of the Sociology of Applied Knowledge* (Chicago: University of Chicago Press).

Gerteis, M.S., Edgman-Levitan, S., Daley, J., and Delbanco, T. (1993) *Through the Patient's Eyes: Understanding and Promoting Patient-Centered Care* (San Francisco: Jossey-Bass).

Haug, M. (1973) 'Deprofessionalization: An Alternative Hypothesis for the Future', *The Sociological Review Monograph*, 20, 195–211.

Hibbard, J. (2007) 'Consumer Competencies and the Use of Comparative Quality Information: It Isn't Just About Literacy', *Medical Care Research and Review*, 64, 379–394.

Institute of Medicine (2001) *Crossing the Quality Chasm: A New Health System for the 21st Century* (Washington DC: National Academies Press).

Jordens, C.F.C., Montgomery, K., and Forsyth, R. (2013) 'Trouble in the Gap: A Bioethical and Sociological Analysis of Informed Consent for High-Risk Medical Procedures', *Journal of Bioethical Inquiry*, 10, 67–77.

Korsch, B. M. (1989) 'Current Issues in Communication Research', *Health Communication*, 1, 5–9.

Little, J.M. (1995) *Humane Medicine* (Cambridge: Cambridge University Press).

Lynn, J., Straube, B., Bell, K., Jencks, S., and Kambic, R. (2007) 'Using Population Segmentation to Provide Better Health Care for All: The "Bridges to Health" Model', *The Milbank Quarterly*, 85, 185–208.

Mezzich, J.E., Snaedal, J., van Weel, C., Botbol, M., and Salloum, I. (2011) 'Introduction to Person-Centered Medicine: From Concepts to Practice', *Journal of Evaluation in Clinical Practice*, 17, 330–332.

Miles, A., and Mezzich, J.E. (2011) 'The Care of the Patient and the Soul of the Clinic: Person-Centered Medicine as an Emergent Model of Modern Clinical Practice', *The International Journal of Person Centered Medicine*, 1, 207–222.

Montgomery, K. and Little, M. (2011) 'Enriching Patient-Centered Care in Serious Illness: A Focus on Patients' Experiences of Agency', *The Milbank Quarterly*, 89, 381–398.

Roter, D.L. and Hall, J.A. (2006) *Doctors Talking with Patients/Patients Talking with Doctors: Improving Communication in Medical Visits* (Westport CT: Prager).

Waitzkin H. and Stoeckle, J.D. (1972) 'The Communication of Information About Illness: Clinical, Sociological, and Methodological Considerations', *Advances in Psychosomatic Medicine*, 8, 180–215.

Ware, J.E., Snyder, M.K., Wright, W.R., and Davies, A.R. (1983) 'Defining and Measuring Patient Satisfaction with Medical Care', *Evaluation and Program Planning*, 6, 247–263.

2
The Continuum of Resident-Centred Care in US Nursing Homes

Nicholas G. Castle and Jamie C. Ferguson-Rome

Introduction

Characteristically, nursing home care in the United States was focused on improving clinical outcomes for residents (Castle and Ferguson, 2010). Much less attention was paid to the living environment and quality of life while delivering this care. However, in the 1990s, some providers began to move nursing home care towards a more home-like environment in which processes were more resident friendly (White-Chu et al., 2009). This became known as person-centred care (or resident-centred care (RCC)) and the ensuing movement that more fully operationalized this process was termed 'culture change' (Rahman and Schnelle, 2008). In this research, we report on the findings from a nationally representative sample of nursing homes examining how embedded RCC practices have become in US nursing homes and identify some factors associated with use of these practices.

Various definitions of RCC exist. The following definition was used in this research, as it seems to summarize the entire realm of what RCC should be: 'resident centered care is an ongoing, interactive process between residents, caregivers and others that honor the residents' dignity and choices in directing their daily life. This is accomplished through shared communication, education and collaboration' (Wisconsin Coalition for Person Directed Care, 2011, p. 1). In general, as part of this concept residents have privacy and choice. Residents' needs and preferences come first with facilities' operations shaped by this awareness (Davis et al., 2005). Residents are given greater control over their daily lives. In addition, the physical and organizational structure of facilities is made less institutional.

RCC practices have gained some momentum over the past decade. There has been growing awareness of RCC practices among professionals and providers in the field. Nationally, in the United States nearly 30 statewide coalitions are in various stages of development working on promoting a RCC approach (Stone et al., 2009). At the federal level, the Centers for Medicare and Medicaid Services (CMS) and the Veterans Affairs (VA) administration have also endorsed RCC (Rahman and Schnelle, 2008). For example, CMS gave directions to 'improve organizational culture' through state Quality Improvement Organizations (QIOs).

Approximately 300 of the 16,000 nursing homes in the United States have undergone full transformation to RCC (Koren, 2010). That is, they use many of the RCC practices advocated by the aforementioned groups. Facilities using many of these RCC practices are often designated as having undergone culture change. Thus, culture change has a somewhat specific meaning in the current US nursing home industry that generally embodies the use of RCC practices.

Nevertheless, some practices of RCC may be implemented in varying degrees by nursing homes. In 2007, The Commonwealth Fund conducted a nationally representative survey of US nursing homes to learn more about the penetration of the culture-change movement (i.e. RCC practices) at the national level and measure the extent to which nursing homes were adopting culture-change principles and practicing RCC. A representative sample of 1,435 nursing homes was surveyed between February and June 2007. Five per cent of nursing homes identified themselves as completely implementing culture change (Koren, 2010). However, the survey identified many other nursing homes as implementing various components of culture change, and using relatively few RCC practices. For example, 29% of nursing homes enabled residents to implement their own daily schedule (Doty et al., 2008).

In this research, data from 2010 are used to further examine how embedded RCC practices have become in US nursing homes. We use recent data, which may be important given the rapidly evolving nature of RCC. In addition, a large nationally representative sample is used. Few prior investigations have examined factors associated with use of RCC practices. The research presented here is significant in that factors such as leadership, cost, size and regulation are examined as factors potentially associated with use of RCC practices.

Conceptual model and hypotheses

In this investigation, the process or series of steps that are implemented by facilities overtime in order to achieve RCC are examined. Thus, the Causal Model of Organizational Performance and Change proposed by Burke and Lewin (Burke, 2008) is used. This Burke–Lewin model proposes the external environment to be transformational, and to foster change in mission, strategy and leadership. This promotes transactional changes in the organization of structure, systems and practices. These transactional and transformational forces work together to alter performance. The model proposes a feedback loop wherein performance can influence the external environment.

The Burke–Lewin model also accounts for the initial characteristics of the leader, organizational resources and prior reinforcing/modifying factors (i.e. the current organizational life). That is, the process of change will likely be more/less successful on the basis of these factors.

The Burke–Lewin model would appear appropriate for investigating the process of culture change in nursing homes. It is likely that culture-change practices in nursing homes are selected on the basis of the unique characteristics of each facility (Sterns et al., 2010). The Commonwealth Fund Survey (noted above) identified cost, size and regulation as major barriers to culture change (Doty et al., 2008). In an evaluation of barriers to culture change coming from 1,147 long-term care specialists, costs, leadership and regulation were rated as the most significant perceived barriers (Miller et al., 2010). Therefore, the factors to be examined in this study of culture change are leadership factors, cost, size and regulation.

A recent literature review identified leadership factors in nursing homes as influential in providing humanistic care to residents (Castle et al., 2009). The elements of humanistic care discussed were analogous to the elements of RCC. Top management turnover was identified as an influential factor impacting leadership. That is, the nursing home administrator (NHA) and/or director of nursing (DON) leaving the facility had an adverse impact on the stability of leadership in the nursing home. With respect to implementing RCC it would seem plausible that top-management stability would be essential to successfully implement and maintain the needed changes. It is hypothesized (H1): Low top-management turnover will be associated with more RCC practices.

As several authors have noted, a favourable business case for RCC would likely be influential in promoting change practices (Sterns et al.,

2010). Given the relative absence of this business case, RCC practices (as deviations from current practice) come with various costs and unknown financial risks. Facilities with the most resources will likely be able to bear the cost and risk of implementing RCC. In this research, direct measures of profits/resources are not available. However, in general, nursing homes with the most private-pay residents (versus residents compensated for by the Medicaid programme) are viewed as the most profitable (Grabowski et al., 2004). It is hypothesized (H2): High private-pay resident occupancy will be associated with more RCC practices.

Facility size (i.e. number of beds) may influence use of RCC. Small nursing homes may not have the staff and resources to implement RCC. Small nursing homes have modest margins of error because they have fewer available resources and are more likely to go out of business than larger ones if risky ventures fail. In addition, small nursing homes may view themselves as already having favourable relationships with residents. Small homes may be better at creating more intimate, nurturing environments that facilitate interaction between staff and residents (Amirkhanyan et al., 2008). Thus, small facilities may not place a high priority of implementing RCC. It is hypothesized (H3): Nursing homes with a large number of beds will be associated with more RCC practices.

As part of the Medicare and/or Medicaid certification process in which almost all US nursing homes partake, deficiency citations can be issued (Castle et al., 2007). Deficiency citations represent deviations from Medicare/Medicaid regulations for providing care and are often used as proxies for poor quality care. Lower quality nursing homes have a higher incidence of deficiency citations. Responding to deficiency citations can be burdensome and may be one reason facilities with high numbers do not implement RCC (and vice versa). It is hypothesized (H4): Nursing homes with low numbers of deficiency citations will be associated with more RCC practices.

Methods

Sample and data

Data used in this research came from several sources. Information regarding the use of RCC practices was obtained from primary data collected from NHAs. In addition, characteristics of the nursing homes (e.g. number of beds, etc.) came from the 2010 Online Survey, System for Certification and Administrative Reporting (OSCAR) data.

NHA questionnaire

Primary data collection from NHAs was used because information on the use of RCC is not available in secondary data sources. Thus, this data was collected through a mail survey. The survey was sent to 4,000 NHAs working in nursing homes. The mail sample was created by using address information from the OSCAR data (described further below). For each survey, the OSCAR facility identification number was also retained, so that facility characteristics of the sample could be subsequently examined.

The sample was randomly chosen from all nursing homes listed in the OSCAR, which includes facilities from every state. The smallest nursing homes (<30 beds) and hospital-based facilities were excluded from the survey sample. This was because very small facilities and hospital-based facilities are considered to be uncharacteristic of the nursing home industry (Castle et al., 2007).

Questionnaire development

Questionnaire items were developed by the research team on the basis of conceptual model and using existing literature. In this research, the intent was to examine both the least complex areas of RCC and some of the more complex areas of RCC. This approach was taken because we believed it was likely that some of the least complex (most simple) areas would be implemented by a greater number of nursing homes than the more complex areas.

Thus, the items from existing questionnaires were collected and collapsed into similar areas (i.e. domains). These similar areas were as follows: 1. care- and resident-related activities are resident directed (RESIDENT); 2. a home-like living environment (ENVIRONMENT); 3. residents, family and staff have close relationships (RELATIONSHIPS); 4. staff respond to residents' needs (STAFF); 5. decentralized decision-making (DECISION-MAKING) and 6. use of measurement and continuous quality improvement (IMPROVEMENT). These areas were previously developed as part of a technical expert panel (Centers for Medicare and Medicaid Services, 2006).

Demographic and job skill information items included in the questionnaire included gender, age, race, education, tenure in nursing home, tenure as NHA, number of NHAs working in the facility in past 3 years and number of DONs working in the facility in past 3 years. These items were included, because in prior research they provided important background information on top management (see review by Castle et al., 2009).

Medicaid reimbursement rates are included in the analyses. This information for each state came from primary data collected by the authors. This primary data collection was independent from the RSC questionnaire. In this case, the data collection followed a process previously used and published by others (Grabowski et al., 2004).

Secondary data

The OSCAR was used as a source of facility characteristics information. The OSCAR contains data collected as part of state/federal nursing home inspections. Facilities that accept residents with Medicare and/or Medicaid payments are surveyed. This includes most (i.e. 97%) nursing homes in the United States. The survey process occurs approximately yearly and includes the recording of many characteristics of the nursing home and aggregate characteristics of residents. The data are commonly used as a secondary source of nursing home characteristics (Castle and Ferguson, 2010).

Dependent and independent variables

A summary score for each domain is used in the analyses. The domain summary scores represent the percentage of nursing homes with positive responses in more than half of the RCC practices in the specific domain. This formulation of the summary score was not based on any existing metric and clearly could benefit from additional research. However, in sensitivity analyses more and less stringent domain summary scores the results presented were relatively stable.

The independent variables included in these multivariate analyses include the facility characteristics of staffing levels, bed size, ownership, chain membership, private-pay occupancy, overall resident census and case-mix (using ADLs), and market characteristics include rural location and number of nursing homes in the county. These variables are shown in Table 2.1.

Analyses

Descriptive statistics for the background variables collected are presented (e.g. demographics and job characteristics). The OSCAR was also used to examine the characteristics of the facility sample (i.e. sample representativeness and non-response). Characteristics of the facility sample are also presented. Descriptive statistics for the individual items in the

Table 2.1 Descriptive characteristics of nursing homes and markets

Variable	Definition	Nursing home respondents ($N = 2,680$) Mean or percentage	Standard deviation	All nursing homes in 2010 OSCAR ($N = 14,093$) Mean or percentage	Standard deviation
Facility characteristics:[a]					
Quality of care deficiency citations	Deficiency citations representing the sum of 25 different deficiency citations (F-tags are: 309 through 353).	62%	–	64%	–
Organizational size	Number of beds	131	(82)	129	(81)
Ownership					
For-profit		65%	–	67%	–
Chain membership	Member of a nursing home chain	54%	–	56%	–
Occupancy	Average daily occupancy rate	89%	(11)	86%	(10)
Medicaid occupancy	Average daily percentage of Medicaid residents	59%	(21)	62%	(20)
Resident case-mix	The average score for three ADLs (eating, toileting and transferring). Constructed by giving a score of 1 for low assistance, 2 for moderate assistance and 3 for high need for assistance summed for each ADL.	1.8	(0.9)	1.9	(0.9)
RN staffing[b]	FTE RNs per 100 residents (including full-time and part-time workers, but not agency staff) in 2007	10.6	(9.2)	NA	NA
LPN staffing[b]	FTE LPNs per 100 residents (including full-time and part-time workers, but not agency staff) in 2007	14.5	(8.1)	NA	NA

Table 2.1 (Continued)

Variable	Definition	Nursing home respondents (N = 2,680) Mean or percentage	Standard deviation	All nursing homes in 2010 OSCAR (N = 14,093) Mean or percentage	Standard deviation
NA staffing[b]	FTE NAs per 100 residents (including full-time and part-time workers, but not agency staff) in 2007	30.1	(9.2)	NA	
Market characteristics:[c]					
Competition	Herfindahl index. The sum of each facility's squared percentage share of beds in the county for all facilities in the county (0–1). Higher values indicate a less competitive market	0.23	(0.3)	0.21	(0.2)
Medicaid reimbursement	The average reimbursement rate for Medicaid residents in the state ($)	122.7	(23.6)	131.1	(22.6)

a. Variables were taken from Online Survey Certification and Reporting (OSCAR) data.
b. Variables were from primary data collection.
c. Variables were taken from the Area Resource File (ARF).
NA = Nurse Aide; RN = Registered Nurse; LPN = Licensed Practical Nurse; FTE = Full-time equivalent; ADL = activities of daily living. Figures from 2010 are shown.

questionnaire are provided. That is, a summary score for each question-naire item is presented. The summary score represents the percentage of positive responses (i.e. Strongly Agree and Agree). This summary score has a range from 0 to 100.

Prior to multivariate analyses, the level of collinearity among the independent variables and multicollinearity using the variance inflation factor (VIF) test was examined. The correlation between these variables was low (i.e. less than $r = .61$).

The scores for the RCC areas examined were somewhat skewed. We accounted for this skew by using negative binomial regression models, which is a generalization of the Poisson regression model for count data that permits for over-dispersion that is evidenced by having facilities with low values. This method also incorporates the sandwich estimator for robust standard errors. The coefficients are reported in incident-rate ratio (IRR) form, which is similar to odds ratios in that estimates greater than 1 represent a positive association between the explanatory variable and the outcome.

Results

A total of 2,680 NHAs returned the questionnaire, giving a response rate of 67%. The response rate varied little across the states, and in general most items on the questionnaire were answered. Missing data occurred in less than 1% of cases and were evenly distributed across questions and states. Also, because we were able to link facilities with OSCAR data, it was determined that no significant differences on facility char-acteristics (i.e. bed size, ownership, chain membership and private-pay census) existed for respondent compared to non-respondent facilities (results not shown). The facility characteristics of the sample are shown in Table 2.1.

Table 2.2 presents the summary scores of the NHAs responses to each of the questionnaire items and domain summary scores. The item scores (using a 0–100 scale) fell into the 13–68 range. The lowest item score was for 'Families are part of the regular and formal part of the man-agement team that makes important decisions affecting the facility' (i.e. score = 13) and the highest item score was for 'All dietary requirements of the residents are considered for meals' (i.e. score = 68). The domain scores (using a 0–100% scale) fell into the 24–42% range. The lowest domain score was for 'RESIDENT' (i.e. score = 24%) and the highest domain score was for 'RELATIONSHIPS' (i.e. score = 42%). Overall, few nursing homes extensively used several RCC practices. Less than 40%

Table 2.2 Descriptive statistics of the RCC items and domains

Items+/Domains[a]	Summary Score + Mean (Standard deviation) N = 2,680
Resident (care- and resident-related activities are resident directed)[a]	**24%**
We offer meal choices to the residents daily	35 (10)
All dietary requirements of the residents are considered for meals	68 (12)
Residents choose the time of day they bathe	21 (12)
Residents can sleep late and still get breakfast	23 (10)
Residents go to bed for the night at any time they want	42 (13)
Environment (a home-like living environment)[a]	**29%**
Nursing home leaders and staff share values and common goals related to a home-like environment	26 (12)
Residents are allowed to bring personal furniture in their rooms	42 (13)
Residents are welcome to decorate their rooms	35 (10)
We provide books and newspapers with large print for the residents	66 (12)
Nurses stations are decentralized	23 (10)
Overhead paging is not used	36 (11)
Relationships (residents, family and staff have close relationships)[a]	**42%**
Visiting hours are flexible for family and friends	59 (7)
Families questions about care are always answered	53 (7)
Families are informed about medical treatments (e.g. tests ordered)	48 (9)
Families are part of the regular and formal part of the management team that makes important decisions affecting the facility	13 (9)
Staff (staff respond to residents' needs)[a]	**29%**
In the past year we have made many changes to adapt to the residents' needs	44 (11)
Team huddles are conducted during the day	23 (11)
We have well-established protocols to enhance care coordination	27 (8)
Staff are trained to do tasks outside of their primary duty	15 (9)
Decision-making (decentralized decision-making)[a]	**27%**
Residents are engaged in decision-making about their care plans	23 (9)
We use consistent assignment	38 (9)

NAs determine their own schedules	14 (12)
We involve all staff in most discussions and meetings	12 (7)
Staff are part of the regular and formal part of the management team that makes important decisions affecting the facility	15 (9)
Improvement (use of measurement and continuous quality improvement)[a]	**26%**
In the past year, we have conducted internal surveys to understand needs of the residents	39 (10)
In the past year, we have conducted internal surveys to understand needs of the family members	23 (9)
In the past year, we have conducted internal surveys to understand needs of the staff $N = 2,680$	39 (12)

Note: + A summary score for each questionnaire item is presented. The summary score represents the percentage of positive responses (i.e. Agree/Strongly Agree). This summary score has a range from 0 to 100. This approach of presenting summary scores is consistent with the method recommended by AHRQ for use with this response scale (www.ahrq.gov/qual/nhsurvey08/nhguide.pdfwww.ahrq.gov/qual/nhsurvey08/nhguide.pdf).
[a]The domain summary score represents the percentage of nursing homes with positive responses in more than half of these RCC practices.

of nursing homes used half of the practices listed. Approximately 22% of nursing homes could be considered as 'culture-change' organizations; whereas, 16% do not use any RCC approaches (not shown).

The results of the regression analyses are displayed in Table 2.3. Six models were used examining each of the RSC domains. The associations with leadership turnover, private-pay occupancy, bed size and deficiency citations were the independent variables of interest. For leadership turnover, four of the six coefficients of interest were significant. That is, in high top-management turnover facilities an association with low RCC practices exists. For example, leadership turnover was associated with the RELATIONSHIPS domain summary score (IRR = 0.36; $p \le 0.05$). These findings provide support for hypothesis 1.

For private-pay occupancy, all six coefficients of interest were significant. That is, in high private-pay occupancy facilities an association with high RCC practices exists. For example, private-pay occupancy was associated with the ENVIRONMENT domain summary score (IRR = 1.55; $p \le 0.05$). These findings provide support for hypothesis 2.

For bed size, five of the six coefficients of interest were significant. That is, in facilities with a large number of beds an association with high RCC practices exists. For example, bed size was associated with the STAFF domain summary score (IRR = 1.76; $p \le 0.01$). These findings provide support for hypothesis 3.

Table 2.3 Regression coefficients examining resident-centred care domains

Independent variables of interest	Resident	Environment	Relationships	Staff	Decision-making	Improvement
NHA and DON turnover (H1)	0.44*	0.21	0.36*	0.37*	0.51	0.34*
	(0.19)	(0.13)	(0.15)	(0.13)	(0.30)	(0.18)
Private-pay occupancy (H2)	1.53**	1.55*	1.73**	1.50**	1.41***	1.50***
	(0.13)	(0.21)	(0.15)	(0.15)	(0.11)	(0.12)
Bed size (H3)	1.94*	1.49***	1.76	1.76**	1.78***	1.31*
	(0.41)	(0.13)	(0.51)	(0.21)	(0.15)	(0.15)
Deficiency citations (H4)	0.60**	0.54*	0.34	0.67*	0.54*	0.62
	(0.18)	(0.20)	(0.25)	(0.24)	(0.23)	(0.51)

Notes: In Columns 1–6 the IRR for negative binomial regressions are presented. Robust standard errors are in parentheses. Regression coefficients for the independent variables of interest are presented for parsimony; all variables in Table 1 were included in each model (results for all variables in the models included in Table 1 are available from the authors).

Domains examined are the following: 1. Care- and resident-related activities are resident directed (RESIDENT); 2. A home-like living environment (ENVIRONMENT); 3. Residents, family and staff have close relationships (RELATIONSHIPS); 4. Staff respond to residents needs (STAFF); 5. Decentralized decision-making (DECISION-MAKING) and, 6. Use of measurement and continuous quality improvement (IMPROVEMENT).

*$p < .05$; **$p < .01$; ***$p < .001$.

$N = 2,680$.

NHA = Nursing Home Administrator; DON = Director of Nursing; H = hypothesis.

For deficiency citations, four of the six coefficients of interest were significant. That is, in facilities with a high number of deficiency citations an association with low RCC practices exists. For example, deficiency citations were associated with the DECISION-MAKING domain summary score (IRR = 0.54; $p \leq .05$). These findings provide support for hypothesis 4.

Discussion

An influential Institute of Medicine (IOM) report (IOM, 2001) noted that care in the US healthcare system should be 'person-centered'. However, implementation of person-centred (i.e. RCC) practices in nursing homes involves a process requiring many changes (Rahman and Schnelle, 2008). Providers do not simply move from having no RCC practices to full RCC. In this research, RCC practices in nursing homes are examined.

We identify approximately 22% of nursing homes to be using many RCC practices such that they could be considered culture-change facilities. These findings are not longitudinal. Nevertheless, based on the prior levels reported in the literature (5%; Koren, 2010), it is likely that RCC practices are becoming more widespread. However, we do note that the number of RCC practices needed to be considered a culture-change facility is not well defined. Our findings should be interpreted with this in mind.

One limitation of our survey is that we may have a greater response rate from 'better' facilities and 'better' responses to RCC practices. As such, the percentage of nursing homes to be using RCC practices nationally may be overestimated, and the individual RCC practices reported to be used likewise may be over-reported (and vice versa). Thus, with 16% of nursing homes (as a possible underestimate) reporting that they are not using any RCC practices, it would seem like we still have a long way to go before RCC becomes mainstream in US facilities. The multivariate analysis results may help give some indication of initiatives that may be useful in further embedding RCC practices in US facilities.

The leadership team of most nursing homes consists of the NHA and DON. Recent research has begun to demonstrate that these top managers have a potentially important influence on the effectiveness of their organizations. For example, empirical investigations have demonstrated that top-management leadership can be associated with better quality of care (Anderson et al., 2003). The findings of this research indicate that they also influence RCC (supporting H1, low top-management turnover will be associated with more RCC practices).

As with our research, nursing home top-management research has tended to focus upon factors such as turnover and tenure. The association of the leadership style of NHAs, as well as that of DONs, to RCC may give some additional insight into implementation of RCC practices. A central tenet of RCC is to allow staff (e.g. nurse aides) to work with the residents to make decisions (Scalzi et al., 2006). This focus on decision-making between caregivers and residents necessitates that top managers give enough decision-making authority to nurse aides. Thus, the goal of implementing RCC appears most compatible with certain leadership styles. Evidence of this would appear to come from Scalzi et al. (2006) who found that culture change was ineffectual when top managers did not involve the nursing staff in culture training and activities.

Different strategies and models for RCC (and culture change) exist, but all change involves rethinking practices. We speculate that top-management leadership may be a fundamental enabler, such that practices can be changed, comes only with top-management leadership.

Nursing homes are able to charge higher rates for private-pay residents compared to the government designated rates of the Medicare and Medicaid programme. Nursing homes with the most private-pay residents likely have the most resources. Some of these resources would seem to be used for RCC. We identified considerable support for H2 (High private-pay resident occupancy will be associated with more RCC practices.). In additional analyses (not shown), the assumed most difficult and most expensive RCC practices were examined. Again, higher occupancy rates for private-pay residents were associated with these practices.

These findings are not causal, and rather than private-pay occupancy enabling the development of RCC it may be that RCC practices attract private-pay residents. We speculate that causality may in fact run in both directions. As such, identification of the benefits of RCC (with respect to profits/private-pay occupancy) would clearly be beneficial. If RCC practices attract residents, then a business case for use of these practices would exist.

It was hypothesized that nursing homes with a large number of beds would be associated with more RCC practices (i.e. H3). Again, some support for this hypothesis was identified. It would be useful in future work to observe care in smaller facilities, as they may already be consistent with many RCC practices (Kim et al., 2009). However, some practices (such as those in the measurement domain) were much less well implemented in small facilities. This may be an impediment to achieving the full potential benefits of RCC (even if some of the RCC practices are already inherent to small size). Given that the average number of beds for US nursing homes is low (i.e. 104), more investigation may be needed on this finding. This would seem especially pertinent given that some models of culture change (e.g. Green House Project) actually use very small facilities.

It was also found that nursing homes with low numbers of deficiency citations were associated with more RCC practices (i.e. supporting H4). Thus, the adoption of RCC practices is likely associated with quality of care. The deficiency citation process may overburden facilities, leading to less RCC implementation.

A further potential interpretation of the findings is that RCC practices do not lead to an increase in deficiency citations. That is, a somewhat beneficial association may exist between RCC and deficiency citations, and this may provide some further momentum to implementation of RCC practices. This may be important, for specific deficiency citations are not used for RCC practices; rather, concern has centred around the reverse case. That is, RCC practices are departures from standard care practices and as such may lead surveyors to levy deficiency citations (Rahman and Schnelle, 2008). Our findings are not causal; however, we find no association between RCC practices and deficiency citations.

Limitations to the study and suggestions for further research

The NHAs reports of RCC may be biased by social desirability. Reports of sensitive behaviours are potentially subject to underreporting as a result of social desirability concerns, perceived invasion of privacy and fear of disclosure to third parties. That is, due to social desirability and other concerns, NHA respondents may have tended to under-report behaviours that reflect poorly on them and over-report behaviours that make them look more favourable (e.g. effort in participating in RCC).

The research presented only examines opinions of NHAs. As noted above, the top-management team consists of the NHA and DON. Examining the opinions of both may give a more representative picture of RCC initiatives. One would assume that the opinions of these managers would be consistent, but some practices may be more familiar to one or other party. Moreover, examining the opinions of residents may also be useful.

Conclusion

RCC practices have been hailed as potentially important measures that can fundamentally improve the quality of US nursing homes. Despite the many advocates and supporters of RCC, implementation of RCC practices could be more widespread. In this research, it was identified that more facilities were using RCC practices than in the past, indicating some progress, but it was also found that many nursing homes have made much less progress.

References

Amirkhanyan, A.A., Kim, H.J., and Lambright, K.T. (2008). Does the public sector outperform the nonprofit and for-profit sectors? Evidence from a national panel study on nursing home quality and access. *Journal of Policy Analysis & Management*, 27(2), 326–353.

Anderson, R.A., Issel, L.M., and McDaniel, R.R. Jr. (2003). Nursing homes as complex adaptive systems: Relationship between management practice and resident outcomes. *Nursing Research*, 52(1), 12–21.

Burke, W.W. (2008). *Organization Change: Theory and Practice*, Thousand Oaks, CA: Sage.

Castle, N.G., Ferguson, J., and Hughes, K. (2009). Humanism in nursing homes: The impact of top management. *Journal of Health and Human Services Administration*, 31(4), 483–516.

Castle, N.G. and Ferguson, J.C. (2010). What is nursing home quality and how is it measured? *The Gerontologist*, 50(4), 426–442.

Castle, N.G., Men, A., and Engberg, J. (2007). Variation in use of nursing home deficiency citations. *Journal for Healthcare Quality*, 29(6), 12–23.

Centers for Medicare and Medicaid Services. (2006). Artifacts of culture change. Sharing innovations in quality. Retrieved September 13, 2006, from http://www.artifactsofculturechange.org/Data/Documents/artifacts.pdf.

Davis, K., Schoenbaum, S.C., and Audet, A.M. (2005). *The Commonwealth Fund New York NY USA*. A 2020 Vision of Patient-Centered Primary Care. Health Policy.

Doty, M.M., Koren, M.J., and Sturla, E.L. (2007). *Culture Change in Nursing Homes: How Far Have We Come? Findings From The Commonwealth Fund 2007 National Survey of Nursing Homes*. The Commonwealth Fund.

Grabowski, D.C., Feng, Z., Intrator, O., and Mor, V. (2004). Recent trends in state nursing home payment policies. *Health Affairs*, Suppl Web Exclusives, W4, 363–373.

Institute of Medicine (2001). *Improving the Quality of Long-term Care*. National Academy Press, Washington, D.C.

Kim, H., Harrington, C., and Greene, W. (2009). Registered nurse staff mix and nursing home quality. *The Gerontologist*, 49(1), 81–90.

Koren, M.J. (2010). Person centered care for nursing home residents: The culture change movement. *Health Affairs*, 29(2), 312–317.

Miller, E.A., Mor, V., and Clark, M. (2010). Reforming long-term care in the United States: Findings from a national survey of specialists. *The Gerontologist,* 50, 238–252.

Rahman, A.N. and Schnelle, J.F. (2008). The nursing home culture-change movement: Recent past, present, and future directions for research. *The Gerontologist,* 48, 142–148.

Scalzi, C.C., Evans, L.K., and Hostvedt, K. (2006). Barriers and enablers to changing organizational cultures in nursing homes. *Nurse Administrator Quarterly,* 30, 368–372.

Sterns, S., Miller, S.C., and Allen, S. (2010). The complexity of implementing culture change practices in nursing homes. *Journal of the American Medical Directors Association,* 11(7), 511–518.

Stone, R.I., Bryant, N., and Barbarotta, L. (2009). *Issue Brief. Supporting Culture Change: Working Toward Smarter State Nursing Home Regulations.* The Commonwealth Fund. 2009.

White-Chu, E.F., Graves, W.J., Godfrey, S.M., Bonner, A., and Sloane P. (2009). Beyond the medical model: the culture change revolution in long-term care. *Journal of the American Medical Directors Association,* 10(6), 370–378.

Wisconsin Coalition for Person Directed Care (2011). Wisconsin Coalition for Person Directed Care. http://www.wisconsinpdc.org.

3
Reconceptualizing Institutional Abuse: Formulating Problems and Solutions in Residential Care[1]

Diane Burns, Paula Hyde and Anne Killett

Introduction

Institutional abuse in the form of neglect, mistreatment and loss of dignity is a global problem. As populations grow older, it has become an increasingly important issue for governments in over 25 countries (CNPEA 2009). In the United Kingdom alone, there are around 6,000 registered care homes providing care for over 400,000 older people, and demand continues to grow (Laing and Buisson 2009). At the same time, abuse has been a significant problem in UK care homes. During 2009–2010, 400 regulated adult care services in England were rated as poor, with 34 care homes and 8 staffing agencies being forcibly shut down and 39 care homes closing voluntarily (CQC 2010a). Abuses related to unsafe management of medicine, lack of medical or nursing care, sanitation and insufficient staff training. A fundamental challenge is how to develop practices that enable the provision of residential care that can safely meet the individual needs of residents.

We use Rittel and Webber's (1973) work on tame (well-defined and solvable) and wicked (ill-defined and difficult to solve) problem analysis as a lens to examine the issue of institutional abuse. We draw on empirical data from a study undertaken as part of a research project to examine the institutional dynamics of respectful care and mistreatment in residential care homes for older people. We show how solutions, often informed by tame formulations of the issue, either generate alternative problems or fail to solve the problem in the long term and offer a reconceptualization of institutional abuse to illuminate its multifaceted and reoccurring wicked characteristics.

To accomplish this, we first review the emerging literature on wicked and tame problems. Then we draw on a more extensive literature that dates back to Goffman (1961), which examines the issue of service failure within institutions such as hospitals and care homes. Following the outline of the research design, an example from empirical research is presented to illuminate the wicked characteristics of institutional abuse in residential care provision. Finally, the chapter concludes by reconceptualizing institutional abuse as a wicked problem.

Problem solving and definition

The concept of wicked problems refers to resistant, complex and recurring issues that are incompletely described and seem to have competing and changing requirements (Rittel and Webber 1973). They use the term wicked 'in a meaning akin to that of "malignant" (in contrast to "benign"), or "vicious" (like a circle) or "tricky" ' (p. 160) rather than denoting ethically unacceptable (evil) problems. Rittel and Webber characterize wicked problems as those (1) with no definitive formulation, (2) an open-ended search for a solution, (3) solutions that are not 'true-or-false', but 'good-or-bad', (4) with no rules to determine the correct explanation of a problem and (5) where every wicked problem is a symptom of another problem. Thus wicked problems involve chains of events that are interlinked and interdependent in spite of their seeming to be unrelated (Conklin 2006). Solutions to one problem tend to generate new problems.

By contrast, tame problems are relatively well defined and stable, have definite stopping points (i.e. one knows when the problem is solved), have solutions that can be objectively evaluated as being right or wrong, belong to a class of similar problems that can be solved in a similar manner and have solutions that can be tried and abandoned.

In relation to the first characteristic of wicked problems – no definitive formulation – there is no definitive definition of institutional abuse (Dixon et al. 2010). Moreover, in a review of 13 public inquiry reports about institutional abuse (Killett et al. 2011), organizational features commonly associated with institutional abuse were identified. These features highlight how the problem of abuse has been formulated as if it were susceptible to definitive formulation and occurred as the result of particular issues with definitive solutions. For instance, inquiries have explained abuse as a problem of weak and ineffective management (solvable by stronger management); inappropriate and inconsistent application of guidelines and policies (solvable by a review of policies), insufficient recording keeping and monitoring (solvable by risk assessments and quality assurance mechanisms), poorly prepared staff (solvable by training); staff shortages and low morale (solvable by increased resourcing and professional development opportunities). However, the problem of institutional abuse has not responded to tame solutions and is notable in its persistence; it is also wicked in that it is commonly considered to be a symptom of other familiar sets of problems (Walshe and Higgins 2002). In addition each problem is linked to a particular recommendation and consequently a definitive formulation of the problem and solution is shown to be elusive.

We argue that institutional abuse in care homes is formulated within care homes as a tame problem requiring linear solutions. We suggest that decision makers may be tempted to treat the problem as if it is tame because each facet of the wicked problem appears reducible to a particular issue or solution.

Institutional abuse

Institutional abuse in care organizations involves repeated acts and omissions due to either the regime within the institutions or abuse perpetrated by a person(s) directed at another individual in that setting (Bennett et al. 1997). More recently UK health policy describes institutional abuse as: 'a lack of positive response to complex needs, rigid routines, inadequate staffing and an insufficient knowledge base within services' (DH/HO 2000: 12). There has been limited research into institutional abuse since Goffman's (1961) study of total institutions. Goffman identified how institutions control their members' needs en masse by bureaucratic means. He proposed that members of a total institution suffer degradation via social and physical abuses, and they are divested of their roles in life and their property. They are subjected to objectifying regimes and procedures. This historic work has been used to identify negative aspects of hospitals and care homes and to identify measures for countering adverse effects. For instance, good practice is associated with the avoidance of batch living; increasing privacy, breaking down institutional regimes and providing care for people in smaller groups (Cantley 2001). Other works examining mistreatment from multiple perspectives, interviewing people from across different groups within the elder care community, showed the effects of established organizational routine in episodes of neglectful care of residents (Wiener and Kaser-Jones 1990, Lee-Treweek 1997, Teeri et al. 2006).

While policy and regulation may deliver improved detection of institutional abuse, formulations of the problem and the solution tend to be of the tame category. We argue that institutional abuse within the contexts of residential care for older people has characteristics associated with wicked problems. Therefore, we apply the lens of wicked problem analysis in this area. Our research examined care provision in eight residential care homes for older people. After describing the research design, we outline an example of institutional abuse that had wicked characteristics.

Research design

Research context

The findings are drawn from case study research at eight care homes that provided residential and nursing care for older people in England.[2] The purposive sample ensured inclusion of care homes varying in size and sector-provider type. Inspection reports from the national regulator show three of the homes had a history of poor care quality and five had good care quality. Drawing on Eisenhardt and Graebnor (2007) comparative case study method, we examined the organization of care in these homes focusing on events, practices and processes leading to good care and to mistreatment.

Data collection

The primary data for this research was collected between November 2009 and May 2011 (following ethical approval 09/H0306/63 from the National Research Ethics Service, Cambridgeshire 3 Research Ethics Committee in October 2009). A total of 294 hours of observations of day-to-day interactions, behaviours and activities (excluding personal care of residents) were carried out. This included observations of communal areas during morning and evening shifts, night shifts and at weekends. There were semi-structured interviews with 86 members of staff and 38 residents, between 30 and 60 minutes long, 99 were digitally recorded, professionally transcribed in full and anonymized. Our formal data was complemented by frequent informal conversations with members of staff, residents and visitors to the home and a wealth of internal documents.

Data analysis

The data was analysed using a process of systematic recursive cycling (Eisenhardt and Graebnor 2007) to identify, establish and test out understandings of the relationship between organizational factors and processes and staff and resident experiences. In the following section, we present data from one care home, 'Honeysuckle Place' to illuminate how problem and solution formulated at the macro-policy level, can create new problems when implemented within the local context of the care home setting. This particular case example is not exceptional, rather it is used to examine in-depth familiar patterns of problem definition and attempted solutions. In this particular case, the problem identification centred around feeding and the solution generated problems for toileting.

Wicked problems and tame solutions

Honeysuckle Place is a two-story purpose built home, run by the local authority and provides residential care for 20 older people. In response to national care standards, the arrangements for feeding residents were changed to improve the range of choices available and to emulate a restaurant service. Although this seemed to work well, meal times had lengthened as a result and there were delays in getting residents to the toilet after meals. This meant that some residents had soiled themselves during their wait to be taken to the toilet. Consequently, residents were keen to get in the queue for the toilets after their meals to avoid any further accidents. This example is presented in detail below.

Formulating the problem and implementing solutions

One characteristic of institutions is batch living where people are grouped and treated in homogenous ways (Goffman 1961). Person-centred philosophies and models of care,[3] enshrined in health policy and regulation may, depending on the extent to which they are enacted in practice, offer a means to counter institutionalization. It has been noted recently that a common feature of poor care has been lack of adequate nutrition and consequent weight loss. In response, Governmental standards of care were introduced, which state that any resident can expect care, treatment and support that meet their needs, leading to outcomes such as choice of meals and adequate nutrition (CQC 2010b).

To this end, three years earlier, Honeysuckle Place had taken part in a local authority supported project to create a 'restaurant style' meals service designed to improve residents' dining experiences and better meet individual nutrition needs. Changes had been made to the dining room so it resembled a commercial restaurant in layout and furnishings. All the meals were freshly prepared on the premises and the menu expanded. The care staff waited on the tables at meal times, they told residents of the options on the menu and asked residents to choose. Staff took residents' orders to the service counter and a chef plated up the orders. The member of staff returned with resident's food and would usually help residents with feeding where needed. Overall residents reported that the menus were a success:

> *The dining room is quite good, it's quite modern and the staff are always on time and the meals are nice. You can fancy any of the meals on offer and I'm a fussy one over food you know. I think we're very lucky.*
>
> (Isobel Resident)

The move to the restaurant style service was also said to have had a positive impact on care beyond the immediate:

> *Quite a few members of staff left when we went to restaurant service. But it was good for them to leave, if that makes sense, because the older entrenched staff, they didn't like being waitresses basically. I think that actually helped change the culture quite a bit in the care staff group and gradually we got better people working here.*
>
> (Evie, Home Manager)

The locally designed solution appeared to create a more person-centred meals service. Moreover, problems such as an increase in staff turnover were said to have had a positive outcome. Whilst the meals were a success, the changes in arrangements lead to related problems detailed in the following section.

Wicked problem analysis

The time-consuming process of helping residents to the dining room for their meals and back to the floor where they live had become heavily routinized. The dining room was located on the ground floor and residents lived on the first floor. All 20 residents needed assistance to walk or had to be wheeled to the floor below by care staff via the use of a small lift. These activities demanded concentrated amounts of staff time. First, the lift had the capacity to accommodate only one member of staff and one resident if using a wheelchair, or two residents if using walking aides. Second, the nearest toilets to the dining room were located on the floor above. Third, organizational rules about when residents could enter and leave the dining room were firmly established.

Staff were not allowed to take residents into the dining room any earlier than 20 minutes before meals were served; and catering staff were not allowed to clear away tables and clean the dining room until all the residents had left. Consequently, staff assisted residents to use the toilets before they were taken to the dining room for meals and again after being taken back to the floor above: '*We don't start toileting until we've got them all up to the top floor because the kitchen staff have got to get on with clearing and they can't do that until all the residents have left*' (Mollie, Care Worker).

The location of the dining room on the ground floor, the reliance on one small lift, the lack of toilet facilities in the dining area and organizational rules combined to delay access to toilets around meal times. Consequently, residents tried to leave early to be near the front of the queue for the toilet. One resident who had lived in the home for several years commented about the need for residents to be ready to fit in with the routine:

> *You've got to do whatever is happening next. You've got to be ready. Now today at half past four, that's when we get started up at the top of the lounge for tea. Across in the wheelchairs they go to the toilets first, and then the people who are first, go down below to the dining room. Automatic this is and then the staff know exactly where one person and their chair will go in the dining room. And then you sit there and you wait.*

> (Reg, Resident)

More importantly perhaps, residents were acutely aware that the routine around meal times prevented them from being able to use a toilet when they needed to:

> *One of the worst things is toileting. Now we have our breakfast in the morning and our medication and then we're sat in a line and as they take you up in the lift you are set in another line in the main circle. You stay there in your chair, no toilet. You can't go until it's your turn after they've brought everybody up to the top floor. Then they decide who was first up and perhaps you're left until last because you're in a wheelchair and can't go yourself. Sometimes you're desperate if you've just had the medication you know, I find that very very difficult.*

> (Emily, Resident)

Changes to the mealtime arrangements impeded timely access to the toilet for residents, contributing to instances of neglect around toileting.

We were told by two residents that delays in being taken to the toilet after meal times had led to soiling.

While senior staff were proud of the home's restaurant style meals service, more junior individual care staff also commented on the difficulties they found with taking the residents to the toilet when they needed to go:

> *After lunch is a particular example of high demand. Everybody wants the toilet but there are only 3 staff and there are 20 residents, so somebody's got to wait. Somebody's got to be last. But everybody's like, 'oh I need to go now' and that's a really stressful time.*
>
> (Ruby, Care Worker)

Residents suggested that the problem was well known to senior staff:

> *Yes the toileting is very difficult but what can the staff do? I don't know. If we say anything to the manager she'll say 'well I'll tell them they should take you when you get to that point where you're frightened you're going to do it in your clothes. For goodness sake, take them don't leave them feeling like that.' But it's never worked. That's a very very sore point with a lot of us if we've got to sit there waiting.*
>
> (Emily, Resident)

This example was a wicked problem in the sense that it also indicated the interconnecting factors contributing to the problem: structural constraints to the architecture and facilities and strict organizational rules combined to generate new problems by encumbering the ability of staff to meet toileting needs and resulting in routinized treatment that denied residents the care they needed, when they needed it. Yet the problem of meeting residents' toileting needs was not linked to the arrangements for providing better feeding. In addition, this example illustrates another wicked characteristic of the problem as the issue was viewed differently by each set of stakeholders. The manager tried to resolve the problem by 'telling' the care staff to take the resident to the toilet. Whereas care staff identified high demands for toileting as the crux of the issue. By contrast, the residents suggested that they had little say in how their care was organized, despite having rich insights into the routine and potential for detrimental effects.

However, senior staff told us about problems arising from the 'routine' of care work for staff: *I don't think my staff have enough time to enjoy their job, a lot of it is routine* (Evie, Care Home Manager). In an attempt to address the problem of residents leaving lunch early and forming a queue to go upstairs the manager had introduced a change to the usual routine around meal times:

> *Time to sit and chat, could be for 2 minutes, just to sit and have a cup of tea or 5 minutes for staff to sit and have a cup of tea with the residents. We're trying that at the meal times, to slow meal times down.*
>
> (Evie, Care Home Manager)

Yet, junior care staff were adamant that activities to extend the lunchtime period caused more problems for them and for the residents:

> *To keep the residents at the dining table longer, the manager's introduced having cups of tea and us staff can sit and have a cup with the residents. She's hoping to last the dinner out a bit longer but they all want to go to the toilet. Then it's all rush to get them upstairs and do the toileting before you leave off duty. That cup of tea after the meal makes a heck of a lot of difference.*
>
> (Mollie, Senior Care Worker)

This attempted linear solution to improve work routines for staff and for residents was treated as if it was separable from the toileting issue. As these extracts demonstrate, a consequence of treating an issue as if it is a tame problem is that the issue is assumed to be discrete and consequently linear-type solutions tend to be proposed. Hence, the way to interrupt rigid routine is to extend the lunch time, and the way to increase interaction is to allow staff to sit down with residents and have a cup of tea. Paradoxically, this increased the necessity for staff to take a more en masse task-based approach to providing care in the time available.

Reconceptualizing institutional abuse

The example we elaborate was not recognized to constitute institutional abuse by managers and other staff members. Moreover, when problems were detected, explanations and responses did not link to other interconnecting components of care provision, so solutions focused on the immediate issue at hand. Consequently, rather than being able to determine whether the correct explanation of the problem had been reached, we argue that, in practice no rules for checking solutions were present. This is how tame solutions aimed at improving care provision can generate problems in other areas. The meal-time solution enhanced a person-centred approach to nutrition with positive impacts for residents at the same time as it encumbered personal care, with detrimental outcomes for residents.

Whilst we recognize that some problems in care quality will be easily solved with no consequential problem development, we argue that institutional abuse has wicked characteristics: it is relatively difficult to define, there are no rules to determine the correct explanation of the problem, it cannot be easily separated into discrete parts nor easily controlled using conventional methods (Grint 2005, Conklin 2006). In Honeysuckle Place, there was no consensus found among staff, managers and residents over what was the best method to solve the problem of toileting, rather conflicting views of the issue were identified. Wiener and Kayser-Jones (1990) showed key differences in the perspectives of doctors, staff and relatives about the problems of care provision in care homes. Despite the different perspectives, each group was argued to be contributing to a downward spiral of care as their powerlessness to change care provision resulted in apathy and the acceptance of poor care standards. Although apathy can be a feature associated with poor care provision, the findings of our study suggest, in the words of Rittel and Webber, more 'malignant', 'vicious' and 'tricky' phenomena are at play (1973: 160).

Notes

1. This chapter is a shortened and adapted version of the paper Burns, D., Hyde, P. and Killett. A. (forthcoming) Wicked problems or wicked people? Reconceptualising institutional abuse. *Sociology of Health and Illness* doi: 10.1111/j.1467-9566.2012.01511.x published by Wiley Blackwell.
2. This study was funded by the Department of Health and Comic Relief (grant number PR-AN-0608-1022). The views expressed in this chapter are not necessarily the views of the Department of Health and Comic Relief.
3. Under Person Centred Care, Standard 2 of the National Service Framework for Older People, people should be treated as individuals and receive appropriate and timely care that meets their needs (SAP 2006).

References

Bennett, G., Kingston, P., and Penhale, B. (1997) *The Dimensions of Elder Abuse: Perspectives for Practitioners*. Basingstoke: Macmillan.
Cantley, L. (2001) Understanding people in organisations, in Cantley, L. (Ed.) *A Handbook of Dementia Care*. Milton Keynes: Open University Press, pp. 220–239.

Canadian Network for the Prevention of Elder Abuse. (2009) In The News. www. cnpea.ca/senior_abuse_in_the_news.htm (last accessed June 13, 2012).

Care Quality Commission (CQC) (2010a) *The State of Care 2009/10*. London: Care Quality Commission.

Conklin, J. (2006) *Dialogue Mapping: Building Shared Understanding of Wicked Problems*. West Sussex, England: Wiley & Sons.

CQC. (2010b) *Guidance about Compliance: Summary of Regulations, Outcomes and Judgement Framework*. London: Care Quality Commission.

Department of Health and Home Office. (2000) *No Secrets: Guidance on Developing and Implementing Multi-Agency Policies and Procedures to Protect Vulnerable Adults from Abuse*. London: Department of Health.

Dixon, J., Manthorpe, J., Biggs, S., Mowlam, A., Tinker, A., and McCreadie, C. (2010) Defining elder mistreatment: reflections on the United Kingdom study of abuse and neglect of older people, *Aging and Society*, 30, 3, 403–420.

Eisenhardt, K. and Graebnor, M. (2007) Theory building from cases: opportunities and challenges, *Academy of Management Journal*, 50, 1, 25–32.

Goffman, E. (1961) *Asylums: Essays on the Social Situation of Mental Patients and Other Inmates*. New York: Anchor Books.

Grint, K. (2005) Problems, problems, problems: the social construction of 'leadership', *Human Relations*, 58, 11, 1467–1494.

Killett, A., Burns, D., Hyde, P., Poland, F., Gray, R., and Kenkmann, A. (2011) *Organisational Dynamics of Respect and Elder Care*. A report prepared for the Department of Health and Comic Relief. London: Department of Health.

Laing and Buisson. (2009) *Occupied places in April 2009. Care of Elderly People: UK Market Survey 2009*. London: Laing & Buisson.

Lee-Treweek, G. (1997) Women, resistance and care: an ethnographic study of nursing auxiliary work, *Work, Employment and Society*, 11, 1, 47–63.

Rittel, H. and Webber, M. (1973) Dilemmas in a general theory of planning, *Policy Sciences*, 4, 155–169.

Teeri, S., Leino-Kilpi, H., and Välimäki, M. (2006) Long-term nursing care of elderly people: Identifying ethically problematic experiences among patients, relatives and nurses in Finland. *Nursing Ethics*, 13, 2, 116–129.

Walshe, K. and Higgins, J. (2002) The use and impact of inquiries in the NHS. *British Medical Journal*, 325, 895–900.

Wiener, C.L. and Kayser-Jones, J. (1990) The uneasy fate of nursing home residents: an organizational-interaction perspective, *Sociology of Health and Illness*, 12, 1, 84–104.

4

The Place of Patient-Centred Care in Medical Professional Culture: A Qualitative Study

Wendy Lipworth, Miles Little, Jill Gordon, Pippa Markham and Ian Kerridge

Background and rationale

Patient-centred care (PCC) has been defined in many ways over the past three decades. Core components of patient-centred care have been identified as: respect for patient preferences and values; emotional support; physical comfort; information, communication and education; continuity and transition; coordination of care; involvement of the family and friends and access to care (Epstein and Street, 2011). The first of these – respect for patients' needs and preferences – has emerged as the most consistent element among the many definitions of patient-centred care (Luxford et al., 2011). This, in turn, entails facilitating patients' involvement in their own care by sharing information with patients, exploring patients' perspectives and values, helping with decision-making, facilitating access to care and enabling patients to follow through with behavioural changes (Epstein et al., 2010).

Advocates of patient-centred care argue that the principles of PCC should not only be understood and respected by practising clinicians but they also need to be part of clinical cultures (Luxford et al., 2011). In this regard, concerns have been raised that the process of enculturation during medical education works against the development of a patient-centred medical culture by encouraging detachment, self-interest and objectivity among students (Coulehan and Williams, 2003). The concern is that some students might be able to resist the forces that undermine patient-centredness, but others adopt a 'technical', 'non-reflective' (Coulehan and Williams, 2003) or even cynically disengaged (White et al., 2009) stance.

While the process of enculturation during clinical training is important, ultimately what matters is whether or not practising clinicians inhabit a patient-centred culture. We know that, when asked directly, clinicians tend to espouse patient-centredness and believe that they themselves engage in PCC, within the bounds of various professional constraints and organizational, personal and patient-derived limitations such as lack of resources and leadership, lack of skill and time and difficulties in communicating with certain groups of patients (Tufano et al., 2008). There is, however, some empirical evidence that health professionals defining PCC actually adopt a model in which professional priorities determine patients' needs (Gillespie et al., 2004) and that adopting a patient-centred ideology can threaten clinicians' sense of status in relation to patients and colleagues (O'Flynn and Britten, 2006).

While this research is helpful, it is limited because doctors' espoused stance towards patient-centred care, whether positive or negative, might not accord with their actual (personal and cultural) values. Similarly, definitions of PCC provided to research participants might differ from the ways in which patient-centred care is actually understood – which is highly likely given the broad variety of definitions of PCC. An alternative approach, which we pursue in this chapter, is to ask practising doctors to describe their values in general terms, and then to 'read for' themes that might reflect a patient-centred culture (or lack thereof). As part of a qualitative study of clinicians' values, we therefore, 'read for' statements that appeared to be related to PCC, with a view to determining whether and how patient-centredness played out in our participants' narratives. We emphasize that we did not ask specifically about patient-centredness, but rather allowed relevant statements to emerge from the data.

Method

In this study, medical doctors associated with the Sydney Medical School were invited to reflect upon the ways in which values matter in their practices and their educational experiences. Interviews were semi-structured, with participants encouraged to reflect on episodes in their careers that had stayed in their minds because of their moral dimensions. They were also asked to talk about specific issues such as the cost of healthcare, the availability of health services, the appropriateness of the medical education programme that they had received or were teaching, the place of evidence and research in medical education and practice, and the impact of role models and mentors. Interviews were conducted by a medical doctor and a psychologist, either together or separately. All interviews were anonymized with coded numbers used for each participant. Ethical clearances were obtained from the University of Sydney. We have withheld detailed demographic details of each doctor to protect anonymity. There were 7 women and 13 men. Ages ranged from 28 to 76 (median 49), and years since graduation from 3 to 52 (median 26). Specialties included general practice, internal medicine, surgery, ophthalmology, radiation oncology, psychiatry, emergency medicine, paediatrics and public health.

Transcripts were thematically coded for statements relating to patient-centredness. We did not attempt to define patient-centredness narrowly as our aim was to be inclusive and open to meanings that might not be captured in formal definitions. Any statements that related to knowing patients, respecting patients and involving patients (as individuals or communities) in medical decision-making were therefore included in our analysis. We were interested primarily in patient-centred clinical decision-making, and so we did not read our data for other form of patient-centred care such as emotional and physical support, access and continuity of care. We categorized the emergent themes into more abstract concepts, using constant comparison and reformulation of research questions and theories (Morse, 1994). Agreement about themes, codes and categories were reached at regular meetings of the research group.

Results

None of our participants spontaneously used the phrase 'patient-centred care', but statements relating to patient-centred care were numerous and emerged almost invariably when participants were asked for their views about evidence-based medicine (EBM). Indeed, questions about EBM seemed to trigger responses that were as much about patient-centredness as they were about evidence. Patient-centredness was thus very closely related, in our participants' minds, to medical knowledge, and our participants seemed to recognize two, coexisting and intertwined forms of medical knowledge: bioknowledge – knowledge about the body – that draws upon many different forms of observational and experimental (including epidemiological) data, clinical experience and clinical anecdote and lifeworld knowledge – which is knowledge of the experience of being human and imbedded in cultural, social and personal contexts (Husserl, 1985; Habermas, 1992). In such a schema, our participants associated bioknowledge with EBM, while lifeworld knowledge (in combination with bioknowledge) was seen as the basis of patient-centred care.

The results are organized as follows: first we demonstrate that, while our participants were advocates of bioknowledge and EBM, they recognized its limitations. Next we illustrate the importance to our participants of certain elements of PCC, which took two forms: communicating bioknowledge and balancing bioknowledge with lifeworld knowledge. We conclude by showing that our participants were aware of the challenges associated with the communication aspects of patient-centredness, but nonetheless expected it of themselves and others.

1. Bioknowledge and EBM are important but have their limitations

All of our participants expressed at least some support for bioknowledge and EBM:

> **P8:** *Well I think it's one of the great revolutions of medical practice. I think it's truly Copernican in its scope; that is the focus has gone from the doctor in the centre of the universe, to evidence guiding practice.*

Bioknowledge, as encoded in EBM, was seen as a powerful validating attribute of medical discourse and as a necessary qualification to enter the community of medical practitioners:

> **P11:** *And so if you want people to come and see us with real or difficult problems, then they're going to have to trust the system, and anything that breaks down that trust is a problem for the profession. In answer to your question about evidence based medicine, I think it makes a valuable contribution to the quality and status of medicine.*

But while bioknowledge and EBM were strongly supported by our participants, they also posed problems for many, simply because of probabilistic outputs and the persistent doubt that data derived from epidemiological studies or clinical trials would apply to the care of individual patients:

> **P3:** *So I now think … the pendulum is a little too far the other way, in that people feel a slave to guidelines. And people in clinical trials fulfil a certain profile, and the individual in front of you often does, but sometimes doesn't.*

And so I find that knowledge of clinical trials tempered by the individual factors, is not an easy equation.

2. Patient-centredness in communication is important

In their talk, participants tended to reflect upon the importance of two (related) kinds of patient-centredness as it relates to decision-making: (a) communicating bioknowledge and (b) balancing bioknowledge with lifeworld knowledge.

(a) Communicating bioknowledge

First, participants emphasized the importance of communicating bioknowledge, in the form of statistics, to patients so that patients were aware of existing data, were cognisant of the limitations of this (or any) data and were more able to participate in shared decision-making:

> *P10: I think it's fair to tell a patient that these are your options, these are the figures, these are the issues, and each individual circumstance is slightly different.*

The process of communicating bioknowledge was, however, acknowledged to be an art in itself:

> *P5: You don't want to just give people a whole list of statistics because I guess the art is trying to use the evidence or the science, and tailor it to that particular situation.*

(b) Balancing bioknowledge with lifeworld knowledge

Without exception, the participants in this study emphasized the importance of incorporating lifeworld knowledge into their clinical decision-making. This included allowing patients to define for themselves what constituted a medical problem, and how such problems should be diagnosed and treated. In each example that follows, the key role of doctor–patient and patient–doctor communication is very clear:

> *P1: You have people come in with menstrual problems in their forties, and they don't know that it's quite normal and it's very common. And it's okay... to say to them 'well actually... a lot of people do go through*

this, it's up to you to what extent that's impairing your quality of life so much that you want to do something about it' – at that point it becomes a medical issue, but it doesn't have to be.

P9: ...it was a lovely woman who had metastatic breast cancer...I thought she would be suitable for this trial that I was doing of chemotherapy, and I thought in three months, six months or some time, that would happen. And as it turned out, she never had chemotherapy...because of choice she just chose not to have it...So it was interesting that I spent a lot of time with her and her family, and talked to her a lot, and put a lot of, effort is not the right word, but it was a lot of thought and stuff.

The goal of incorporating lifeworld knowledge into the clinical encounter was not to replace EBM with lifeworld knowledge, but rather to find some way of balancing the two in clinical decision-making:

P9: I think drawing that EBM picture with the evidence and the person's circumstances and their preferences ...I think that's actually quite a good model. And I think the thing is, the less compelling or clear the high-quality research is, the more influential the patient's values and things become...and so the more finely balanced that decision, the greater the extent of the person's kind of philosophy and attitudes and things.

3. Patient-centredness is important, but difficult to achieve

It was, however, recognized that lifeworld knowledge may be simply unattainable in some contexts because of the cultural gap between patient and doctor. P10, an oncologist, described how much easier it was to invoke lifeworld knowledge when dealing with an educated, English-speaking patient than with someone with whom communication was difficult:

P10: ...The other patient I saw was a 79-year-old Indian gentleman, who had a very, very high risk prostate cancer...Now his English was marginal, his son was interpreting, but his son's understanding wasn't great: 'There's cancer there Doc'. And in the end, I just said 'this is the treatment we recommend....And I made the executive decision that if I tried to explain the pros and cons and the issues, far too complex. So occasionally I'll make executive decisions, and do what I think is best.

It was also recognized that some doctors are better than others at eliciting lifeworld knowledge and incorporating it into their clinical decisions. Some people were seen to be particularly good at learning and deploying bioknowledge/EBM, while others were seen to be more skilled at knowing and understanding their patients and deploying lifeworld knowledge/PCC:

> *P15: Um, I guess there are people who probably know all the facts and probably all the different chemical pathways in the body, and would probably be able to quote any sort of thing out of a textbook.*

> *P9: there was a guy called Dr B, who was a very old world general physician... and had this completely implausible ability to remember the personal details of all his patients... and it just used to astound me how much he knew about their kind of personal experiences and idiosyncrasies and things.*

Doctors were, however, expected to master and deploy both their bioknowledge and their lifeworld knowledge with skill, relevance and sensitivity, even if they were better at one than the other. Failure to at least make the effort was viewed with severe disapproval:

> *P15: I think you need both. I think everybody has a bit of both, then obviously there are some that lean more one way than the other. And I think they've both got their virtues, you can't really say the perfect person would have more of one feature than the other. People with more science are often good at what they're doing, and the ones with more of an arty background succeed in what they're doing, it's different styles. I don't think I could say one is better than the other.*

> *P9: I remember when I was training there was a particular person that I found particularly annoying... basically it was somebody who I thought didn't really take their responsibilities very seriously. So with the difficult decision, whereas the appropriate response might have been 'look this is difficult, there are pluses or minuses, your views and values are going to be really important in making this decision, what do you think about it?' That might be the right thing to say, but this person would say 'well you tell me what you're going to do.' And I saw it was like a perversion of the shared decision-making model.*

Discussion

This study provides insights into the current status of patient-centred medicine, as it relates to patient involvement in decision-making, from the perspective of doctors.

Our participants did not need to be prompted to speak about PCC and, although none used the specific phrase, all described patient-centred values and practices. This suggests that patient-centredness is part of the professional culture of medicine – that is, it is one of the profession's 'shared basic assumptions... that has worked well enough to be considered valid and, therefore, to be taught to new members as the correct way to perceive, think and feel...' (Schein, 1992, p.12). While our participants did not use the phrase 'patient-centred care', this is to be expected as shared cultural understandings are often unstated (Martin, 2002).

On reflection, it is not surprising that patient centredness should be an integral part of medical professional culture. After all, the idea that medicine cannot be reduced simply to appropriate prescribing and good surgical technique is evident from the earliest writings about medicine to the present day. Values-based medicine (Fulford, 2011), narrative medicine (Charon, 2001), culturally competent medicine (Hasnain-Wynia, 2006), humanistic medicine (Little, 1995), person-centred medicine (Fulford, 2011) and a host of others have been proposed as alternatives to a narrow, reductionist approach to medicine. Even patient-centred care itself now has a long history. Michael Balint is believed to have introduced the term in the 1950s (Balint, 1957), and it has been in use ever since.

Patient-centred medicine was discussed most frequently in the context of discussions about EBM. This suggests that the idea of patient-centredness is deeply embedded in the culture as part of its epistemic value system and its pragmatically acquired and applied 'social knowledge' (Hakli, 2007). It is interesting to note, however, that EBM and patient-centred medicine, while both clearly part of the social knowledge of the medical profession, were viewed by our participants as separate concepts – one based on bioknowledge and the other on lifeworld knowledge. This suggests that, despite EBM's avowed inclusion of patient values, narrative, clinical expertise and so on (Sackett et al., 2000), EBM has generally preserved its association with epidemiology and biostatistics; qualitative knowledge of preferences and values was set apart. Our participants, despite retaining a narrow definition of EBM, freely and proudly gave lifeworld knowledge a place alongside bioknowledge. This suggests that practising doctors do not view EBM as an exclusive discourse, pitched against other, supposedly inferior, forms of medical knowledge and practice. Viewed this way, it seems that some of the concerns about medical dominance, hegemony and resistance to change (Jones, 2004) might be overly simplistic, for medicine is at once person-centred, culturally grounded, values-based and reliant on different conceptions of 'evidence'.

Whether and how this understanding and appreciation of patient-centredness translates into actual practice is a separate question, given that culture refers not only to behaviour but also to what guides behaviour (Alvesson and Sveningsson, 2008). But these findings do at least suggest patient-centredness is already a part of medical culture and that further education alone may not address whatever gaps exist between culture-in-theory and culture-in-practice. In other words, clinicians already possess the knowledge and values required for patient-centred practice. If it is true that doctors, for the most part, both understand and value patient-centredness, then it follows that advocates of increased patient-centredness will need to address organizational and structural barriers to its enactment rather than (just) educating health professionals regarding its merits. Steps will need to be taken not so much to convince doctors to be patient-centred and explain to them what it means, but rather to ensure that they have the resources, support and time to practise it and recognition for doing so. The fact that what is required are systemic and structural reforms, rather than cultural change, is both reassuring and challenging. Reassuring because changing culture is difficult and challenging because systemic change requires both resources and political will (Braithwaite et al., 2010).

Acknowledgement

This study was supported by a grant for values-based medicine research awarded by the Sydney Medical School Foundation, University of Sydney.

References

Alvesson, M. and S. Sveningsson (2008) *Changing Organizational Culture. Cultural Change Work in Progress* (New York: Routledge).

Balint, M. (1957) *The Doctor, His Patient and the Illness* (London: Pitman Medical).

Braithwaite, J., P. Hyde, C. Pope (2010) *Culture and Climate in Health Care Organizations* (London: Palgrave Macmillan).

Charon, R. (2001) 'Narrative medicine: A model for empathy, reflection, profession, and trust.' *Journal of the American Medical Association* 286(15): 1897–1902.

Coulehan, J. and P. Williams (2003) 'Conflicting professional values in medical education.' *Cambridge Quarterly of Health Care Ethics* 12: 7–20.

Epstein, R., K. Fiscella, L. Lesser (2010) 'Why the nation needs a policy push on patient-centered care.' *Health Affairs* 29: 1489–1495.

Epstein, R.M. and R.L. Street, Jr (2011) 'The values and value of patient-centered care.' *The Annals of Family Medicine* 9(2): 100–103.

Fulford, K. (2011) 'Bringing together values-based and evidence-based medicine: UK Department of Health Initiatives in the "Personalization" of care.' *Journal of Evaluation in Clinical Practice* 17(2): 341–343.

Gillespie, R., D. Florin, S. Gillam (2004) 'How is patient-centred care understood by the clinical, managerial and lay stakeholders responsible for promoting this agenda?' *Health Expectations* 7(2): 142–148.

Habermas, J. (1992) *Moral Consciousness and Communicative Action* (Cambridge: Polity Press).

Hakli, R. (2007) 'On the possibility of group knowledge without belief.' *Social Epistemology* 21(3): 249–266.

Hasnain-Wynia, R. (2006) 'Is evidence-based medicine patient-centered and is patient-centered care evidence-based?' *Health Services Research* 41(1): 1–8.

Husserl, E. (1985) *The Crisis of European Sciences and Transcendental Phenomenology* (United States: Northwestern University Press).

Jones, R.K. (2004) 'Schism and heresy in the development of orthodox medicine: The threat to medical hegemony.' *Social Science and Medicine* 58(4): 703–712.

Little, M. (1995) *Humane Medicine* (Cambridge: Cambridge University Press).

Luxford, K., D.G. Safran, T. Delbanco (2011) 'Promoting patient-centered care: A qualitative study of facilitators and barriers in healthcare organizations with a reputation for improving the patient experience.' *International Journal for Quality in Health Care* 23(5): 510–515.

Martin, J. (2002) *Organizational Culture. Mapping the Terrain* (Thousand Oaks, CA: Sage Publications).

Morse, J.M. (1994) *Critical Issues in Qualitative Research Methods* (Thousand Oaks, CA: Sage Publications).

O'Flynn, N. and N. Britten (2006) 'Does the achievement of medical identity limit the ability of primary care practitioners to be patient-centred? A qualitative study.' *Patient Education and Counseling* 60(1): 49–56.

Sackett, D.L., S. Straus, W. Richardson, W. Rosenberg, R. Haynes (2000) *Evidence-Based Medicine: How to Practice and Teach EBM* (New York: Churchill Livingstone).

Schein, E. (1992) *Organizational Culture and Leadership* (San Francisco: Jossey-Bass).

Tufano, J.T., J.D. Ralston, D. Martin (2008) 'Providers' experience with an organizational redesign initiative to promote patient-centered access: A qualitative study.' *Journal of General Internal Medicine* 23(11): 1778–1783.

White, C.B., A.K. Kumagai, P. Ross, J. Fantone (2009) 'A qualitative exploration of how the conflict between the formal and informal curriculum influences student values and behaviors.' *Academic Medicine* 84(5): 597–603.

Part II

Coordinating for Patient-Centred Care

5
Capacity for Care: Meta-Ethnography of Acute Care Nurses' Experiences of the Nurse–Patient Relationship

Jackie Bridges, Caroline Nicholson, Jill Maben, Catherine Pope, Mary Flatley, Charlotte Wilkinson, Julienne Meyer and Maria Tziggili

Introduction

This chapter reports findings of a meta-ethnography of published qualitative research on nurses' experiences of nurse–patient relationships in acute settings, reported in detail in Bridges et al. (2012a). Concerns are growing that modern healthcare delivery is lacking in compassion and is failing to provide the individualized care required by, for instance, older people with complex needs (Firth-Cozens and Cornwell, 2009). Promoting meaningful connections with patients in which practitioners see each patient 'as a person to be engaged with rather than a body to do things to' (Nicholson et al., 2010, p. 12) requires nurses and others to be able to articulate and appreciate the nature of these connections and their impact on patient outcomes, along with an understanding of the factors that can promote or inhibit therapeutic relationships. Nurses and nursing are now often portrayed as lacking in compassion and being distracted from these aspects of care (Flatley and Bridges, 2008). A range of high-profile reports in the United Kingdom into the quality of in-patient care for older people suggest that many of the reported problems centre on a lack of humanity in hospital staff, particularly nurses. While good practice does exist, we understand little about the conditions in which high-quality, compassionate in-patient care is delivered. Insight into nurses' experiences as they engage with patients is therefore critical to understand how best to support existing good practice and to focus service improvement initiatives. This focus is of particular importance in acute settings where patient throughput, service configuration and staffing patterns reduce contact time between staff and patients. In addition, we lack understanding about how nurse–patient relationships, the act of caring and engagement in therapeutic relationships impact on nurses themselves.

There are an increasing number of primary qualitative studies relevant to this topic, but a systematic overview of this work has not been previously conducted. This chapter uses meta-ethnography to integrate findings from qualitative research studies focused on nurses' experiences of the nurse–patient relationship in acute in-patient hospital settings.

Methods

Synthesis was conducted using the meta-ethnographic method described by Noblit and Hare (1988), and a full description of methods used can be found in Bridges et al. (2012a). This meta-ethnography aimed to provide the deeper insight needed into nurse–patient relationships by synthesizing research that explores the experiences of nurses in these relationships. Systematic search and quality appraisal procedures were used to ensure a final sample of items that were conceptually rich and potentially able to make a contribution. Synthesis began with repeated readings of the studies to identify key categories and to determine relationships between individual studies. A list of key categories was thus generated and used as the basis for comparing and sorting interpretations, and then integrating these within a new ('third-order') interpretation that applies across the studies, referred to as a 'line-of-argument' (Noblit and Hare, 1988).

Results

Eighteen papers reporting 16 unique studies were included in the synthesis. Eight studies were set in critical care. Six were set on general ward settings (medical, surgical, cancer, care for older people) and two included nurses from critical care and general settings. Twelve had a sample that included nurses with 10 or more years of nursing experience, one focused on newly qualified nurses and three did not specify experience. All the studies used qualitative interviews as the sole form of data collection.

The synthesis produced a line-of-argument which stated that nurses' capacity to build and sustain therapeutic relationships with patients is strongly influenced by the organizational conditions at a unit level; the organizational conditions in critical care units enhance nurses' capacity, while the conditions on general wards appear to inhibit nurses' capacity to build therapeutic nurse–patient relationships. This line-of-argument is illustrated through the third-order construct: influence of setting on capacity for caring, and builds on three second-order constructs identified through the synthesis (nurses' characterizations of relationships, relationship-building strategies, emotional impact on nurses). The second-order constructs are summarized here first.

Nurse–patient relationships (characterizations and strategies)

The synthesis findings enabled an overview of how nurses characterize their relationships with patients and the strategies they employ to build relationships with patients. Nurses in the individual studies consistently reflected characterizations of nurse–patient relationships as therapeutic or potentially therapeutic through the potential to support informed decision-making and treatment-response assessment; to provide the medium through which tailored care, comfort and support is provided; to guide and support patient decision-making; to reconcile differing perspectives between patient, family and professionals and to act as patient advocate.

In addition to nurses perceiving the relationship as therapeutic and as the medium for the delivery of high-quality care, the findings also reflected a range of strategies used by nurses to build relationships with patients. The studies consistently reflect that nurses aspire to make meaningful connections with patients, to gain a thorough knowledge of individual patients and their personal characteristics and to involve patients and families in a meaningful way in decisions made. These aspirations for a therapeutic relationship held true across studies that include different clinical settings and nurses with varied professional experience.

> You can make a difference for the patient when you take into account what they are experiencing and perhaps what it means to be them. So I try to get as close as I can.
>
> (Hawley and Jensen, 2007, p. 666)

Emotional impact on nurses

In addition to nurses' characterizations of and strategies for building nurse–patient relationships, a number of the primary studies reported on the emotional impact for nurses of being in the nurse–patient relationship. If nurses are able to deliver care of a quality that matches their personal aspiration and that is seen as the best for that patient, they experience feelings of gratification, personal enrichment and privilege.

> When the patient dies, you do feel a sense of loss. I enjoyed being a part of the process… You need and you want to be part of that experience.
>
> (Calvin et al., 2007, p. 145)

However, if nurses are not able to meet their aspirations, they experience guilt, regret and frustration.

> I heard he (the patient) had died earlier on the Sunday morning and I personally found that very difficult… hard that I hadn't told him he was dying, which he asked me to, I hadn't been there when he was dying, which I felt, I might have liked to have been, or to have some part of it, and that my last interaction was, I was too busy to stop.
>
> (Quinn, 2003, p.169)

The findings from this synthesis affirm findings from individual primary studies that nurses perceive a therapeutic potential to the nurse–patient relationship and that the degree to which the relationship can be achieved can have a strong emotional impact on nurses.

Influence of clinical setting on capacity to care

This final section of the findings introduces a novel line-of-argument that nurses' capacity to build and sustain therapeutic relationships with patients is strongly influenced by the organizational conditions at unit level. This line-of-argument is illustrated through an analysis of the influence of setting on capacity for caring and builds on three second-order constructs identified in the previous sections.

Studies reviewed reflected a range of factors perceived by nurses as influencing their ability to form a therapeutic relationship with patients, including nurses' and patients' personal characteristics, but organizational factors beyond the control of the individual nurse were the primary influence identified. A clear contrast was identified between the perceptions of capacity of nurses in critical care settings and general settings, indicating that the nature of the clinical setting is a key determinant of nurses' capacity to build and sustain therapeutic relationships with patients.

For nurses working in critical care settings, the most common issue reported related to the doctor's superior role in the team hierarchy. Nurses reflected that they do not always share the same goals for patient care that the doctors hold, with doctors often focusing solely on the curative aspects of treatment. Nurses saw their role as helping doctors understand what suffering and symptoms mean to individual patients and relatives but reported that doctors did not always accept nurses' judgements and overruled their views (Table 5.1). This issue reflects that critical care nurses often can and do form sufficiently close relationships with patients to feel able to act as their advocates in treatment decisions but that the relationship with medical colleagues determined whether or not this advocacy role could be realized. Following a situation where a physician sited an intravenous cannula into a patient's arm against her clearly expressed wish, a nurse in Gutierrez's (2005) study reflects that not acting as the patient's advocate had a deleterious impact on her relationship with the patient:

> It all happened very quickly. It wasn't until after the look crossed her face that I realized how violated she felt...It was a time when I should have been the patient's advocate and I wasn't on my toes, I didn't realize what was going on. And the loss of trust with that patient...in me. She looked at me when he left and wrote on her (communication) board 'How could you let that happen?' She never fully trusted me again after that...It's something you knew down here, in your gut. It was an awful loss.
>
> (Gutierrez, 2005, p. 234)

By contrast, general ward nurses commonly reflected a lack of capacity to form therapeutic relationships with patients (Table 5.1). Key issues reported here were lack of time and a lack of organizational value attributed to nurse–patient relationships. These issues related to the level and acuity of nursing work coupled with inadequate staffing and

Table 5.1   What does the synthesis add?

How does the clinical setting influence nurses' capacity for caring?
Critical care nurses frustrated that their intimate knowledge of the patient did not influence physician treatment plan (Halcomb et al., 2004; Gutierrez, 2005; De Bal et al., 2006; Hov et al., 2007).

Critical care nurses more likely to report moral distress associated with contributing to unnecessary suffering (Söderberg, 1999; Hopkinson et al., 2003; Halcomb et al., 2004; Gutierrez, 2005; De Bal et al., 2006; Calvin et al., 2007; Hov et al., 2007).

Nurses on general wards more likely to report frustrations in building and sustaining relationships (Söderberg, 1999; Eriksson and Saveman, 2002; Hopkinson and Hallett, 2002; Quinn, 2003; Wilkin and Slevin, 2004; Nordam et al., 2005; Nolan, 2006, 2007; Mackintosh, 2007).

Nurses on general wards more likely to report lack of time to build relationships (Söderberg, 1999; Eriksson and Saveman, 2002; Hopkinson and Hallett, 2002; Quinn, 2003; Wilkin and Slevin, 2004; Nordam et al., 2005; Mackintosh, 2007; Nolan, 2007).

Nurses on general wards report lack of organizational value attributed to building relationships (Eriksson and Saveman, 2002; Nordam et al., 2005; Nolan, 2006, 2007; Mackintosh, 2007).

Nurses on general wards report moral distress associated with patient autonomy being constrained (Eriksson and Saveman, 2002; Nolan, 2006).

Nurses on general wards more likely to report active disengagement from nurse–patient relationship (see below) (Eriksson and Saveman, 2002; Hopkinson and Hallett, 2002; Nordam et al., 2005; Nolan, 2006, 2007; Mackintosh, 2007).

Disengagement from the nurse–patient relationship
Avoiding over-involvement with patients (Hopkinson et al., 2003; De Bal et al., 2006; Nolan, 2006, 2007)

Reluctance to return to work (Gutierrez, 2005)

Being a different person at work (Mackintosh, 2007)

Avoiding certain patients and families (Gutierrez, 2005)

Reluctance to care for patients at all (Gutierrez, 2005)

Block out feelings/try to forget (Hov et al., 2007)

Frustrated aspirations lead to stress, burnout, patient abuse (Nordam et al., 2005)

Ignoring patients (Eriksson and Saveman, 2002)

---

appeared to be particularly associated to patients with complex needs such as older patients and patients with dementia.

> What we lack is the possibility to sit down and to figure out, in a reasonable way, how to best help and treat the demented patient. But it can't be done here in an acute ward, we have our routines and everything is already fixed. We just have to carry on to make the work run as smoothly as possible. There isn't any time for solving conflicts. Instead you find yourself running away from them. Nor do we have the time to find out how to behave towards the demented person.
> (Eriksson and Saveman, 2002, p. 82)

On the general wards, organizational value was attributed to maintaining 'fixed' 'routines' (Eriksson and Saveman, 2002, p. 82) at the expense of attending to complex patient needs.

> Talking to patients is important. But there has to be opportunities to communicate, and that is the problem. As a nurse, you feel ill at ease with that lack of time. You would like to spend some time with that patient, but you are hindered. It is a 'lack of being' instead of a lack of time. You aren't able to be there for your patient.
> (De Bal et al., 2006, p. 594)

This lack of support for caring activities appears linked with individual nurses choosing not to employ the strategies identified as being required to build a therapeutic relationship but to employ instead strategies to actively disengage from the nurse–patient relationship in order to protect themselves (Table 5.1). The need to use these strategies is linked with a reduced capacity for caring and was more commonly reported in general ward settings. For instance, Mackintosh (2007) found that nurses working in surgical areas developed coping mechanisms as their professional experience grew, the most common of which was 'ability to switch off' (p. 986). Nurses reported developing a work persona that included switching off/withdrawal, loss of caring beyond a certain acceptable level and depersonalization of individuals and situations.

> I think it is like a plastic shield that you put up, and I think if you stick at it long enough, and you're in the job long enough, it becomes a natural way.
> (Mackintosh, 2007, p. 986)

Other studies reflected this disengagement:

> At the same time as we face the suffering we try to roll down our blinds. It is very brutal. If I am to cope with this and not distress myself, I have to forget it.
>
> (Hov et al., 2007, p. 207)

> It's a good thing if you can make the patient take a sedative after lunch, then they'll hopefully sleep until the evening meal and I'll have time to do my job and report to the evening staff in peace and quiet.
>
> (Eriksson and Saveman, 2002, p. 81)

Across the studies and regardless of setting, nurses described the main source of their emotional support as informal support from nursing colleagues. Few studies mentioned the existence of more formal support services and, where they did exist, nurses tended not to see them as helpful.

In summary, the synthesis findings (summarized in Table 5.2) reflect that, while nurses share an aspiration for a therapeutic relationship with patients, the organizational setting at a unit level can strongly influence

Table 5.2   Synthesis, including second- and third-order interpretations

Categories	Second-order interpretations	Third-order interpretations
Nurses' characterizations of relationships with patients Nurses' strategies to build relationships with patients Emotional impact of relationship on nurses Influencing factors	(a) Relationships are therapeutic or potentially therapeutic to the patient; (b) Nurses identify particular strategies that promote relationship: unique position, intimate knowledge, being 'present', nature of engagement; (d) Degree to which aspirations can be met . dictates emotional impact: moral distress/satisfaction	(c) Some nurses use strategies to limit their emotional engagement with patients if their capacity to care is constrained by organizational conditions (e) Organizational conditions at unit level strongly influence nurses' capacity to build and sustain therapeutic relationships

nurses' capacity to build and sustain such relationships. The findings also show that nurses working in organizational conditions that inhibit their capacity to care may then employ self-protection strategies which may further reduce their caring capacity.

Discussion

The synthesis identified three second-order constructs and one third-order construct – the influence of setting on capacity for caring. The findings reflect that nurses aspire to an emotionally intimate therapeutic relationship with patients, that they attempt particular strategies to ensure that these relationships are therapeutic and that the degree to which their aspirations can be realized can have a strong emotional impact on nurses. These findings closely match the nursing mandate or contribution repeatedly advanced by and for the nursing profession over the past 25 years or so (Dingwall and Allen, 2001). They offer a reassuring message that counters concerns within the profession and among the general public that nurses are not as compassionate as they were in the past. These findings help us better understand that nurses also benefit from developing and sustaining therapeutic relationships with patients, and this is an important finding in a context in which negative emotions often attract greater attention (Dewar, 2010). However, where nurses' aspirations are not achieved, they can experience distress and a desire to withdraw, either from caring for a particular patient, or from caring work altogether. Other empirical work has confirmed that there is often a difference between what nurses think they ought to be doing and what actually happens in practice, and have linked this theory-practice gap with morale, job satisfaction and retention difficulties in nursing (Maben et al., 2007).

Our unique contribution has been to identify through the meta-ethnographic method how the nature of the organizational setting at unit level can be a primary influencing factor on nurses' capacity to build and sustain therapeutic relationships with patients. The results show two clear organizational types, with nurses from general ward settings more frequently reflecting an impaired capacity to form therapeutic relationships with patients. The deliberate disengagement behaviours described for some general ward nurses contrast with the ideal of the nurse being 'present' in a relationship, that is bringing self to the relationship and exposing oneself fully to the experiences in the relationship. They are associated with the distress inherent in nursing work, and this links with findings from other studies that nurses can use a range of defensive strategies against the anxiety raised by the painful feelings invoked by nursing work (Menzies, 1960). But the meta-ethnography findings also illustrate that the disengagement behaviours result from the moral distress arising from an inability to provide adequate care. Lack of time and an adherence to routine constrain general ward nurses' capacity to care. Williams et al. (2009) identified a key tension in acute care systems between 'pace' (the desire to discharge people as quickly as possible) and 'complexity' (taking account of the complex interaction between medical and social issues). While nurses have not relinquished direct control over nursing care, they are increasingly working in a man-agerialist environment with less autonomy over the conditions in which care is delivered and in which 'pace'dominates (Adams et al., 2000; Williams et al., 2009). Nursing is then conceptualized as solely technical and physical work, while the more complex but less codifiable rela-tional aspects of care are ignored or viewed as a 'luxury' by healthcare planners and managers (Dingwall and Allen, 2001; Iles and Vaughan Smith, 2009). The meta-ethnography findings indicate that the impact of these organizational conditions at a unit or ward level can result in moral distress for nurses because they cannot deliver the care they aspire to. Nurses then withdraw from attempting to emotionally engage with patients, having not received the support they need in the form of the right organizational conditions. We also found that, while nurses in critical care settings also have difficulty attaining their aspirations, espe-cially as patient advocates, they do apparently have more capacity than nurses working on general wards to form therapeutic relationships with patients. Certain organizational conditions in critical care settings may help to explain the difference, for instance richer skill-mix and one-to-one (or one-to-two) nursing, both of which could enhance contact time between patients and nurses, and thus capacity to care.

Conclusion

The findings of this meta-ethnography reflect the importance of nurses and nursing openly acknowledging the complexity, struggle and moral dilemmas inherent in nursing work. Nurses need to refocus current debate on the relational aspects of care, exploring and articulating their benefits and the conditions in which they can be successfully deliv-ered (Williams et al., 2009; Bridges et al., 2010). The findings that contrast nurses' experiences in critical care and general ward settings highlight the importance of unit-level conditions in shaping nursing work and indicate the conditions in which relational work by nurses can flourish, although more research is needed to inform the development of suitable interventions. The nursing profession also needs to articulate how registered nurses can promote and best supervise relational care, when others, such as nursing assistants, may have more direct contact with patients. Other healthcare professions need to consider this review's findings and establish the relevance of them for their own practice. Acute care organizations and wider healthcare systems need to establish cultures that more visibly value and support therapeutic professional–patient relationships across organizations and at individual unit level and that reflect the emotional dimensions for all parties involved in healthcare delivery. Managers need to improve nurses' control over the conditions in which they work, optimize contact time between registered nurses and patients and ensure that clinical supervision and peer support is routinely available and accessible to all nursing staff, including nursing support workers.

We see the findings from this meta-ethnography as a contribution to an ongoing debate by nurses and nursing about what nurses do and as a resource for acute care organizations about how to support nurses in this work. The findings from this meta-ethnography make a contribution, through nurses' voices, not only to articulating the less visible aspects of nursing care in acute settings but also to recognizing the organizational conditions in which patients and nurses fare best.

References

Adams, A., Lugsden, E., Chase, J., Arber, S., and Bond, S. (2000). Skill-mix changes and work intensification in nursing. *Work, Employment and Society,* 14, 541–555.

Bridges, J., Flatley, M., and Meyer, J. (2010). Older people's and relatives' experiences in acute care settings: systematic review and synthesis of qualitative studies. *International Journal of Nursing Studies,* 47, 89–107.

Bridges, J., Nicholson, C., Maben, J., Pope, C., Flatley, M., Wilkinson, C., Meyer, J., and Tziggili, M. (2012). Capacity for care: meta-ethnography of acute care nurses' experiences of the nurse-patient relationship. *Journal of Advanced Nursing,* 69, 760–772.

Calvin, A.O., Kite-Powell, D.M., and Hickey, J.V. (2007). The neuroscience ICU nurse's perceptions about end-of-life care. *Journal of Neuroscience Nursing,* 39, 143–150.

De Bal, N., Dierckx de Casterlé, B., Beer, T.D., and Gastmans, C. (2006). Involvement of nurses in caring for patients requesting euthanasia in Flanders (Belgium): A qualitative study. *International Journal of Nursing Studies,* 43, 589–599.

Dewar, B. (2010). *Caring about caring: an appreciative action research study that explores and develops compassionate care in an acute care setting for older people.* Edinburgh Napier University.

Dingwall, R. and Allen, D. (2001). The implications of healthcare reforms for the profession of nursing. *Nursing Inquiry,* 8, 64–74.

Eriksson, C. and Saveman, B.I. (2002). Nurses' experiences of abusive/non-abusive caring for demented patients in acute care settings. *Scandinavian Journal of Caring Sciences,* 16, 79–85.

Firth-Cozens, J. and Cornwell, J. (2009). *Enabling compassionate care in acute hospital settings.* London: The King's Fund.

Flatley, M. and Bridges, J. (2008). Promoting the art of caring for older people. *International Journal of Nursing Studies,* 45, 333–334.

Gutierrez, K.M. (2005). Critical care nurses' perceptions of and responses to moral Distress. *Dimensions of Critical Care Nursing,* 24, 229–241.

Halcomb, E., Daly, J., Jackson, D. and Davidson, P. (2004). An insight into Australian nurses' experience of withdrawal/withholding of treatment in the ICU. *Intensive and Critical Care Nursing,* 20, 214–222.

Hawley, M.P. and Jensen, L. (2007). Making a difference in critical care nursing practice. *Qualitative Health Research,* 17, 663–674.

Hopkinson, J. and Hallett, C. (2002). Good death? An exploration of newly qualified nurses' understanding of good death. *International Journal of Palliative Nursing,* 8, 532–533.

Hopkinson, J.B., Hallett, C.E. and Luker, K.A. (2003). Caring for dying people in hospital. *Journal of Advanced Nursing,* 44, 525–533.

Hov, R., Hedelin, B. and Athlin, E. (2007). Being an intensive care nurse related to questions of withholding or withdrawing curative treatment. *Journal of Clinical Nursing,* 16, 203–211.

Iles, V. and Vaughan Smith, J. (2009). *Working in health care could be one of the most satisfying jobs in the world – why doesn't it feel like that?* [Online]. http://www.reallylearning.com/Free_Resources/MakingStrategyWork/working inhealthcare.html. [Accessed 21.05.2012].

Maben, J., Latter, S. and Clark, J.M. (2007). The sustainability of ideals, values and the nursing mandate: evidence from a longitudinal qualitative study. *Nursing Inquiry,* 14, 99–113.

Mackintosh, C. (2007). Protecting the self: A descriptive qualitative exploration of how registered nurses cope with working in surgical areas. *International Journal of Nursing Studies,* 44, 982–990.

Menzies, I.E.P. (1960). *The functioning of social systems as a defence against anxiety.* London: Tavistock Institute of Human Relations.

Nicholson, C., Flatley, M., Wilkinson, C., Meyer, J., Dale, P. and Wessel, L. (2010). Everybody matters 2: promoting dignity in acute care through effective communication. *Nursing Times,* 106, 12–14.

Noblit, G.W. and Hare, R.D. (1988). *Meta-ethnography: synthesizing qualitative studies.* Newbury Park: Sage.

Nolan, L. (2006). Caring connections with older persons with dementia in an acute hospital setting – a hermeneutic interpretation of the staff nurse's experience. *International Journal of Older People Nursing,* 1, 208–215.

Nolan, L. (2007). Caring for people with dementia in the acute setting: a study of nurses' views. *British Journal of Nursing,* 16, 419–422.

Nordam, A., Torjuul, K. and Sørlie, V. (2005). Ethical challenges in the care of older people and risk of being burned out among male nurses. *Journal of Clinical Nursing,* 14, 1248–1256.

Quinn, B. (2003). Exploring nurses' experiences of supporting a cancer patient in their search for meaning. *European Journal of Oncology Nursing, 7,* 164–171.

Wilkin, K. and Slevin, E. (2004). The meaning of caring to nurses: an investigation into the nature of caring work in an intensive care unit. *Journal of Clinical Nursing, 13,* 50–59.

Williams, S., Nolan, M. and Keady, J. (2009). Relational practice as the key to ensuring quality care for frail older people: discharge planning as a case example. *Quality in Ageing and Older Adults, 10,* 44–55.

6

Creating an Enriched Environment of Care for Older People, Staff and Family Carers: Relational Practice and Organizational Culture Change in Health and Social Care

Mike Nolan

Introduction

Despite a number of major initiatives over a sustained period of time, including the National Service Framework for Older People (DoH 2001), the Dignity Challenge (DoH 2006) and The Modernising Adult Social Care (MASC) programme (Newman and Hughes, 2007), the quality of care provided to frail older people remains seriously inadequate. Indeed such was the level of concern that in 2011 there was a perceived need for a 'Commission on Dignity' in care instigated by Age UK, The National Health Service (NHS) Confederation and The Local Government Association in order to try and 'understand how and why older people's care is failing in dignity and what will drive improvement'.

In suggesting an answer to this question, this chapter argues that the roots of this failure can be traced to the emergence of modern day medicine with its focus on 'cure' rather than 'care' such that those with long-term needs are seen as 'failures' of the system. It is further argued that the disadvantaged position of frail older people has been exacerbated by the present policy emphasis on autonomy and individuality and the 'target-driven' culture that shapes the delivery of health and social care. Such a focus fails adequately to recognize and address the multiple and diverse needs of frail older people, raising, it is suggested, fundamental tensions between 'pace', as exemplified in the rapidity of acute treatment and the 'complexity' of need among frail older people and their family carers (Williams et al. 2009, Patterson et al. 2010). The widespread political response to the above challenge has been a call for 'culture change', which seems to be the preferred, if rather rhetorical, solution whether the problem lies within health and social care systems, or the current global financial and banking crisis.

However, culture change is inherently complex and requires long-term and deep-rooted action. With respect to improving the quality of care for older people, this chapter draws primarily on a programme of research conducted over a 25-year period, initially at the University of Wales, Bangor and for the last 15+ years at the University of Sheffield. This has resulted in the development, application and testing of the 'Senses Framework' (Nolan et al. 2002, 2006) as a model to drive improvements in the quality of care for frail older people and their family carers. Underpinning this framework is the belief that an 'enriched environment' of care will only be created when there is a refocusing of health and social systems towards 'relationship-centred' (Tresolini and Pew Fetzer Foundation 1994) as opposed to 'person-centred' care. Rather than addressing the needs of a particular individual, as in 'person-centred care', the Senses Framework and relationship-centred care recognize that the needs of all groups (patients, staff and family carers) have to be considered if high-quality care is to be achieved. How this can be realized is illustrated with reference to a major recent study exploring culture change in acute health care for older people (Patterson et al. 2010).

Background

Concerns about the quality of health and social care for frail older people are long-standing and initially prompted the emergence of geriatric medicine after the Second World War (see Wilkin and Hughes 1986 for an insightful account). Despite the pioneering efforts of early Geriatricians who did much to promote the value and status of work with older people and introduced the concept of rehabilitation for older people who could not be cured of their condition (Wilkin and Hughes 1986), problems remain and have been exacerbated over time. Such problems are complex and relate not only to the tensions created by a healthcare system which predominately focuses on cure and discharge, when the needs of increasing numbers of older people are not consistent with such a model, but also concern wider societal attitudes towards older people and indeed ageing itself.

Therefore, despite innumerable initiatives to improve care for older people over the last 60 years scandals recur with predictable regularity (Norton et al. 1962, RCN/BGS/RCP 1987, HAS 1998, 2000, Abraham 2011) with the Health Service Ombudsman in England recently highlighting the 'ignominious failure' of the NHS to live up to its core value of compassion (Abrahams 2011) and the Older Persons' Commissioner for Wales describing the hospital care for some older people as 'shamefully inadequate' (OPCW 2011). Both of these reports called for 'fundamental change' in the attitudes and practices of staff.

Debates about the root cause of this seemingly intractable problem have focused on the increasing emphasis placed on 'technical' as opposed to 'affective' care (Berdes and Eckert 2007). Consequently, it has been argued that recent 'impressive technical advances' in treatment fail at the human and emotional level (Youngson 2008). Such tensions have been increased by the 'quick-fix and target-driven' culture of the NHS (RCN 2008, NMC 2009) with its reliance on 'technocratic solutions' (incentives, penalties, regulations) that 'fundamentally miss the point' (Goodrich and Cornwell 2008). Herein lie all the characteristics of a 'wicked' problem as defined by the Australian Public Services Commission (2007) who consider that a 'wicked' problem:

- Is difficult to define clearly
- Has complex interdependencies
- Is unstable and evolving
- Has no clear or correct solution
- Proposed solutions have uncertain effects
- Is socially complex and involves several stakeholders
- Crosses organizational boundaries
- Solutions require considerable behavioural change

In the face of such challenges, the response is often to call for 'culture change' which according to some commentators has become the 'buzzword' of the twenty-first century (Stone 2003) achieving the status of a 'social movement' (Meyer and Owen 2008). But as the characteristics of a 'wicked' problem suggest such culture change is far from simple to achieve. A meta-analysis of efforts to introduce quality improvement programmes within healthcare organizations worldwide concluded that there was little chance of success unless considerable attention was paid to the 'complex social interactions' that characterize relationships in such organizations (Powell et al. 2009).

In understanding these complex social interactions much recent attention has been focused on what have been termed 'relational practices' (Parker 2008). Relational practices have been defined as those activities necessary to develop and sustain interpersonal relationships between patients, families and staff based on an understanding of each individual's circumstances and their contexts (Parker 2008). Parker suggests that the success or otherwise of relational practice depends not only on the skills of individuals but also on the extent to which the organization of which they are part values and supports such practices, she sums this up as follows:

> Relational work in caregiving organisations thus depends, not only on the skills of individual practitioners and care workers, but also on the extent to which the workgroup and the organisation are structured and operated in ways that are supportive of relational work behaviours (p. 206).

Several recent studies on the quality of care for older people, whilst not explicitly coining the term 'relational practice', have elaborated upon the types of social interactions needed to provide high-quality care (see e.g. Bridges et al. 2009, Dewar and Nolan 2012). These, and other studies, stress the need for staff to be supported in their efforts if relational practices are to flourish, with Williams et al. (2009) suggesting that there are three prerequisites for successful relational practice:

- Such work has to be accorded value and status.
- There have to be sufficient resources for staff to engage meaningfully with patients/clients.
- Staff must be emotionally supported themselves.

Unfortunately, in the dominant target driven culture of the NHS, such 'relational practices' are not explicitly acknowledged or accorded value, and as such there is little incentive for staff to engage with them. Following a major recent study on dignity in care for older people Tadd et al. (2011) concluded that staff must be treated with dignity and respect by colleagues, managers, patients and carers if they are to provide dignified care themselves. Such a belief underpins the 'Senses Framework' and relationship-centred care which, it is argued, provide a way towards addressing the 'wicked' problem of how to improve the quality of care provided for frail older people.

The origins of the 'Senses Framework'

The 'Senses Framework' has emerged over a period of some 25 years starting with what might be called an 'intellectual itch'. This emerged from both my clinical practice as a Charge Nurse working with older people and my initial forays into the literature around care for older people. From both these sources it became clear that if work with older people generally was accorded little value and status that with frail older people with ongoing needs was even further denigrated. This is perhaps most succinctly, if pithily, summarized in a phrase that I came across but have never been able to attribute to an appropriate source:

> If geriatrics is the Cinderella of services, long-term care is the ugly sister.

If the terminology now appears dated, the sentiment, unfortunately, remains all too relevant. The question that perplexed me was 'What provides a sense of therapeutic direction from which to derive job satisfaction and meaning for people working in long-term care'? For those who work in acute settings 'cure' is the goal and when, as is often the case with older people, cure is not an option then rehabilitation becomes the primary aim. However, for many older people neither cure nor rehabilitation is an option, and there often then exists a therapeutic vacuum. Over the years successive authors have struggled to define goals for what was called 'long-term' care. Evers (1981) described it as 'aimless residual care' and somewhat later Reed and Bond (1991) coined the term 'good geriatric care' which essentially comprised efforts to keep frail older people clean, well-fed and tended for. There was little aspiration beyond these goals and as reports over the years attest even these modest ambitions were all too often not met. After many years of thinking and reading, and informed by such ideas as 'therapeutic reciprocity' (which defines the need for 'give and take' in caring relationships) (Marck 1990) and the 'therapeutic quadrangle' (which focuses attention on the needs of the disabled person, family carer and service system in to response to a particular condition) (Rolland 1988) ideas began to crystallize and these formed the intellectual building blocks of the 'Senses Framework'. Things came together when I was asked to present a keynote address to a European Older People's Nursing Conference on the future of long-term care. In this presentation, I suggested that there was a need to articulate what a good long-term care environment should look like and argued that this was one in which older people should experience six 'senses'. These, modified following several years subsequent work involving older people, family carers and practitioners, are outlined below:

A positive, later termed an 'enriched', environment (Nolan et al. 2006) is one in which older people experience a 'Sense' of:

- Security – to feel safe physically, psychologically, existentially
- Belonging – to feel part of a valued group, to maintain or form important relationships
- Continuity – to be able to make links between the past, present and future
- Purpose – to enjoy meaningful activity, to have valued goals
- Achievement – to reach valued goals to satisfaction of self and/or others
- Significance – to feel that you 'matter' and are accorded value and status

Although initially the 'Senses' were seen to apply to older people, it soon became apparent that if staff were to create these senses for older people then they too had to work in an environment that created the 'senses' for them. Therefore, unless staff felt that they were secure (e.g. to raise concerns about poor standards of care), that they 'belonged' and so forth then it was unreasonable to expect them to create the 'senses' for older people. This was summarized succinctly by Tom Kitwood (1997) when writing about staff working with people with dementia:

> If employees are abandoned and abused, probably clients will be too. If employees are supported and encouraged they will take their sense of well-being into their day-to-day work.
>
> (Kitwood 1997, p. 103)

Furthermore, while the 'senses' were originally developed for a longer term care setting additional empirical and theoretical work over a number of years has demonstrated their usefulness in both acute care and community settings (see Davies et al. 1999, Nolan et al. 2006). Subsequent work has also extended the concept of an enriched environment to the learning experience of student practitioners, arguing that if they are to choose to work with older people when they qualify then they need to experience an 'enriched' learning environment during their training (see Nolan et al. 2006, Brown et al. 2008 for further details). Therefore, current thinking about the nature of an enriched

Table 6.1   Characteristics of an enriched environment as captured by the 'Senses Framework' (Nolan et al. 2006)

Senses \ Stakeholder	Older person	Staff	Family carers	Students
Security				
Belonging				
Continuity				
Purpose				
Achievement				
Significance				

environment of care is one in which all major groups experience the 'senses' as captured in Table 6.1.

As the 'senses' were further developed, it became apparent that there were tensions between the rhetoric of 'person-centred' care underpinned by the values of autonomy and individuality for the older person that lie at the heart of recent policy and the interdependence that characterizes the 'senses' (see Nolan et al. 2004 for a fuller discussion). This interdependence is more fully reflected in the notion of 'relationship-centred care'. This phrase was first coined by Tresolini and the Pew-Fetzer Task Force (1994) who undertook a major review of the American healthcare system. They concluded that it was not 'fit for purpose' as it was primarily focused on acute care when the major challenges come from people with long-term conditions. They argued that if health care was to respond to future challenges then it needed to adopt a relational approach that recognized the interdependencies between the givers and receivers of care inherent in health, and I would add social care, encounters. However, they did not identify an approach that would allow this philosophy to be achieved in practice, and this is where the 'senses' come in.

Recent work (Patterson et al. 2010) has applied the 'Senses Framework' in a study exploring the nature of culture change in acute hospital settings for older people. Based on in-depth case studies and extensive survey work in four purposively selected acute hospital trusts, the study clearly demonstrated the value of the 'senses' in unpicking the predominant culture in operation at the various sites and the impact of the culture on shaping the experiences of older people, family carers and staff. Using sophisticated statistical modelling and in-depth analysis of extensive volumes of qualitative data, the study highlighted the critical leadership role of the Ward Sister in creating an enriched environment for all concerned. In the presence of positive leadership by the Ward Sister, staff applied a consistent philosophy of care that valued and prioritized the relational dimensions of interactions with older people and family carers whilst demonstrating excellent teamwork and a supportive culture for colleagues. On such units, older people and family carers reported significantly improved levels of satisfaction with care whilst staff demonstrated improved morale and job satisfaction and lower levels of burnout.

The leadership style adopted by Ward Sisters on these units was characterized by the following behaviours:

Sisters:

- instilled pride in their staff by highlighting what they did well
- improved staff confidence by providing positive feedback on their work
- engaged all the team when making important decisions
- consulted widely before introducing any change
- set clear and explicit standards of care that promoted excellence
- made themselves readily available to staff and demonstrated a caring and supportive attitude
- worked with staff on an individual basis to provide coaching and mentorship
- were highly visible on the ward and regularly involved in the delivery of 'hands-on' care

The critical role of the Ward Sister in creating a positive culture of care has been described in several other studies (see Davies et al. 1999 for a more detailed discussion), but this work gives the most detailed account yet of the type of behaviours that create an 'enriched' environment in which everybody can flourish. These behaviours can be seen as advanced forms of 'relational' practice and whilst these are clearly highly effective if they are to flourish it is essential, as Parker (2008) notes that the wider organization is 'structured and operated in ways that are supportive of relational work behaviours'. However, I would go further and suggest that it is not just the organization that needs to be supportive of such behaviours but the entire health and social care system, and indeed society as a whole. We therefore might wish to ask ourselves a series of searching questions which are challenging but essential to address if the care of frail older people is to achieve the standard that they have a right to expect. Such questions raise serious concerns about the 'quick-fix and target-driven culture' of the NHS (RCN 2008, NMC 2009). Fundamentally if the type of 'compassionate care' that has become the new rhetoric is to be achieved then the types of relational practices described above have to be recognized as being essential skills for all staff and accorded status and value. In terms of the 'senses' they have to be seen as significant, but it also needs to be recognized that in applying relational practices staff are potentially emotionally vulnerable and need a 'secure' environment where such vulnerability is not only recognized but also supported. We therefore might wish to consider some of the following questions:

- Does present government policy for health and social care promote an enriched environment of care?
- Does a 'pace'-driven agenda where change follows change create the sort of continuity needed for culture change to be successfully achieved?
- Does a target-driven and largely punitive culture create the sense of security necessary for people to feel safe to take risks and innovate?
- Do organizations and professions providing health and social care have a shared sense of purpose and belonging?
- Do we celebrate and reward the achievement of relational practice?
- Fundamentally, what values really drive health and social care, and what counts as significant?

In the conclusion to their study, Patterson et al. (2010) argued that there currently exists a 'perform or perish' culture in the NHS which is dominated by a short-term, top-down agenda with a largely punitive culture with a focus on the 'metrics' of care. Within such a culture the needs of frail older people will inevitably be compromised on the altar of greater efficiency and productivity. If things are to improve, there is a need to refocus the health and social care system towards a 'relational and responsive' culture (Patterson et al. 2010). This promotes a longer term perspective that adopts a bottom–up approach in which everybody's views are solicited and seen as important. An empowering model that encourages innovation is supported and failures are recognized as learning opportunities. In essence the emphasis is on the meaning and not on the metrics of care.

Culture change is a long-term objective, and if it is to become more than political rhetoric it has to be recognized, as Boyd and Johnson (2008) note, that it is 'a journey not a destination'. It has been suggested

(Nolan 2010) that if society uses the 'Senses Framework' as an analytic lens then what we see as significant and how we define the senses of purpose and achievement gives a clear indication of the direction in which we wish to travel. As a potentially frail older person myself in the future, I believe that there is a need for a serious reappraisal of what society sees as significant and how it defines purpose and achievement in relation to health and social care. Similarly the senses of security, belonging and continuity are essential if staff are to create the conditions necessary to achieve an enriched environment of care. As Guba and Lincoln (1989) so cogently noted, 'It is certainly possible to coerce people into compliance, but is it impossible to coerce them into excellence'.

A 'perform or perish' culture needs to be transformed into 'relational and responsive' one: the 'Senses Framework' offers one means to achieve this reorientation of care away from personalized models to ones that recognize the needs of all those both giving and receiving care.

References

Abraham, A. (2011) *Care and compassion: A report on 10 investigations into the care of older people*. The Stationary Office, London.

Australian Public Services Commission (2007) *Tackling wicked problems: A public policy perspective*. Commonwealth of Australia, ACT.

Berdes, C. and Eckert, J.M. (2007) The language of caring: Nurse's aides use of family metaphors conveys affective care. *Gerontologist*, 47(3): 340–349.

Boyd, C. and Johansen, B. (2008) A cultural shift: Resident-directed care at providence mount St. Vincent in Seattle places elders at the center of the Universe. *Health Program*, 89(1): 37–42.

Bridges, J., Flatley, M. and Meyer, J. (2009) *Best practice for older people in acute care settings (BPOP): Guidance for nurses*. RCN/City University.

Brown, J., Nolan, M., Davies, S., Nolan, J. and Keady, J. (2008) Transforming students' views of gerontological nursing: Realising the potential of 'enriched' environments of learning and care: A multi-method longitudinal study. *International Journal of Nursing Studies*, 45: 1214–1232.

Davies, S., Nolan, M.R., Brown, J. and Wilson, F. (1999) *Dignity on the ward: Promoting excellence in the acute hospital care of older people*. Report for Help the Aged/Order of St John's Trust.

Department of Health (2001) *The national service framework for older people*. Department of Health, London.

Department of Health (2006) *The dignity challenge*. Department of Health, London.

Department of Health (2007) *Releasing time to care integrated service improvement programme*. The Stationery Office, London.

Dewar, B. and Nolan, M. (2012) Caring about caring: developing a model to implement compassionate relationship centred care in an older people setting, *International Journal of Nursing Studies*, Published online April 2012.

Evers, H.K. (1981) Multidisciplinary teams in geriatric wards: Myth or reality? *Journal of Advanced Nursing*, 6, 205–214.

Guba E and Lincoln Y (1989), *Fourth Generation Evaluation*. Newbury Park, CA. Sage.

Goodrich, J. and Cornwell, J. (2008) *Seeing the person in the patient: The point of care review*. The King's Fund, London.

HAS. 2000 (1998) '*Not because they are old': An independent inquiry into the care of older people on acute wards in general hospitals*. Health Advisory Service, London.

Kitwood, T. (1997) *Dementia reconsidered: The person comes first*. Open University Press, Bucks.

Marck, P. (1990) Therapeutic reciprocity: A caring phenomenon, *Advances in Nursing Science*, 13(1), 49–59.

Meyer, J. and Owen, T. (2008) Calling for an international dialogue on quality of life in care homes. *International Journal of Older People Nursing*, 3(4): 291–294.

Newman, J. and Hughes, M. (2007) *Modernising adult social care: What's working?* Department of Health, London.

Nolan, M.R. (2010) Relationship centred care, the senses framework and culture change: moving beyond the interpersonal, Opening Keynote address to the Inaugural International Conference on Compassionate Care, Edinburgh, June 2010.

Nolan, M.R., Davies, S., Brown, J., Keady, J. and Nolan, J. (2002) *Longitudinal study of the effectiveness of educational preparation to meet the needs of older people and carers: The AGEIN (Advancing gerontological education in nursing) project*. English national board for nursing, Midwifery and Health Visiting, London (p. 320).

Nolan, M.R., Davies, S., Brown, J., Keady, J. and Nolan, J. (2004) Beyond person centered' care: A new vision for gerontological. *International Journal of Older People Nursing*, 13(3a), 45–53.

Nolan, M.R., Brown, J., Davies, S., Nolan, J. and Keady, J. (2006) *The senses framework: Improving care for older people through a relationship-centred approach*. Getting Research into Practice (GRIP) Series, No. 2, University of Sheffield.

Norton, D., McLaren, R. and Exton-Smith, A.N. (1962). *An investigation of geriatric nursing problems in hospital*. London: National Corporation for the Care of Old People, reprinted in 1976 by Churchill Livingstone.

Nursing and Midwifery Council (2009) *Guidance for the care of older people*. Nursing and Midwifery Council, London.

Older Peoples' Commissioner for Wales (2011) *Dignified Care: The experiences of older people in hospital in Wales, Older Peoples'*. Commissioner for Wales, Cardiff

Parker, V.A. (2008) Connecting relational work and workgroup context in caregiving organizations. *The Journal of Applied Behavioural Science*, 38(3): 276–297.

Patterson, M., Nolan, M., Rick, J., Brown, J., Adams, R. and Musson, G. (2010) 'From metrics to meaning: Culture change and quality of acute hospital care for older people'. Report for the National Institute for Health Research Service Delivery and Organisation Programme.

Powell, A.E., Rushmer, R.K. and Davies, H.T.O. (2009) *A systematic narrative review of quality improvement models in health care*. NHS Quality Improvement, Scotland.

RCN/BSG/RCP (1987) *Improving the care of elderly people in hospital*, Royal College of Nursing, London.

Reed, J. and Bond, S. (1991) Nurses' assessment of elderly patients in hospital. *International Journal of Nursing Studies*, 28, 55–64.

Rolland, J.S. (1988) A conceptual model of chronic and life threatening illness and its impact on families. In Chilman. C.S., Nunnally, E.W. & Cox, F.M. (eds) *Chronic Illness and disabilities*, pp. 17–68, Sage, Beverley Hills.

Royal College of Nursing (2008) *Defending dignity – challenges and opportunities for nursing*. Royal College of Nursing, London.

Stone, R.L. (2003) Selecting a model of choosing your own culture. *Journal of Social Work in Long-Term Care*, 2(3/4): 411–422.

Tadd, W., Hillman, A., Calnan, S. et al. (2011) *Dignity in practice: A exploration of the care of older people in acute NHS Trusts*, HMSO, London.

Tresolini, C.P. and the Pew-Fetzer Task Force (1994) *Health professions education and relationship-centred care: A Report of the Pew-Fetzer Task Force on advancing psychosocial education*. Pew Health Professions Commission, San Francisco.

Wilkin, D. and Hughes, B. (1986) The elderly and the health services. In: Phillipson, C. & Walker, A. (Eds) *Ageing and policy: A critical assessment*, pp. 163–183. Gower, Aldershot.

Williams, S., Nolan, M. and Keady, J. (2009). Relational practice as the key to ensuring quality care for frail older people: Discharge: Planning as a case example. *Quality in Ageing*, 10 (3), 44–55.

Youngson, R. (2008). *Compassion in healthcare: The missing dimension of healthcare reform?* The NHS Confederation, www.debatepapers.org.uk, accessed 21/5/09.

7
Promoting Patient-Centred Health Care: An Empirically Derived Organizational Model of Interprofessional Collaboration

David Greenfield, Peter Nugus, Joanne Travaglia and Jeffrey Braithwaite

Introduction

In an era where there has been an unprecedented expansion of evidence-based medicine, clinical guidelines and healthcare standards, patients continue to receive care below levels judged to be appropriate (McGlynn et al. 2003; Hunt et al. 2012; Runciman et al. 2012). Interprofessional collaboration (IPC), a fluid mix of interprofessional learning (IPL) or interprofessional education (IPE) and interprofessional practice (IPP), is advocated as being a driver to promote and improve patient-centred health care. The argument being prosecuted is that IPE is the basis for IPP, which in turn enhances communication, strengthens professional relationships and improves teamwork (Braithwaite et al. 2007c; Greenfield et al. 2011b). These are believed to be critical elements necessary for patient-centred care (International Alliance of Patients' Organisations 2007).

Further, IPC is advocated as being able to provide benefits such as: more creative, integrated services (Phillips et al. 2002; Greenfield 2007); improved communication and trust amongst clinical groups (Oandasan et al. 2004); better collaborative skills for individuals (Engeström et al. 2003); more positive professional relationships (Atwal and Caldwell 2002); an improved approach to teamwork (Sexton et al. 2000) and an associated reduction in between-professional rivalries (Hughes et al. 2005; Nugus et al. 2010). These potential outcomes are recognized as being necessary to achieve high-quality and safe healthcare organizations that promote patient-centred health care (Hammick 2000; Hindle et al. 2006; Varpio et al. 2008; Greenfield et al. 2011c).

To achieve these outcomes, and the ongoing enactment of patient-centred health care, requires personal, interpersonal, interprofessional and organizational skills and resources. Improvements in communication, collaboration, teamwork and the integration of services cannot be realized without them (Gittell et al. 2010). However, the strength of individual components, and how they integrate together to enable IPC and patient-centred health care require investigation. Hence, questions occupying the minds of academics and practitioners are as follows: how do we conceptualize and model IPC? Do we continue to borrow from existing theories or do we need new approaches (The Faculty Advisory Group on Interprofessional Learning and Education, (FAGILE) 2007)? We can, of course, continue productively to draw upon a range of ideas including, for example, community of practice (Wenger 1998), knotworking (Engeström et al. 1999), relational coordination (Gittell et al. 2010) and teamwork (Sheard and Kakabadse 2000). Individually and collectively they help us understand the benefits and challenges of professionals working together. Those interested in IPC seemingly draw on various literatures, often 'cherry picking' the strengths of each. But we need to go one step further. If we are to realize more fully the benefits of IPC and model its contribution to patient-centred health care, we need to be able to recognize it in the environment of health organizations and expose what attitudes, behaviours and structures promote, or inhibit, its enactment.

Drawing upon empirical data, from a study articulated specifically to investigate IPC longitudinally (Braithwaite et al. 2007c), we report on the development of a conceptual model to represent the enactment of IPC in health organizations. To develop our model, we examined the understandings of IPC held collectively by a community of health professionals. We examined commitment expressed, or not expressed, in action – what our participants did as well as what they said, and the structures, both formal and informal, through which they enacted their practice with or without their interprofessional peers.

Methods

Design and organizational setting

We conducted a large-scale collaborative action research study, the details of which are published elsewhere, examining the extent to which IPL and IPP are being used to improve IPC (Braithwaite et al. 2007c). The study used a multi-method longitudinal design to investigate change across the whole health system (Braithwaite et al. 2007b; Benn et al. 2010). The project involved over 20 research, policy and practice investigators. Action research (Reason and Bradbury 2001) was used to generate a collaborative approach involving health professionals and a university research team. Central to the approach was an iterative dynamic whereby literature, improvement activities and reflections on progress drove the study. The intention was to produce information and knowledge that can be applied to benefit IPC across the health system (Braithwaite et al. 2007c). The participating organization was Australian Capital Territory Health (ACT Health), an autonomous bounded health jurisdiction in Australia. ACT Health provides a wide range of tertiary and community-based services. Approval for the study was provided by the ethics committees of both the university and health organization (HREC 07002(PI)/Panel Ref 9-03–81and ETH.3/07.274).

Theoretical framework

We developed a purpose designed tool to assess the organization's progress with IPC. The tool was labelled the 'interprofessional praxis audit framework' (IPAF) (Greenfield et al. 2010). The IPAF measures an organization's culture and the attitudes and behaviour of health professionals to ascertain engagement, or disengagement, with IPC. The IPAF contains sections which: assess the complexity of social-organzational contexts; allows for inclusion of multiple perspectives; uses multi-method data collection and, promotes engagement and collaboration between researchers and organizational staff (Greenfield et al. 2010).

Data sources and analysis

To administer the IPAF within our chosen site, we sought a healthcare setting that would serve as an exemplar in order to strengthen transferability of findings to other health settings. We applied three criteria. First, the sample site should cover both acute and sub-acute care. Second, health professionals from medical, nursing, allied health and corporate services were required to be organizationally and physically located within care settings in the site. Third, the site needed to be perceived by participants as a healthcare setting that exemplified IPC. The Aged Care and Rehabilitation Division (ACRD) met these criteria.

We used mixed methods to collect the data and investigator triangulation to analyse it (Rosenfield et al. 2011). We conducted 27 interviews, of which 11 were individual and 16 were group interviews, involving 112 participants. We performed 71 hours of ethnographic observations and over 30 hours of document analysis. Participants had the study explained to them and gave verbal consent. Data analysis was a three-step process (Pope et al. 2000). The strength of this process is that combined assessments of teams are noted to result in more consistent quality assessments (Gawel and Godden 2008). First, three researchers independently conducted a thematic analysis of the data, using the constant comparative approach (Braithwaite et al. 2007a; Rosenfield et al. 2011). Drawing on the themes from praxis theory (Zuber-Skerritt 2001), we constructed a list comprising attitudes, values and conduct, and organizational structures that reflected IPC. Second, the researchers met to collectively review and construct a common list of items; differences were resolved though comparison and discussion. Finally, the common list was then analysed collectively by the researchers. The items were examined and thematically recategorized into interpersonal skills, clinical abilities, interprofessional orientation, organizational aptitude and contextual factors.

Results

Data were organized into five categories. The groupings are as follows: interpersonal skills; clinical abilities; interprofessional orientation; organizational aptitude; and contextual factors. We present below an explanation of the categories and, in the associated tables, examples of the items that comprise them.

Interpersonal skills

A range of interpersonal skills were identifiable in the data. They were noted as necessary to enable individual clinicians to interact positively with their colleagues and patients and their families; conversely their absence was considered to contribute to interpersonal difficulties in clinical, team and organizational forums (Table 7.1). The skills include: the capacity to communicate effectively; respect for the contribution of others; having a positive approach to team work; management of stress; and the willingness to resolve differences and conflict. The data suggest that these skills are the foundation upon which IPC, teamwork and networks are built.

Clinical abilities

Within the data clinical abilities that promote and enable IPC were recognizable. These abilities involve individuals developing expertise in their own clinical field, including focusing on learning about conditions

Table 7.1   Interpersonal skills that are the foundation for IPL and IPP

Interpersonal skills: examples of attitudes, behaviours and interactions
- Introduce self using first name
- Willing to listen to the concerns of others
- Learn from others (professions, students and clients)
- Seek to develop good relationships
- Ability to communicate effectively
- Positive approach to the work
- Respect the contribution of other staff
- Identify and respond to different cultural needs

Table 7.2   Clinical abilities that enable IPL and IPP

Clinical abilities: examples of attitudes, behaviours and interactions
- Ongoing development of clinical knowledge and skills
- Pride in, but not arrogance about, work and speciality
- Patient-centred focus
- Documentation of professional activities clearly and timely
- Learning about and valuing each professional role
- Recognition of health care by a multidisciplinary team
- Ask for and provide advice, share knowledge and information and support
- Involve the patient/family in care-planning and decision-making
  (as appropriate)

and their treatment from the perspective of other disciplines (Table 7.2). A key learning is the recognition of the importance of multidisciplinary teamwork which focuses on providing patient-centred care. Additionally, seeking patient involvement in decision-making is an important skill, for both individuals and care teams.

Interprofessional orientation

An interprofessional orientation that facilitates IPC could be discerned from the data set (Table 7.3). This orientation involves individuals simultaneously enacting their interpersonal skills and clinical abilities in clinical and organizational settings. The purpose of this is to establish trust, form positive professional networks and work in collaborative teams across professional, service and organizational boundaries. Interprofessional skills include the following: the ability to collaborate over care delivery; the capacity to undertake joint decision-making,

Table 7.3 Interprofessional orientation that facilitates IPL and IPP

Interprofessional orientation: examples of attitudes, behaviours and interactions

- Belief that professional groups should exercise autonomy over input into client care
- Encourage team work and collaboration by others
- Ability to engage and converse with other professionals
- Awareness of and capacity to deal with power differentials (personal, professional, organizational)
- Seek to coordinate patient care and encourage others to do so
- Value self and team reflection on practice
- Ability to cope with change to traditional roles
- Display permeable boundaries (professional, service and organizational)
- Identify and model positive interactions (personal and clinical)

---

as clinically appropriate; the display of distributed leadership and the management of care transitions for patients and staff.

Organizational aptitude

An organizational aptitude towards IPC was observed in the data. This is the propensity to work collaboratively with other professionals to construct a culture and network that promotes inclusion of and collaboration with staff to provide the environment that delivers high quality care. It is the participation in activities necessary for a complex bureaucracy to address human resource, financial and clinical governance requirements (Table 7.4). Activities include participation in: service (team) meetings; quality improvement projects; family and

Table 7.4 Organizational aptitude that demonstrates IPL and IPP

Organizational aptitude: examples of attitudes, behaviours and interactions

- Participation in team activities, for example staff meetings, quality improvement projects
- Participation in collaborative clinical activities, for example case conferences, family conferences, discharge planning, ward rounds, informal conversations
- Participation in organizational activities, for example clinical governance meeting, risk registers, policy and guideline reviews
- Ability to identify and acknowledge tribalism
- Deal with complaints

---

clinical case conferences; clinical governance meetings; and policy and guideline reviews.

Contextual factors

A number of contextual factors ranging from the service setting to the broader organizational climate were noted as shaping the enactment of IPC (Table 7.5). In individual services the stability or instability of staff enhanced or inhibited the enactment of IPC. Services with ongoing staffing issues, such as staff turnover, vacant positions, the rotation of staff, or staff acting in higher positions, were continually in a state of flux. Participants reported that providing clinical services was a challenge and they did not have the team relationships to do so in an interprofessional manner. Those services which had full complements of staff, and the time to form and work as teams, reported engaging in IPC when providing care. Additionally, organizational policies were acknowledged to limit or enhance IPC. For example, when the organization instituted a policy that aimed to reduce the patient's length of stay in hospital, this restricted the capacity of some professionals to complete assessments and treatments. Medical issues became prioritized over therapeutic issues so that once patients' medical treatments were completed there was significant, normally irresistible, pressure to discharge them. Requirements such as these define practice so as to focus primarily upon medical issues, thereby limiting, reducing or excluding the contribution of some professions. Conversely, the existence of a clinical governance policy that required a collaborative review of services promoted interaction and learning across professions. Furthermore physical space was recognized as a factor that shaped the opportunity for interactions,

Table 7.5   Contextual factors that influence IPL and IPP

Contextual factors: examples of factors

- Increased stability of organization, services and staff promotes and instability inhibits (i.e. staff turnover, empty positions, rotating staff, higher duties, restructuring of services)
- Organizational policies and guidelines
- Physical space: co-location promotes interactions and learning
- Access to resources (physical and adequate staffing levels)
- Leadership (senior managers) that promotes and displays collaboration and inclusion
- Access to supervisors, senior professionals, managers and directors
- Transparency of decisions from senior managers

leaning and teamwork. The co-location of staff is an important platform for the development of relationships and informal interactions of both a clinical and social nature. Teamwork and collaborative learning emerged in the physical and emotional space people occupied.

Discussion

Using the five components identified, a schematic diagram representing the enactment of IPC is presented. We have named the model the 'organizational model of interprofessional collaboration' (OMIC); see Figure 7.1. This model is an empirically grounded contribution to the field amongst a sea of theory and speculation, and, we believe, will resonate with many commonly held beliefs of practitioners and academics. OMIC, which is predicated upon a social theory of learning (Wenger 1998), underscores how interpersonal skills and abilities are the foundation for the development of an individual's clinical abilities and an interprofessional orientation to patient-centred health care. These components influence each other, and, individually and together, shape the organizational aptitude of individuals and teams to enacting patient-centred health care. The black arrows represent the flow of practice or 'knowing' and the dashed arrows represent the feedback that occurs individually and collectively across professionals, teams and the organization. The learning flows through to shape interprofessional

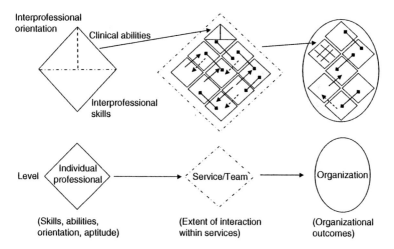

Figure 7.1 Organizational model of interprofessional collaboration (OMIC)

behaviour, reinforcing or undermining individual and team clinical and organizational activities that promote patient-centred health care. The strength of IPC is represented by the closeness or distance between individuals and teams at the respective levels. Organizational aptitude and contextual factors that enhance or inhibit the enactment of IPC are manifest in the lines with solid ends; these facilitate networking and reinforce interprofessional conduct between individuals and services to realize organization with culture promoting IPC and patient-centred health care.

For IPC and patient-centred health care to become the cultural norm of a service, it is necessary for the four internal components to be simultaneously displayed by a majority of staff, from across professions in a service, a majority of the time. The fifth component, the contextual factors, need to be considered by the service team and their potential positive impacts heightened and negative impacts minimized. The enactment of IPC may, at times, depending on the circumstances, involve some but not every profession and most but not all members. The non-participation of one group or individual does not prevent learning and collaboration by others. However, the level of participation and relative clinical and organizational positioning, will shape the extent to which IPC and patient-centred health care become embedded in the culture of the service. Alternatively, if the components of OMIC are not operationalized then the potential benefits of IPC and patient-centred health care will not be realized. For example, if one professional group was not to participate in clinical or policy reviews or support these through a display of their organizational attitudes, then the learning and practice improvements would have difficulty flowing back through to shape conduct in team or clinical settings.

OMIC locates in the one model a schematic snapshot of IPC and patient-centred health care. Few now doubt that the capacity of health professionals to provide appropriate, high-quality and safe care is improved by strengthening interprofessional skills (McAllister et al. 2001; Braithwaite et al. 2006; Gittell et al. 2010). The benefits of effective communication, teamwork and collaboration (Litaker et al. 2003), and the willingness to form professional relationships in order to break down knowledge silos (Philbin 1999), are to be promoted. The IPC logic suggests that interpersonal skills and attitudes need to be developed in clinical and team settings. Expertise is enhanced as, individually and collectively, professionals learn and deliver services together; they are engaging in conduct termed 'relational coordination' to improve organizational outcomes (Gittell et al. 2010). In doing so they collectively refine and improve their diagnostic abilities (Rosenfield et al. 2011), skills in patient-centred health care (Gaines et al. 2008), the display of distributed leadership (Greenfield 2007) and the management of care transitions for patients and staff (Gaines et al. 2008). These skills and behaviours, collated and labelled within the model as 'interprofessional orientation', accumulates with participation in clinical and service meetings to assess, plan and review care systems and outcomes for clients (Greenfield et al. 2011b; Naylor et al. 2011). The benefits that are realized through this approach are known to be improved clinical outcomes (Braithwaite et al. 2006; Hindle et al. 2006), better continuity of care (Berg 2005; Greenfield et al. 2011a) and increased patient satisfaction with the quality of care (Tattersall 2002).

Through deriving a model of IPC, this study challenges readers to examine IPC in their healthcare contexts and to reflect upon how the interactions and behaviours of health professionals and the structures in which they work shape patient care. The study contributes to the ongoing discussion of how to close the gap between recommended and provided patient care. There is the potential for the OMIIC and its components to be tested and refined in different healthcare settings and organizations. Health professionals and researchers could use the model to diagnose the presence or absence of IPC within different environments and identify remedial strategies to improve IPC and patient-centred health care. These activities could contribute to the furthering of collaborative learning and practice and drive improvements in patient care.

Conclusion

Many healthcare organizations are pursuing a goal of patient-centred health care to achieve care that is of high quality and safe for patients. IPC promotes inclusive and collaborative activities to accomplish these ends. The OMIC provides a high-level framework by which to recognize, name and identify the impact of the complex interwoven mix of skills, abilities, attitudes, behaviours and organizational structures that can promote or inhibit IPC. The model can be used to expose these characteristics for discussion and reflection, allowing critical examination as to whether and the extent to which progress in improving IPC and patient care is being made.

References

Atwal, A., and Caldwell, K. 2002. Do multidisciplinary integrated care pathways improve interprofessional collaboration? *Scandinavian Journal of Caring Sciences* 16(4):360–367.

Benn, J., Burnett, S., Parand, A., Pinto, A., Iskander, S., and Vincent, C. 2010. Studying large scale programmes to improve patient safety in whole care systems: Challenges for research. *Social Science & Medicine* 69(12): 1767–1776.

Berg, S. 2005. The well-informed patient: A new breed of health consumer. The advantages (and pitfalls) of seeking health information. *Asthma Magazine* 10(4):28–30.

Braithwaite, J., Greenfield, D., and Pawsey, M. 2007a. *Accreditation: Assessing the Evidence. ISQua 24th International Conference on Quality in Health Care.* Boston: United States.

Braithwaite, J., Travaglia, J., and Nugus, P. 2007b. *Giving a Voice to Patient Safety in New South Wales.* Kensington: Centre for Clinical Governance Research in Health, UNSW.

Braithwaite, J., Westbrook, J., Foxwell, R., Boyce, R., Devinney, T., Budge, M., Murphy, K., Ryall, M-A., Beutel, J., Vanderheide, R. et al. 2007c. An action research protocol to strengthen system-wide inter-professional learning and practice [LP0775514]. *BMC Health Services Research* 7:144.

Braithwaite, J., Westbrook, J., Pawsey, M., Greenfield, D., Naylor, J., Iedema, R., Runciman, B., Redman, S., Jorm, C., Robinson, M. et al. 2006. A prospective, multi-method, multi-disciplinary, multi-level, collaborative, social-organisational design for researching health sector accreditation [LP0560737]. *BMC Health Services Research* 6:113–123.

Engeström, Y., Engeström, R., and Kerosuo, H. 2003. The discursive construction of collaborative care. *Applied Linguistics* 24(3):286–315.

Engeström, Y., Engeström, R., and Vähäaho, T. 1999. When the center does not hold: The importance of knotworking. In: Chaiklin, S., Hedegaard, M., and Juul Jensen, U. (eds.). *Activity Theory and Social Pratice: Cultural-Historical Approaches.* Aarhus University Press, pp. 345–374, Denmark.

Gaines, R., Missiuna, C., Egan, M., and McLean, J. 2008. Educational outreach and collaborative care enhances physician's perceived knowledge about Developmental Coordination Disorder. *BMC Health Services Research* 8(21). doi: 10.1186/1472-6963-8-21.

Gawel, R., and Godden, P. 2008. Evaluation of the consistency of wine quality assessments from expert wine tasters. *Australian Journal of Grape and Wine Research* 14:1–8.

Gittell, J., Seidner, R., and Wimbush, J. 2010. A relational model of how high-performance work systems work. *Organization Science* 21(2):490–506.

Greenfield, D. 2007. The enactment of dynamic leadership. *Leadership in Health Services* 20(3):159–168.

Greenfield, D., Nugus, P., Travaglia, J., and Braithwaite, J. 2010. Auditing an organisation's interprofessional learning and interprofessional practice: The interprofessional praxis audit framework. *Journal of Interprofessional Care* 24(4):436–449.

Greenfield, D., Nugus, P., Fairbrother, G., Milne, J., and Debono, D. 2011a. Applying and developing health service theory: An empirical study into clinical governance. *Clinical Governance: An International Journal* 16(1):8–19.

Greenfield, D., Nugus, P., Travaglia, J., and Braithwaite, J. 2011b. Factors that shape the development of interprofessional improvement initiatives in health organisations. *BMJ Quality and Safety* 20:332–337.

Greenfield, D., Pawsey, M., and Braithwaite, J. 2011c. What motivates health professionals to engage in the accreditation of healthcare organizations? *International Journal for Quality in Health Care* 23(1):8–14.

Hammick, M. 2000. Evidence form the past to guide the future. *Medical Teacher* 22(5):461–467.

Hindle, D., Braithwaite, J., Travaglia, J., and Iedema, R. 2006. *Patient Safety: A Comparative Analysis of Eight Inquiries in Six Countires.* Sydney: University of New South Wales: Centre for Clinical Governance Research in Health.

Hughes, J.L., Hemingway, S., and Smith, AG. 2005. Interprofessional education: Nursing and occupational therapy – could old rivals integrate? *Nurse Education in Practice* 5(1):10–20.

Hunt, T.D., Ramanathan, S.A., Hannaford, N.A., Hibbert, P.D., Braithwaite, J., Coiera, E., Day, R.O., Westbrook, J.I., and Runciman, W.B. 2012. CareTrack Australia: Assessing the appropriateness of adult healthcare: protocol for a retrospective medical record review. *BMJ Open* 2(1).

International Alliance of Patients' Organisations. 2007. *What is patient-centred healthcare? A review of definitions and principles.* London: IAPO.

Litaker, D., Mion, L.C., Planavsky, L., Kippes, C., Mehta, N., and Frolkis, J. 2003. Physician and nurse practitioner teams in chronic disease management: The impact on costs, clinical effectiveness, and patients' perception of care. *Journal of Interprofessional Care* 17(3):223–237.

McAllister, L., Lawson, M., Teo, K.K., and Armstrong, P.W. 2001. A systematic review of randomised trials of disease management programmes in heart failure. *American Journal of Medicine* 110:378–384.

McGlynn, E.A., Asch, S.M., Adams, J., Keesey, J., Hicks, J., DeCristofaro, A., and Kerr, E.A. 2003. The quality of health care delivered to adults in the United States. *New England Journal of Medicine* 348(26):2635–2645.

Naylor, J., Mittal, R., Greenfield, D., Milne, J., Ko, V., Harris, I., and Adie, S. 2011. Scope for a 'one size fits all' rehabilitation approach after knee replacement? Heterogeneity in patient preferences makes this unlikely. *International Journal of Person Centred Medicine* 1(2):260–267.

Nugus, P., Greenfield, D., Travaglia, J., Westbrook, J., and Braithwaite, J. 2010. How and where doctors exercise power: Interprofessionalism, collaboration and leadership across a health system. *Social Science & Medicine* 71: 898–909.

Oandasan, I., D'Amour, D., Zwarenstein, M., Barker, K., Purden, M., Beaulieu, MD., Reeves, S., Nasmith, L., Bosco, B., Ginsburg, L. et al. 2004. *Interdisciplinary Education for Collaborative, Patient-centred Practice: Research and Findings Report.* Ottawa: Health Canada.

Philbin, E.F. 1999. Comprehensive multidisciplinary programme for management of patients with chronic heart failure. *Journal of General Internal Medicine* 14:130–135.

Phillips, R.L., Jr., Harper, D.C., Wakefield, M., Green, L.A., and Fryer, G.E., Jr. 2002. Can nurse practitioners and physicians beat parochialism into plowshares? A collaborative, integrated health care workforce could improve patient care. *Health Affairs* 21(5):133–142.

Pope, C., Ziebland, S., and Mays, N. 2000. Qualitative research in health care: Analysing qualitative data. *BMJ* 320(7227):114–116.

Reason, P. and Bradbury, H. 2001. *Handbook of Action Research.* London: Sage.

Rosenfield, D., Oandaasan, I., and Reeves, S. 2011. Perceptions versus reality: A qualitative study of students' expectations and experiences of interprofessional education. *Medical Education* 45:471–477.

Runciman, W., Hunt, T., Hannaford, N., Hibbert, P., Day, R., Coiera, E., Westbrook, J., McGlynn, E., Hindmarsh, D., and Braithwaite, J. 2012. CareTrack: Assessing the appropriateness of healthcare delivery in Australia. *Medical Journal of Australia* 197(2): 100–105.

Sexton, J.B., Thomas, E.J., and Helmreich, R.L. 2000. Error, stress, and teamwork in medicine and aviation: Cross sectional surveys. *BMJ* 320(7237):745–749.

Sheard, A. and Kakabadse, A. 2000. From loose groups to effective teams: The nine key factors of the team landscape. *Journal of Management Development* 21(2):133–151.

Tattersall, R. 2002. The expert patient: A new approach to chronic disease management for the twenty-first century. *Clinical Medicine* 2(3):227–229.

The Faculty Advisory Group on Interprofessional Learning and Education (FAGILE). 2007. *Models of Interprofessional Learning.* Nottingham: University of Nottingham.

Varpio, L., Hall, P., Lingard, L., and Schryer, C.F. 2008. Interprofessional communication and medical error: A reframing of research questions and approaches. *Academic Medicine* 83(10):S76–S81.

Wenger, E. 1998. *Communities of Practice: Learning, Meaning and Identity.* Cambridge: Cambridge University Press.

Zuber-Skerritt, O. (2001) Action learning and action research: Paradigm, praxis and programs. In Sankaran, S., Dick, B., Passfield, R. and Swepson, R. (eds.), *Effective Change Management Using Action Research and Action Learning: Concepts, Frameworks, Processes and Applications* (pp. 1–20). Lismore, Australia: Southern Cross University Press.

8
From a Project Team to a Community of Practice? An Exploration of Boundary and Identity in the Context of Healthcare Collaboration

Roman Kislov

Background

Communities of practice (CoPs) have been used both as a theoretical heuristic to analyse inter-group knowledge-sharing in health care (Ferlie et al., 2005) and as a knowledge mobilization tool enabling learning, innovation and problem-solving within and across healthcare organizations (Ranmuthugala et al., 2011). This chapter aims to enhance our understanding of CoPs by providing an empirical account of an emergent, multiprofessional, knowledge-brokering community which developed from a project team functioning alongside other project teams in a large-scale healthcare partnership. By discussing the practical implications of the team-to-CoP conversion for intra-organizational processes, such as boundary spanning and identity construction, the chapter provides useful insights for those intent on cultivating CoPs within their own organizations to enhance communication, coordination and innovation in patient-centred care.

A CoP is defined as 'a group of people who share a concern, a set of problems, or a passion about a particular topic, and who deepen their understanding and knowledge of this area by interacting on an ongoing basis' (Wenger et al., 2002, p. 4). CoPs are characterized by mutual engagement, joint enterprise and shared repertoire (Wenger, 1998) and could be distinguished from project teams along several dimensions (Table 8.1). Wenger and Snyder (2000) emphasize that the main factor

Table 8.1 Distinctions between CoPs and project teams

Characteristic	Communities of practice	Project teams
Purpose	To build and exchange knowledge and to develop individual capabilities	To accomplish a specified task
Membership	Self-selection based on expertise or passion for a topic	Employees assigned by senior management
Boundaries	Fuzzy	Clear
What holds them together	Passion, commitment and identification with the group and its expertise	The project's goals and milestones
Life cycle	Evolve and end organically (last as long as there is relevance to the topic and interest in learning together)	Predetermined ending (when the project has been completed)

Source: Adapted from Wenger and Snyder (2000); Wenger et al. (2002).

defining a CoP is shared practice, whereas a project team is characterized by the coordination of tasks the group has to accomplish. At the same time, it has been suggested that, under certain conditions, a project team may develop CoP characteristics and hence become a 'true' CoP (Hildreth, 2004). This premise has, however, received little empirical attention.

Knowledge-sharing across CoPs is often analysed through the notion of a boundary representing, on the one hand, a barrier between different practices and, on the other hand, an opportunity for cross-fertilization and discovery of different perspectives (Wenger, 2000). Tagliaventi and Mattarelli (2006) argue that barriers to knowledge-sharing at the boundaries between CoPs are expected to prevail, being raised by the specificity of practice of a given community and a strong collective identity among its members. Similarly, Ferlie et al. (2005) show that CoPs in health care are predominantly unidisciplinary, tend to seal themselves off from neighbouring professional communities and are highly institutionalized, which enables a relatively easy flow of knowledge within these CoPs but causes the 'stickiness' of knowledge across boundaries and hence retards the innovation spread. A more optimistic view on knowledge-sharing between co-located CoPs maintains that boundaries between them can be successfully bridged by knowledge brokers (both individuals and groups), boundary objects and boundary interactions among the members of neighbouring CoPs (Wenger, 1998, 2000). It should be noted that previous research has mainly focused on the boundaries of uniprofessional CoPs, while knowledge-sharing across the boundaries of multiprofessional communities remains underresearched.

Although multiprofessional CoPs may show over time the same characteristics as the organic, naturally occurring, uniprofessional CoPs (Gabbay et al., 2003), the formation of cohesive and functional multidisciplinary CoPs in health care may be problematic since healthcare contexts are notorious for their interprofessional power struggles, traditional dominance of the medical profession and strong inter- and intraprofessional boundaries (Kislov et al., 2011). At the same time, participation in a multiprofessional and multi-agency CoP would imply some degree of identification with the community, that is at least partial reconciliation of pre-existing and concurrent professional, organizational and workplace identities into one coherent sense of self (Handley et al., 2006). While it has been argued that our ability to suspend and engage identities determines our ability to productively deal with boundaries (Wenger, 2000), the effects of shared identities on knowledge-sharing across the boundaries of multiprofessional CoPs remain empirically unexplored.

The chapter will therefore address the following three research questions:

1. What are the mechanisms and consequences of the conversion from an organizational project team to a multiprofessional CoP?
2. How is knowledge shared across the boundary separating such a CoP from its neighbouring extra- and intra-organizational communities?
3. How does identification with a multiprofessional CoP influence the process of knowledge-sharing at the CoP boundary?

Case and method

This chapter presents a brief summary of a research project conducted within the implementation strand of a collaborative partnership ('Collaboration') between a university and 20 local National Health Service (NHS) Trusts aiming to support the translation of research evidence into clinical practice. It focuses on one of the four implementation teams operating within the Collaboration, namely the heart failure (HF) team comprising six people (a senior nursing academic, a management academic, a manager, a specialist nurse and two full-time change agents, one with a managerial and the other with a nursing background) and aiming to improve HF services in primary care in line with existing scientific evidence. The HF team is analysed in this chapter as a single holistic qualitative case study looking at both the intra-organizational

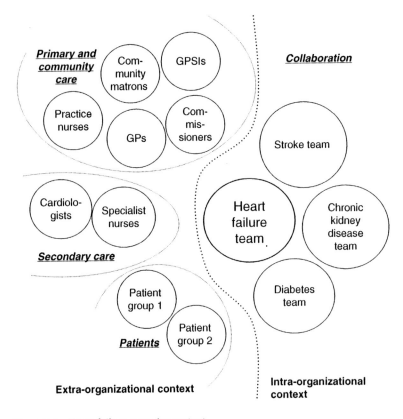

Figure 8.1 Heart failure team in context

context in which the HF team functioned, that is its interactions with the other three teams in the Collaboration's implementation strand, and extra-organizational context, that is its interactions with various external professional groups providing services to HF patients in the NHS (Figure 8.1). The case study comprises 28 semi-structured interviews and 45 hours of direct observation undertaken between September 2010 and September 2011.

Findings

Team interactions, roles and autonomy

An essential part of the practice of the HF team was getting together for a fortnightly team meeting, which normally lasted around two hours and was used as a forum to collectively discuss various work-related issues in an open, friendly and informal atmosphere. The meetings did not have a dedicated agenda or structure, and the team often discussed issues that were only indirectly related to their immediate tasks but formed part of their wider interest in heart disease. There was also room for exchanging jokes and news about things not related to work itself, some of the favourite themes being football, leisure activities of the team members and TV programmes.

The way the team was set up presumed a clear distribution of roles, with the clinical lead responsible for clinical guidance and leadership, programme manager being in charge of finances and administration and academic lead providing academic input. In reality, it did not, however, transform the team into a top-down, command-and-control hierarchical structure. Some team members described their roles as vaguely defined and flexible, with role boundaries blurred. Although the roles of the team members differed, a new shared practice was forming in the team around service improvement in the field of HF care. This practice was markedly different from (although informed by) the practices of research, nursing and management in which the team members were engaged in their other roles outside the team.

In doing their work, change agents were given quite a lot of autonomy with only some guidance from the other members of the team. This approach seemed at least to some extent to be determined by the style of the clinical lead, which was, in turn, seen by many as stemming from her nursing background. It was also felt that there was a match between the personalities of the team members in terms of their shared preferences towards the 'organic', emergent approach to joint working and autonomous, egalitarian style of intra-team interaction. At the level of the Collaboration as a whole, the HF team was also given considerable autonomy to plan, design, implement and evaluate their programme of work. The team devised their own project plan which specified targets, components and deadlines of the project. It was not, however, followed literally, with the sequence of actions, deadlines and scope of work changing continuously throughout the project.

Knowledge-sharing across boundaries

What remained stable throughout the project was the team's affinity for building relationships and engaging with stakeholders to involve them in all stages of the project. As the team's main aim was the facilitation of evidence-based implementation in the field of HF, the external groups involved included patients, academic researchers, NHS commissioners, cardiologists, specialist HF nurses, general practitioners (GPs), GPs with special interest (GPSIs), practice nurses, practice managers and other healthcare professionals. Their knowledge and experience were crucial for shaping up the content of the project in its planning stage, which took more than a year and included numerous consultations with stakeholders. Furthermore, the representatives of these groups were actively involved in designing, piloting and applying the products produced by the team. Bidirectional knowledge exchange occurred between the HF team and the groups mentioned above as well as between different professional and organizational groups brought together for stakeholder events or educational sessions (Table 8.2).

Table 8.2   Examples of boundary interactions and boundary objects used by the HF team as part of their boundary spanning activities

Category	Example	Purpose
Boundary interactions	Stakeholder engagement events	Sharing knowledge about existing problems and ways to solve them; identifying potential supporters, opinion leaders, gatekeepers and blockers; reaching consensus
	Practice visits	Performing heart failure register audits together with the practice staff. providing feedback on the audit results
	Educational sessions	Bringing together specialists (heart failure specialist nurses) and generalists (GPs and practice nurses)
	Face-to-face meetings with stakeholders	Sharing ideas, maintaining relationships, looking out for possible solutions
Boundary objects	Heart failure audit tool and education pack	Codification of secondary-care specialist knowledge for use in primary care
	Heart failure alert card	Improving communication between patients, primary and secondary care
	Website	Raising awareness of different heart failure services available; providing information relevant to patients, carers and healthcare professionals

Spanning the boundaries between the team and targeted extra-organizational groups was successful: not only was knowledge exchanged and transformed, but the actual practices of all communities involved became directly influenced by this process. This can be explained by a number of factors. First, although the change agents were seen as the main people involved in boundary spanning activities, knowledge brokering and boundary spanning formed an essential part of the team's shared practice. Second, in the process of aligning the team's strategy with agendas, expectations and priorities of professional and organizational groups involved, team members invested a lot of time and effort in building trustful relationships with these groups' gatekeepers and opinion leaders. Finally, relevant knowledge was transformed into the products produced by the team, which fulfilled the function of boundary objects (Table 8.2). These were designed either to bridge the gaps between different groups of healthcare professionals (e.g. website and patient alert card) or to combine the explicit, specialist, evidence-based knowledge about HF management with largely tacit, highly context-specific knowledge about how primary-care staff manage these patients in the real world (e.g. audit tool).

Interestingly, knowledge-sharing processes developed differently at the interface between the HF team and other multidisciplinary teams operating within the Collaboration. All of the teams had the same over-arching objectives, partially shared stakeholders, and, at least according to the organizational documents, were supposed to implement the same methodological approach. At the same time, despite a shared focus on service improvement, their practices developed largely independently from each other. So-called 'learning and sharing sessions' for change agents across the Collaboration were established to enable knowledge exchange; there were also regular meetings for academic members. However, it was felt that these meetings were not sufficient for cross-boundary learning. Although the majority of the HF team members had some information about what and how the other teams were doing, this information was often incomplete. Some techniques and methods utilized by other teams were repeatedly mentioned in the meetings (e.g. 'we could use those tips in our work') but never used in actual practice; some were rejected straight away as 'too formalised' and, therefore, unsuitable for the 'organic' approach taken by the HF team. If some mutual cross-boundary learning was happening between the teams, it took the form of 'enlightenment' and did not seem to result in direct and identifiable impact on the teams' practices.

Shared values and identity

Contrary to initial expectations, the multiprofessional nature of the team and team members' concurrent affiliations with different organizations did not lead to major identifiable intra-team tensions which would negatively affect joint working. For instance, a specialist nurse seconded from secondary care to do the audit in primary-care settings admitted that the work she was doing with the HF team aimed at reducing hospital admissions and could thus potentially have negative financial implications for secondary-care settings. This potential tension, however, was resolved by her by prioritizing patient benefit over organizational revenues.

Other values shared by the team members included an 'organic', emergent approach to teamwork, the importance of building and maintaining relationships with stakeholders and achieving consensus with multiple parties without imposing anything on them. These values to a large extent determined the practice co-created by the team, which centred around exchanging knowledge with other communities, discussing the results of this exchange during team meetings and other intra- and intercommunity interactions, and further transformation of shared meanings into a number of boundary objects. Having developed a distinct practice of their own, team members perceived their team as being different from, rather than similar to, other teams within the Collaboration in terms of contexts, stakeholders, personalities and leadership styles. Although certain similarities between the teams were being noted by the team members, the discussion of those formed a relatively insignificant part of the team's shared discourse.

Strong identification with the team and its practice had a number of consequences. First, it may explain knowledge stickiness at the intra-organizational boundaries between the teams, where evidence accumulated and systematized by other teams was perceived as irrelevant by the members of the HF team, the latter preferring their own experiential evidence on the same topics. Second, it complicated the integration of all Collaboration implementation teams into a unified 'vascular theme', which was planned by the Collaboration leadership as a response to financial difficulties faced by the organization. Instead of finishing their project and joining the vascular unit, the HF team were trying their best to secure additional funding which would allow them to continue their HF work. Finally, development of a strong identification with the team and its practice led to a strong sense of ownership over the team's products and posed a potential risk of becoming uncritical of their work, which was, albeit partially, recognized by team members.

Discussion

A project team or a community of practice?

The analysis of the HF team characteristics along the five dimensions presented in Table 8.1 leads to the conclusion that this team is a hybrid form between the 'pure' project team and 'pure' CoP (Figure 8.2). Although conceived as a formal project team within an organization, it acquired a number of features typical for a harmonious CoP with sustained mutual relationships, fast propagation of knowledge within its boundaries, strong collective identity and a number of shared routines, artefacts and stories. In other words, the team described in this chapter has developed the defining CoP characteristics of mutual engagement, joint enterprise and negotiated repertoire. It could thus be suggested that a formal project team and a CoP are not mutually exclusive entities, that there is a multiplicity of transitional forms between the 'pure' versions of a team and a CoP as defined by Wenger and colleagues and

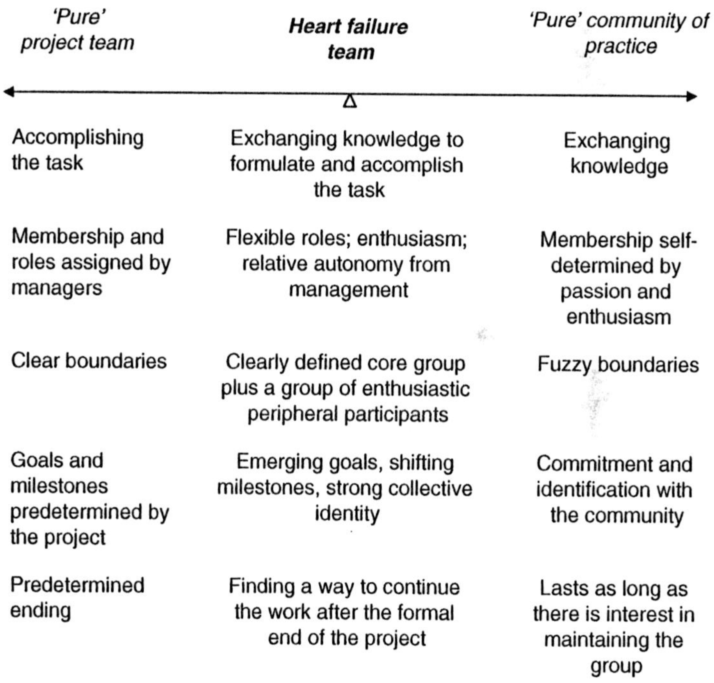

'Pure' project team	Heart failure team	'Pure' community of practice
Accomplishing the task	Exchanging knowledge to formulate and accomplish the task	Exchanging knowledge
Membership and roles assigned by managers	Flexible roles; enthusiasm; relative autonomy from management	Membership self-determined by passion and enthusiasm
Clear boundaries	Clearly defined core group plus a group of enthusiastic peripheral participants	Fuzzy boundaries
Goals and milestones predetermined by the project	Emerging goals, shifting milestones, strong collective identity	Commitment and identification with the community
Predetermined ending	Finding a way to continue the work after the formal end of the project	Lasts as long as there is interest in maintaining the group

Figure 8.2 Heart failure team on the team-CoP continuum

Table 8.3 Factors that might explain the conversion from a project team to a CoP

Organizational factors	Autonomy within the organization
	Absence of strict top-down deadlines and targets
	Nature of the task/purpose/mission of an organization
Team-level factors	Facilitative leadership style
	Informal, egalitarian atmosphere enabling mutual learning and knowledge exchange
	Autonomy within the team
	Regular interaction within the team
	Shared practice
Individual factors	Shared dispositions to collaborative working
	Passion for the area of work
	Common values

that team/CoP distinction should be presented as a continuum rather than a dichotomy.

Factors that may account for the conversion from a formal organizational team to a more informal CoP operate at multiple levels (Table 8.3). At the organizational level, relative autonomy of a team within the organization is important, with the team playing a significant role in determining their own deadlines, targets and outcomes. At the group level, a facilitative leadership and management style, creating an open, egalitarian and informal atmosphere for knowledge-sharing, is crucial. It should not be forgotten that shared practice, enabled in this team by discussing and doing things together, is a necessary prerequisite and takes a certain time to develop. Individual-level factors include sharing similar dispositions to collaborative work, common values, enthusiasm and passion for the area of interest. It should be emphasized, however, that not all CoPs are harmonious and, therefore, it may well happen that a different configuration of factors will lead to the formation of a more conflictual and dysfunctional community, which may render boundary spanning and knowledge-sharing problematic.

In the case study presented here, a CoP developed from a project team organically, without a conscious effort from the organizational or team leadership. However, if the CoP approach is used as a deliberate organizational strategy and if a project is chosen as a crystallization point for the potential CoP, the multiplicity of factors enabling the team-to-CoP conversion should be taken into account. When cultivating CoPs in a project-based organization, an organizational climate supportive of autonomous, self-governing teams needs to be complemented by an adequate team leadership and a mix of team members that would be able to effectively work together. In addition, in those teams who find themselves moving towards the CoP end of the continuum, the team-CoP duality is likely to manifest itself in a number of tensions. These tensions are the result of the contradiction between a CoP's natural inclination to determine its own agenda, focus on learning and find its own way of doing things, on the one hand, and externally predefined roles, goals and deadlines set up for the project by the organization, on the other. It could be assumed that most successful project teams would be able to move between the two ends of the team-CoP continuum depending on the nature of the task at hand and the current contextual factors, but to what extent this is feasible remains to be explored.

The duality of team-CoP interplay was also reflected in the process of knowledge brokering and boundary spanning actively embraced by the team. By virtue of their formal role and the overarching mission of the organization they represented, the team members had to achieve an identifiable and measurable impact on the external CoPs they were interacting with, but at the same time they wanted to avoid intruding into those communities or imposing anything on them. This dilemma was not an insoluble one: the team managed to resolve the tension by a combination of context-specific boundary interactions involving a range of stakeholders as well as by the transformation of knowledge acquired through continuous boundary spanning into a set of products (Table 8.2). These, in turn, provided reification of the team's shared meanings (Wenger, 1998), served as effective boundary objects (Star and Griesemer, 1989), and met the team's regime of accountability: both vertical accountability to the organization and horizontal accountability to a range of external communities involved.

Selective permeability of boundaries and collective identity

The most surprising discovery of this study is the notion of selective permeability of CoP boundaries in relation to different sources of knowledge. The study demonstrated that information was flowing relatively easily in both directions between the HF team and extra-organizational groupings representing various NHS stakeholders involved in the project. At the same time, intra-organizational knowledge-sharing between the HF team and other multidisciplinary teams within the Collaboration was much less visible, perceived both by insiders and outsiders as problematic and did not appear to have a significant effect on the practice of the HF team although a number of formalized inter-team communication channels had been set up by the organization. To conclude, the boundaries of the newly formed CoP were more permeable for extra-organizational than for intra-organizational knowledge-sharing.

Limited permeability of boundaries has traditionally been attributed in the literature to inevitable differences between CoPs in terms of practice, epistemic cultures, value systems and, ultimately, to the development of strong collective identity shared by the community members. A more detailed analysis is, however, required to explain why in this case extra-organizational boundary spanning became prioritized over intra-organizational knowledge-sharing. First, the decision to engage in relationship-building with stakeholders was made by the team members themselves, became one of the team core values and was seen by them as crucial for the success of the whole enterprise, whereas intra-organizational knowledge flows between the Collaboration teams had a top-down nature, were organized along more traditional uniprofessional channels and were not perceived as crucial for fulfilling the team's mission. Second, there was a recognized lack of operational proximity between the teams within the Collaboration (cf. Tagliaventi and Mattarelli, 2006), which significantly decreased opportunities for informal, 'coffee-room' knowledge-sharing seen as fundamental for enabling knowledge exchange (Gabbay and le May, 2011). Finally, there was an inherent competition for achievement and recognition, especially given the fact that the Collaboration experienced significant financial difficulties and the existing programmes of work were under threat.

The findings of the study also show that the development of a shared CoP identity included focusing on in-group similarities (articulating similar personality traits, values, etc.) and out-group differences, whereby other teams were seen as different from the HF team in terms of their preferred approaches to change, stakeholders involved and contextual factors, with these differences possibly being exaggerated. These findings resonate with the social identity theory (Tajfel and Turner, 1979), which holds that (1) social identities are maintained primarily by intergroup comparisons, (2) groups have a vested interest in perceiving greater differentiation between themselves and referent out-groups, especially when the in-group identity is insecure (e.g. because of a threat to its domain or resources) and (3) organizational subunits tend to be the primary focus for inter-group conflict (Ashforth and Mael, 1989). It could be assumed that the processes of differentiation with referent out-groups are likely to be more acute in those organizational groupings that display such characteristics of a CoP as relatively high degrees of collective identification and strength of ties between its members.

The emphasis on in-group similarities and development of shared practice-in-the-making, which was different from the professional practices of the team members, prevented the formation of dysfunctional intra-team tensions related to the multidisciplinary nature of the team, with potential role conflicts being resolved by referring to salient shared values. This was probably aided by the fact that the core team membership was represented by nurses, managers and researchers, with no direct involvement of medics, traditionally perceived as the most dominant group in health care (Harrison and McDonald, 2008).

Conclusion

The contribution of this chapter to the analytical perspective on CoPs is twofold. First, it has demonstrated that project teams and CoPs are not mutually exclusive entities; that a project team can develop typical CoP characteristics, including mutual engagement, shared repertoire, negotiated enterprise, strong collective identity and an emphasis on learning; and that the team-to-CoP conversion is possible in the presence of a combination of certain individual, group-level and organizational factors. Second, it has analysed boundary processes taking place at the interface between a multiprofessional CoP and other extra- and intra-organizational groupings and introduced a concept of selective permeability of CoP boundaries to indicate that a CoP boundary may enable certain knowledge flows while impeding others, which is mediated by the formation of a shared CoP identity through developing shared practice, referring to common values and contrasting themselves with referent out-groups.

As far as the instrumental perspective on CoPs is concerned, this chapter suggests a more nuanced approach to deliberate CoP cultivation for patient-centred care. Although the conversion from a project team to a harmonious CoP is possible in principle, its probability in an organizational setting is likely to be limited by the multiplicity of factors required for this conversion to happen and an inherent tension between the formalized, task-oriented nature of project-based work and the learning-focused philosophy of CoPs. Due to their autonomous and independent nature, CoPs as a knowledge management tool might be ill-suited to settings driven by predetermined targets, deadlines and procedures. It should also be remembered that a tendency to develop their own shared practice and a shared sense of belonging may lead to the formation of a strong boundary blocking intra-organizational knowledge exchange and spread of innovation between the CoP and the rest of the organization.

To counterbalance these challenges, the following steps can be taken. Enhancing organizational identification around the shared values of patient-centred care can act as a buffer to the potentially detrimental effects of group identification on inter-group knowledge-sharing. Another important implication is the need to shift from the tokenistic, 'ritualised' use of formal inter-group learning mechanisms to a more productive dialogue focusing on actual knowledge-sharing, which needs to be supported by the organization. As part of such support, introducing incentives for inter-group learning as well as promoting joint projects may be required to counterbalance the negative effects of inter-group competition. Finally, bridging inter-group boundaries to achieve the objectives of patient-centred care is only possible if the patients' views are used to inform the activities of teams and CoPs involved in service improvement projects and activities.

References

Ashforth, B. E. and Mael, F. (1989). 'Social Identity Theory and the Organization', *Academy of Management Review*, 14, 20–39.

Ferlie, E., Fitzgerald, L., Wood, M. and Hawkins, C. (2005). 'The Nonspread of Innovations: The Mediating Role of Professionals', *Academy of Management Journal*, 48, 117–134.

Gabbay, J. and le May, A. (2011). *Practice-Based Evidence for Healthcare: Clinical Mindlines*. Oxon: Routledge.

Gabbay, J., le May, A., Jefferson, H., Webb, D., Lovelock, R., Powell, J. and Lathlean, J. (2003). 'A Case Study of Knowledge Management in Multiagency Consumer-Informed 'Communities of Practice': Implications for Evidence-Based Policy Development in Health and Social Services', *Health*, 7, 283–310.

Handley, K., Sturdy, A., Fincham, R. and Clark, T. (2006). 'Within and Beyond Communities of Practice: Making Sense of Learning through Participation, Identity and Practice', *Journal of Management Studies*, 43, 641–653.

Harrison, S. and McDonald, R. (2008). *The Politics of Healthcare in Britain*. London: SAGE.

Hildreth, P. M. (2004). *Going Virtual: Distributed Communities of Practice*. London: Idea Group Publishing.

Kislov, R., Harvey, G. and Walshe, K. (2011). 'Collaborations for Leadership in Applied Health Research and Care: Lessons from the Theory of Communities of Practice', *Implementation Science*, 6, 64.

Ranmuthugala, G., Plumb, J. J., Cunningham, F. C., Georgiou, A., Westbrook, J. I., and Braithwaite, J. (2011). 'How and Why Are Communities of Practice Established in the Healthcare Sector? A Systematic Review of the Literature', *BMC Health Services Research*, 11, 273.

Star, S. L. and Griesemer, J. R. (1989). 'Institutional Ecology, 'Translations' and Boundary Objects: Amateurs and Professionals in Berkeley's Museum of Vertebrate Zoology, 1907–39', *Social Studies of Science*, 19, 387–420.

Tagliaventi, M. R. and Mattarelli, E. (2006). 'The Role of Networks of Practice, Value Sharing, and Operational Proximity in Knowledge Flows between Professional Groups', *Human Relations*, 59, 291–319.

Tajfel, H. and Turner, J. C. (1979). 'An Integrative Theory of Intergroup Conflict'. In W. G. Austin and S. Worchel (eds), *The Social Psychology of Intergroup Relations*. Monterey, CA: Brooks/Cole.

Wenger, E. (1998). *Communities of Practice: Learning, Meaning and Identity.* Cambridge: Cambridge University Press.

Wenger, E. (2000). 'Communities of Practice and Social Learning Systems', *Organization*, 7, 225–246.

Wenger, E. C. and Snyder, W. M. (2000). 'Communities of Practice: The Organizational Frontier', *Harvard Business Review*, 78(1), 139–146.

Wenger, E., McDermott, R., and Snyder, W. M. (2002). *Cultivating Communities of Practice*. Boston, MA: Harvard Business School Press.

Part III

Communication in Patient-Centred Care

9

Is Poor Quality of Care Built into the System? 'Routinising' Clinician Communication as an Essential Element of Care Quality

Ros Sorensen, Glenn Paull, Linda Magann and Jan Maree Davis

Introduction

Patients with non-malignant disease often receive sub-optimal end-of-life care. Thus, there is increasing recognition of the need to expand end-of-life care models to the management of end-stage non-malignant diseases in general hospital wards.

This chapter introduces a study of the communication methods health professionals use to obtain information about current medical care for patients at end of life. Using an organizational framework, we report on the study, investigating whether health professionals who share patient care recognize the importance of gathering comprehensive information on patient status as the basis for sound care-planning decisions.

The chapter includes a brief review of the literature, an outline of the main care objectives, challenges to implementing them and strategies to improve care outcomes. It concludes that a comprehensive method of information gathering, disclosure and consensus is foundational to good care planning and patient outcomes.

Review of the literature

Much of the focus and expertise of end-of-life care for people with malignant disease is now being directed towards those with non-malignant conditions, such as end-stage respiratory, cardiac, renal and neurological disease. Regardless of disease type, the standard of end-of-life care has generally been described as sub-optimal with poor communication between health professionals recognized as a major contributor (McQuillan et al., 1998; Øvretveit, 2009). The often varied and individualistic methods of communication used by medical, nursing and allied health clinicians to ascertain information on patient care and communicate medical treatment plans for patients at end of life can result in incomplete information being available for decision-making and care-planning purposes. Patients and families are often left dissatisfied with their care, with clinicians often unaware of the causes of poor patient outcomes and what to do about them. Understanding how information about care is produced and communicated between multidisciplinary clinicians at end of life is an important area of research, particularly in the context of interdisciplinary team care.

Objectives in end-of-life care

The need to improve end-of-life care is well recognized in healthcare policy (Bennett et al., 2010), and end-of-life care objectives are now well established. Policy objectives include the need for health professionals in the treating team to take a collaborative approach to decision-making in the patient's best interests (NSW Health Department, 2005), that includes the patient in decisions that affect them. These ideals are reflected throughout the literature, with research into their implementation via changes in practice falling into two main categories: firstly, early recognition of futility of life sustaining treatment with referral to palliative care services to assist patients and family members come to terms with impending death (Aslakson and Pronovost, 2011); secondly, understanding the challenges clinicians face in attempting to provide the care they believe is required for dying people and their families. Implementing these research findings presents challenges for healthcare teams.

Challenges to enacting care objectives

The challenges that clinicians face in enacting policy ideals primarily relate to recognition of when end-of-life care is indicated. Although much of the early work concentrated on malignant conditions, research is now focusing on non-malignant end-stage chronic disease (Alsop, 2010; Woo et al., 2011). Research findings demonstrate that patients with terminal non-malignant disease experience deficiencies in care-planning and symptom palliation (Walling et al., 2010). Of concern is that people with non-malignant conditions are being treated in hospital wards without access to specialist palliative services (Crawford, 2010; Davison, 2010; Jacobs et al., 2010; Payne et al., 2010; Walling et al., 2010; Pekmezaris et al., 2011; White et al., 2011).

One of the barriers to enacting a palliative model of care is the shortage of medical clinicians with the required skills (Abrahm, 2011). A similar shortage of skills must also be overcome for nursing clinicians based on evidence that nurses often diagnose futility earlier than their medical colleagues (Frick et al., 2003) and interact more frequently with conscious patients and family members. Allied health professionals, including social workers who support family members, also require expertise in end-of-life care to positively influence the patient's end-of-life experience (McCormick et al., 2010).

Using clinical pathways to systematize care processes

The common elements of good end-of-life care are well established. Communication is central, as is patient and family-centred decision-making, continuity of care, attention to emotional and spiritual support and support for treating health professionals (Efstathiou and Clifford, 2011). The complex needs of families and patients at this time requires a comprehensive understanding of diagnosis, care planning and treatment by the diverse array of treating clinicians achieved through systematically planned interventions (Coombs, 2010). Clinical pathways exemplify this method of guiding health professionals in the collaborative care of patients acting to reduce variation in treatment and care, assisting in decision-making and identifying key questions and appropriate responses (Alsop, 2010). Communication can be structured within the pathway to gather information on the patient's status and can include opportunities for disclosing pertinent information as well as building a consensus about diagnosis, prognosis and care planning. Although pathway effectiveness is now well substantiated (Ellershaw et al., 1997; Ellershaw and Ward, 2003; Ellershaw and Wilkinson, 2003) there remains some resistance and scepticism (Duffy et al., 2011; Phillips et al., 2011), with many clinicians preferring to rely on their own experience to inform practice (Efstathiou and Clifford, 2011).

Strategies for change

As well as structuring communication around patient care planning, pathways also structure communication around treatment effectiveness. Measuring performance and benchmarking outcomes over multiple data collection cycles can improve quality (Campion et al., 2011). Therefore, performance reporting helps structure the discussions of multidisciplinary treating clinicians around what care is effective, why some treatment approaches are better than others and from where treatment effectiveness has derived. Finding answers to these questions allows treating clinicians to modify the care-planning process to ensure that the objectives of care are achieved.

A number of strategies other than systematizing care can improve practice and outcomes at end of life. Efstathiou and Clifford (2011) suggest that offering nurses educational opportunities will address a knowledge deficit (Efstathiou and Clifford, 2011); Jacobs et al. (2010) and Schulman-Green et al. (2011) assert that specifically recognizing the contribution of all professionals as specialists within the team will improve end-of-life care (Jacobs, et al., 2010; Schulman-Green et al., 2011). Pekmezaris et al. (2011), Bowers et al. (2010) and Bloomer et al. (2010) found that developing specific communication interventions improved communication competence, especially where tools encouraged practice change in end-of-life care, and if a consultative approach was taken to promote palliation (Bloomer et al., 2010; Bowers et al., 2010; Pekmezaris, et al., 2011). By contrast, Tan and Cheong (2011) promote the importance of personal qualities, such as reflection and insight, as central to professional development in care delivery (Tan and Cheong, 2011).

Research objectives

Based on the foregoing review, the capacity of the multidisciplinary team to structure communication around patient care planning and review of treatment and care outcomes was identified as an effective approach to improvement. Thus, we sought to assess the methods clinicians used to find out about the medical care required for a patient at end of life, to understand whether the forms of communication clinical disciplines used were conducive to improving and sustaining quality.

Method

Our project was conducted at a 680 bed public tertiary referral hospital in Sydney, Australia; part of a broader study into quality of care at end of life. Relevant ethics approval was obtained. The project was undertaken from December 2005 to December 2008.

We surveyed 109 clinicians, proportionately selected from the medical records of a random sample of 411 patients who had died in the preceding six months. The 109 clinicians surveyed comprised: 14 medical clinicians (8 specialist physicians, 4 registrars and 2 interns); 77 nursing clinicians (34 registered nurses, 21 clinical nurse specialists, 10 enrolled nurses, 4 clinical nurse consultants, 4 nurse managers and 4 casual full time nurses) and 21 allied health clinicians (8 social workers, 5 physiotherapists, 4 dieticians, 1 pharmacist and 1 occupational therapist).

The survey comprised six parts, namely:

- the organization of the clinical care process for care at end of life
- patient involvement in decisions about their care
- the ways clinicians communicated about patient care
- how performance was reported
- how performance was reviewed
- how the care process was improved.

In this chapter, we report on the third part of the survey: ways clinicians communicated about patient care. The related survey questions are presented in Table 9.1 as follows:

Table 9.1 Survey

I find out what medical care is required through:							
informal discussions with medical clinicians	1	2	3	4	5	DK	NA
formal meetings with medical clinicians	1	2	3	4	5	DK	NA
medial protocols	1	2	3	4	5	DK	NA
information that is transmitted verbally in ward rounds	1	2	3	4	5	DK	NA
referring to consultant/specialist individual preferences	1	2	3	4	5	DK	NA
the patient's medical record	1	2	3	4	5	DK	NA
my own expertise and experience	1	2	3	4	5	DK	NA
talking with the patient	1	2	3	4	5	DK	NA
a written clinical pathway	1	2	3	4	5	DK	NA

Note: By circling the appropriate response on the scale provided, indicate the extent to which you use the methods listed below to find out what medical care is required or a patient of this case type.
1. Always; 2. Frequently; 3. Sometimes; 4. Seldom; 5. Never, Don't know, Not applicable.

The data were entered into an excel database and the frequency of responses for each clinical groups analysed, namely from nursing, medicine and allied health clinicians. The data are presented in Table 9.2, accompanied by our interpretation of the results.

Interpretation of results

As the data show, medical, nursing and allied health clinicians used widely differing methods of eliciting information about medical care for patients for whom they cared at end of life. Not only did each clinical profession use different methods to find out information about medical care, methods also varied within each clinical profession, suggesting fragmentation of information sources and a variety of forms within which the information was presented and accessed by clinicians of the same disciplinary background.

The categories of communication in the survey range between informal opportunistic modes of communication (informal discussions with medical clinicians, information transmitted verbally via ward rounds, referring to the consultant/specialist individual preferences, own experience and talking with the patient) and formal systematized modes of communication (formal meetings with medical clinicians, medical protocols, the patient's medical record and a written clinical pathway). Our data reveal that clinicians from different health disciplines used very different modes of communication. While this may be expected in view of the different roles and cultures within the treating team, there are implications for comprehensive information accessible to all team members as they plan patient care.

Specifically, informal methods of information gathering were used predominantly by doctors. However, there was some variation among medical clinicians with those methods used most frequently, including referring to the individual preferences of consultants or specialists (8%*; refer the note to Table 9.2), informal discussions with medical clinicians (7.1%), talking with the patient (6.2%) and information transmitted verbally in ward rounds (6.2%). These data suggest that doctors were attuned to the views and preferences of their medical colleagues, potentially senior and more experienced medical consultants or their peers in the absence of senior advice. Medical clinicians less 'frequently' used *information transmitted verbally in ward rounds* (6.2%) where multidisciplinary patient assessments would most likely occur or *talked to the patient* (6.2%) themselves.

Table 9.2 Extent that methods listed are used to find out that medical care is required for a patient

I find out what medical care is required through	Always* All clinician groups %				Frequently All clinician groups %				Sometimes All clinician groups %				Seldom All clinician groups %				Never/Don't know All clinician groups %			
	N	M	AH	T	N	M	AH	T	N	M	AH	T	N	M	AH	T	N	M	AH	T
Informal discussions with medical clinicians	21.4	1.8	6.2	29.5	26.8	7.1	7.1	41.1	14.3	1.8	.9	17	2.7	–	–	2.7	3.6	1.8	4.5	9.8
Formal meetings with medical clinicians	7.1	.9	.9	8.9	10.7	2.7	4.5	17.9	16.1	5.4	6.2	27.7	17.9	.9	.9	19.6	17	2.7	6.2	25.9
Medical protocols	20.3	.9	2.9	24.1	26.8	6.2	7.1	40.2	15.2	2.7	3.6	21.4	3.6	.9	.9	5.4	2.7	1.8	4.5	8.9
Information that is transmitted verbally in ward rounds	20.5	.9	2.7	24.1	26.8	6.2	7.1	40.2	15.2	2.7	3.6	21.4	3.6	.9	.9	5.4	2.7	1.8	4.5	8.9
Referring to consultant/specialist individual preferences	10.7	–	–	10.7	15.2	8.0	1.8	25.0	16.1	2.7	6.2	25.0	8.0	–	2.7	10.7	18.7	1.8	8.0	28.7
The patient's medical record	38.4	1.8	11.6	51.8	17.7	5.3	2.7	25.9	3.6	2.7	.9	7.1	4.5	.9	–	5.4	4.5	1.8	3.6	9.8
My own expertise and experience	18.7	4.5	.9	24.1	30.3	4.5	3.6	38.4	12.5	.9	5.4	18.7	3.6	.9	1.8	6.2	3.6	.9	7.1	12.5
Talking to the patient	23.3	3.6	1.8	28.6	23.2	6.2	3.6	33.0	14.3	.9	8.1	23.2	5.4	–	.9	6.2	2.7	1.8	4.5	8.9
A written clinical pathway	22.3	–	–	22.3	17.0	2.7	–	19.6	15.2	.9	4.5	20.5	8.0	4.5	1.8	14.3	6.2	4.5	12.5	23.2

Note: *The highest possible score for nurses = 68.75%, medical clinicians = 12.5%, allied health clinicians = 18.75% = the total of 100% of clinicians surveyed.

Medical clinicians less 'frequently' referred to the patient's medical record (5.3%), where comprehensive information about patient status and ongoing care treatment and planning is intended to be recorded. Less 'frequently' did medical clinicians use systematized methods, such as a written clinical pathway (2.7%). This may be because pathways are generally regarded as a nursing tool (Degeling et al., 2001). This finding, coupled with the 'seldom' use of medical protocols by a significant proportion of doctors (.9%) indicates that they are either not using or not referring to evidence-based treatment protocols. Rather, the preferences of individual senior clinicians were the usual method employed, from a potentially uncertain evidence base.

By contrast, the majority of nurses (38.4%) reported 'always' using more permanent, explicit and systematic methods, such as the patient's medical record. Notably, 30.3% of nurses relied on their own expertise and experience. Following this, nurses relied on informal methods that included informal discussions with medical clinicians (26.8%) and information transmitted verbally in ward rounds (26.8%), and medical protocols (26.8%).

As with nurses, the majority of allied health clinicians in the sample (11.6%) 'always' referred to the patient's medical record. Allied health clinicians reported less 'frequently' using informal discussions with medical clinicians (7.1%), information transmitted verbally in ward rounds (7.1%) and medical protocols (7.1%). A majority of allied health clinicians (12.5%) 'never' referred to a written clinical pathway.

Our data suggest that the mode of medical communication to find out what medical care was required for a patient was largely exclusive of other disciplines. Medical clinicians' use of more informal and personal methods of communication often excluded nurses and allied health clinicians who employed a range of communication methods to find out about patient care. The data reveal the infrequency with which a written clinical pathway was used by all three disciplines to organize and communicate about shared patient care.

Discussion

Interdisciplinary team care is a complex and, at times, problematic concept in health care – an idealized phenomenon not without its challenges (Berlin and Carlström, 2010). The different interdisciplinary models found in the healthcare literature are largely normative, that is they detail what teams should do, rather than what they actually do (Alimo-Medcalfe, 2008; Fitzgerald and Davidson, 2008). The inclusion of patients' views appeared to be more a default measure by nurses in particular to find out about medical decisions rather than as a purposeful mechanism to include patients in decisions about their care. Recent literature describes a team leadership role as building social identification among team members (Young et al., 2010), but this was not the type of team that emerged from our study. Rather, we found a series of 'teams', comprising loosely connected individuals who shared the care of the patient at different times and in different places. We did not find cohesive, tightly coupled, multidisciplinary, patient-centred teams with effective, collaborative communication methods.

Based on these findings, we comment here on the likely impact of strategies identified in the literature to improve end-of-life care. Efstathiou and Clifford's strategy (2011) to educate nurses so as to change practice and improve outcomes, being discipline-specific, impacts only on nurses. A similar problem occurs in extending education to all trauma professionals, as Jacobs et al. (2010) Bloomer et al. (2010) and Schulman-Green et al. (2011) advocate. Education and consultation, being both passive approaches to clinical practice improvement are only part of the solution if they seek solely to elicit clinician agreement on care objectives rather than also on their ultimate achievement in practice.

Recent work by Lansdell and Beech (2010) identified an emerging clinician confidence from their increased understanding of psychosocial care (Lansdell and Beech, 2010), suggesting that providing the logic for change and the skills to do so precede action on remedial strategies. As Gray (2011) notes, aspects of care that are not well performed, such as pain and other distress management and failure to respect patients' preferences, are aspects of good care that are not necessarily resolved by systematizing clinical work (Gray, 2011). Other strategies are needed to help physicians recognize when patients are entering a trajectory that may end in death to provide options other than active treatment. The personal development strategies advocated by Tan and Cheong (2011) to promote clinicians' reflection and insight may be useful in this regard in assisting clinicians to recognize the limits of their curative skills and hence the value of other options.

Such reflection and insights will be effective only if they are based on evidence of outcomes. The tools advocated by Bowers et al. (2010) that include end-of-life care pathways (Ellershaw and Wilkinson, 2003) can provide the tangible evidence on which evaluation of outcomes can be made. In the absence of integrated 'routinized' pathway processes, the informal and personalized methods of finding out what medical care is required for a patient at end of life that we found in our study will not provide the evidence clinicians need to discriminate between different treatment types, on which improved care planning can be based. The location of such tools in nursing domains is a limitation of this strategy. Further work is required to demonstrate the collective nature of care delivery and evidence of outcomes that we believe is a precondition for the reflexivity that Tan and Cheong (2011) advocate.

Conclusion

Our study highlights health professionals' relatively infrequent use of systematized forms of communication about patient care to plan, deliver and evaluate care at end of life, notwithstanding evidence that systematized and standardized models of care also have the potential to measure and benchmark care outcomes. Data about what worked and why and who contributed to care effectiveness is instrumental in assisting clinicians initiate the types of communication around care planning that our study suggests is required. Both practice evidence and policy are clear about the cross-disciplinary nature of healthcare interventions where patients themselves are part of the team, sharing essential information about diagnosis and treatment preferences at critical times in the episode of care. Only where disclosure, diversity of opinion and consensus are valued, can high-quality decisions be made in the patient's best interest. Good quality of care can be built into the healthcare delivery system at end of life through patient and caregiver consultation within the planning, evaluation and improvement cycle that pathways promote.

References

Abrahm, J. L. (2011). Advances in palliative medicine and end-of-life care. *Annual Review of Medicine, 62*, 187–199.

Alimo-Medcalfe, B. (2008). The impact of engaging leadership on performance, attitudes to work and wellbeing at work: A longitudinal stgudy. *Journal of Health Organization and Management, 22*(6), 586–598.

Alsop, A. (2010). Collaborative working in end-of-life care: Developing a guide for health and social care professionals. *International Journal of Palliative Nursing, 16*(3), 120–125.

Aslakson, R., and Pronovost, P. J. (2011). Health care quality in end-of-life care: Promoting palliative care in the intensive care unit. *Anesthesiology Clinics, 29*(1), 111–122.

Bennett, M. I., Davies, E. A., and Higginson, I. J. (2010). Delivering research in end-of-life care: Problems, pitfalls and future priorities. *Palliative Medicine, 24*(5), 456–461.

Berlin, J., and Carlström, E. (2010). From artefact to effect: The organising effects of artefacts on teams. *Journal of Health Organization and Management, 24*(4), 412–427. doi: 10.1108/14777261011065011.

Bloomer, M. J., Tiruvoipati, R., Tsiripillis, M., and Botha, J. A. (2010). End of life management of adult patients in an Australian metropolitan intensive care unit: A retrospective observational study. *Australian Critical Care, 23*(1), 13–19.

Bowers, B., Roderick, S., and Arnold, S. (2010). Improving integrated team working to support people to die in the place of their choice. *Nursing Times, 106*(32), 14–16.

Campion, F. X., Larson, L. R., Kadlubek, P. J., Earle, C. C., and Neuss, M. N. (2011). Advancing performance measurement in oncology. *American Journal of Managed Care, 17 Suppl 5 Developing*, SP32–36.

Coombs, M. A. (2010). The mourning before: Can anticipatory grief theory inform family care in adult intensive care? *International Journal of Palliative Nursing, 16*(12), 580–584.

Crawford, A. (2010). Respiratory practitioners' experience of end-of-life discussions in COPD. *British Journal of Nursing, 19*(18), 1164–1169.

Davison, S. N. (2010). End-of-life care preferences and needs: Perceptions of patients with chronic kidney disease. *Clinical Journal of The American Society of Nephrology: CJASN, 5*(2), 195–204.

Degeling, P., Kennedy, J., and Hill, M. (2001). Mediating the cultural boundaries between medicine, nursing and management – the central challenge in hospital reform. *Health Services Management Research, 14*, 36–48.

Duffy, A., Payne, S., and Timmins, F. (2011). The liverpool care pathway: Does it improve quality of life? *British Journal of Nursing, 20*(15), 942–946.

Efstathiou, N., and Clifford, C. (2011). The critical care nurse's role in end-of-life care: Issues and challenges. *Nursing in Critical Care, 16*(3), 116–123.

Ellershaw, J., Foster, A., Murphy, D., Shea, T., and Overill, S. (1997). Developing an integrated care pathway for the dying patient. *European Journal of Palliative Care, 4*(6), 203–207.

Ellershaw, J., and Ward, C. (2003). Care of the dying patient: The last hours or days of life. *British Medical Journal, 326*, 30–34.

Ellershaw, J., and Wilkinson, S. (2003). *Care of the Dying: A Pathway to Excellence.* Oxford: Oxford University Press.

Fitzgerald, A., and Davidson, G. (2008). Innovative health care delivery teams: Learning to be a team player is as important as learning other specialised skills. *Journal of Health Organization and Management, 22*(2), 129–146.

Frick, S., Uehlinger, D., and Zenklusen, R. (2003). Medical futility: Predicting outcome of intensive care unit patients by nurses and doctors – A prospective comparative study. *Critical Care Medicine, 31*(2), 456–461.

Gray, B. H. (2011). England's approach to improving end-of-life care: A strategy for honoring patients' choices. *Issue Brief (Commonwealth Fund), 15*, 1–15.

Jacobs, L. M., Burns, K. J., and Jacobs, B. B. (2010). Nurse and physician preferences for end-of-life care for trauma patients. *Journal of Trauma-Injury Infection & Critical Care, 69*(6), 1567–1573.

Lansdell, J., and Beech, N. (2010). Evaluating the impact of education on knowledge and confidence in delivering psychosocial end-of-life care. *International Journal of Palliative Nursing, 16*(8), 371–376.

McCormick, A. J., Curtis, J. R., Stowell-Weiss, P., Toms, C., and Engelberg, R. (2010). Improving social work in intensive care unit palliative care: Results of a quality improvement intervention. *Journal of Palliative Medicine, 13*(3), 297–304.

McQuillan, P., Pilkington, S., Allan, A., Taylor, B., Short, A., Mortan, G.,…Smith, G. (1998). Confidential inquiry into quality of care before admission to intensive care. *British Medical Journal, 316*(20 June), 1853–1858.

NSW Health Department. (2005). *Guidelines for end-of-life care and decision-making* (p. 17). Sydney: NSW Health Department.

Øvretveit, J. (2009). Understanding and improving patient safety: The psychological, social and cultural dimensions. *Journal of Health Organization and Management, 23*(6), 581–596. doi: 10.1108/14777260911001617.

Payne, S., Burton, C., Addington-Hall, J., and Jones, A. (2010). End-of-life issues in acute stroke care: A qualitative study of the experiences and preferences of patients and families. *Palliative Medicine, 24*(2), 146–153.

Pekmezaris, R., Walia, R., Nouryan, C., Katinas, L., Zeitoun, N., Alano, G.,…Steinberg, H. (2011). The impact of an end-of-life communication skills intervention on physicians-in-training. *Gerontology & Geriatrics Education, 32*(2), 152–163.

Phillips, J. L., Halcomb, E. J., and Davidson, P. M. (2011). End-of-life care pathways in acute and hospice care: an integrative review. *Journal of Pain & Symptom Management, 41*(5), 940–955.

Schulman-Green, D., Ercolano, E., Lacoursiere, S., Ma, T., Lazenby, M., and McCorkle, R. (2011). Developing and testing a web-based survey to assess educational needs of palliative and end-of-life health care professionals in Connecticut. *American Journal of Hospice & Palliative Medicine, 28*(4), 219–229.

Tan, Y. S., and Cheong, P. Y. (2011). Experiences in caring for the dying: A doctor's narratives. *Singapore Medical Journal, 52*(3), 140–145.

Walling, A. M., Asch, S. M., Lorenz, K. A., Roth, C. P., Barry, T., Kahn, K. L., and Wenger, N. S. (2010). The quality of care provided to hospitalized patients at the end of life. *Archives of Internal Medicine, 170*(12), 1057–1063.

White, P., White, S., Edmonds, P., Gysels, M., Moxham, J., Seed, P., and Shipman, C. (2011). Palliative care or end-of-life care in advanced chronic obstructive pulmonary disease: A prospective community survey. *British Journal of General Practice, 61*(587), e362–370.

Woo, J., Lo, R., Cheng, J. O. Y., Wong, F., and Mak, B. (2011). Quality of end-of-life care for non-cancer patients in a non-acute hospital. *Journal of Clinical Nursing, 20*(13–14), 1834–1841.

Young, S., Bartram, T., Stanton, P., and Leggat, S. (2010). High performance work systems and employee well-being. *Journal of Health Organization and Management, 24*(2), 182–199. doi: 10.1108/14777261011047345.

10
Giving Voice in a Multi-Voiced Environment: The Challenges of Palliative Care Policy Implementation in Acute Care

Geralyn Hynes, David Coghlan and Mary McCarron

Introduction

Health service research, particularly that emanating from sociology, has long recognized the hierarchical nature of the hospital environment. Issues concerning power, empowerment, participation and different kinds of knowledge are highlighted with the voices of some groups being silenced or dominated by others. Such issues are also of central concern in action research and determinants of the quality of an inquiry process (Bradbury and Reason, 2003; Reason, 2006). Thus, how we give voice to patients or different kinds of knowledge is a primary focus in healthcare-related action research. The purpose of this chapter is to show how the idea of heteroglossia or multi-voicedness may help in understanding what underlies persistent difficulties in implementing a well-supported palliative care policy. We explore the idea of voices as world views and multiple narratives rippling through the practice environment and inquiry process. We see these as ever present in how we hear and address other points of view, values and beliefs. The idea of multiple voices in action at any given moment shifts the focus from representing the individual(s) to how we consciously or unconsciously represent voices or narratives that flow through the inquiry process.

This chapter has three sections. In Section 1, we first introduce the idea of voices in health care and link this to national palliative care policy implementation. We then explore the idea of heteroglossia in which voice is neither singular nor static but rather, might be understood as reflecting multiple narratives that are often competing with one another for privilege (Hynes et al., 2012b). In Section 2, we draw on our experience of a two-phased action-research project aimed at embedding palliative care in nursing practice to illustrate the contribution which the idea of heteroglossia brings to policy implementation. For the purposes of this chapter, we focus on Phase 2 of the project. Our starting point is acknowledging the hospital environment as a melting pot of voices or differing and often hierarchical world views in which all are continually interacting with one another. Different positions reflect a particular emphasis on interpreting the nature of evidence and underpinning values (Kleinman, 1988; Opie, 1997; Puustinen, 1999; Charon, 2006). In the final section of this chapter, we draw on the idea of heteroglossia to suggest possible reasons why the implementation of a well-supported palliative care policy is complex and sometimes doomed. However, heteroglossia may also offer organizations and practitioners a means to begin to address the barriers to this same policy.

Recognizing voices in health care

Voices in health care

The study of chronic illnesses has given rise to a substantial body of work that distinguishes disease from illness perspectives and meaning-making (Kleinman, 1988; Cassell, 1991; Martin and Peterson, 2009). A disease-oriented perspective here refers to a world view that focuses on the biomedical, reducible or measurable aspects of a condition. This is in contradistinction to an illness-oriented view that embraces the experience of living with a life-limiting illness. A disease-oriented perspective underscores reductionism in acute hospital care in which disease guidelines and protocols govern criteria for decision-making and organization of care with predetermined expected bed stay, discharge planning and outpatients care.

An illness-oriented world view, on the other hand, addresses the physical, emotional, cultural and lifeworld experiences of living with the condition. Illness-oriented care places an emphasis on the individual's sense of self and the impact of a condition on his or her meaning-making and place in the world. Treatment of acute exacerbations of chronic illnesses is often underpinned by a disease-oriented philosophy of care. This is in sharp contrast with an illness-oriented care philosophy which might, in the hospital environment, be best exemplified in the idea of palliative care.

Within the disease/illness continuum, different disciplines, such as medicine and nursing, each bring their own knowledge base, values and positionality in relation to the reductionism of biomedicine, and psychosocial and existential dimensions of illness. Since the system as a whole and acute environment specifically, favour reductionism in management and care delivery, those disciplines such as medicine and management that are most associated with disease-oriented care are often hierarchical to those disciplines that favour a more illness-oriented knowledge and value base. Disciplinary positionality is reflected in their respective voices which are different to but continuously engaging with one another in a way that brings complementarity and tensions to engagement (Hynes et al., 2012a). Into this mix, patients and their carers bring their positionality in respect of illness experiences.

Policies and philosophies of care

The modern concept of palliative care is underpinned by the notion of total pain or suffering in advanced illness. Total pain recognizes that pain is multidimensional with physical, psycho-social, emotional and existential dimensions. These are interdependent so that to focus on one dimension only, such as the physical, is to deny a person's total pain or suffering. In advanced chronic obstructive pulmonary disease (COPD) for example, patients' illness accounts refer to living a life of COPD in which exacerbations are seen in terms of the overall illness trajectory (Elkington et al., 2004; Fraser et al., 2006; Goodridge, 2006; Goodridge et al., 2008). Loss of mobility, social interaction, roles and identities are part and parcel of this advanced illness trajectory. Thus, care delivery that focuses on management of exacerbations as discrete episodes of pneumonia fails to acknowledge patients' total pain or suffering and therefore palliative care needs.

In Ireland, as in other countries, there is a national policy for palliative care provision. This requires that palliative care be provided at different levels of expertise from specialist to basic. At basic level, the policy requires that every healthcare worker should have at least basic knowledge of palliative care. The policy also states the right of every patient to have access to palliative care while recognizing that for most patients, specialist palliative care will not be required. In essence, the policy requires that the principles of palliative care should be embedded in clinical practice and not left exclusively to those working in specialist palliative care. However, evidence points to failure in implementing policy in Ireland and elsewhere despite widespread support for change (Irish Hospice Foundation, 2010; Gott, Seymour et al., 2011).

Embedding palliative care in everyday practice is not about supplanting one care approach with another. Rather, from a policy perspective, palliative and acute care in advanced chronic illness should coexist in a complementary way. In the hospital environment, different world views are expressed through articulation of care needs and approaches, assessments of care process and organization of care. Attention to a patient's suffering experience reflects a different understanding of care needs to one which focuses on biomedical parameters. This implies a complex interaction of all and often competing world views that underpin approaches to and determinants of care on a moment-to-moment basis (Hynes et al., 2012a). Palliative care policy implementation therefore requires complex organization development that fosters difference rather than hegemony in chronic disease/illness management in our acute care settings.

Heteroglossia

The idea of heteroglossia is associated with Mikhail Bakhtin (1895–1975) and describes the stratification of language into a particular genre, dialect, sociolect, discipline/profession-specific jargon, and so on. These complex stratifications each with their particular associations are integral to our everyday life (Bakhtin et al., 1981). Each stratification as a language within languages with its underpinning values and beliefs is continually evolving. Thus, in a hospital setting, the voices of biomedicine, health informatics, medical authority, care recipients, different dialects and sociolect are continually evolving as they intersect one another in a given interaction. Even our titles for these voices are themselves stratifications of language with underpinning values and beliefs. Pathology investigations and reports, health-related quality of life, biochemistry, bed management, procedures, protocols are all familiar terms within any hospital environment, but each reflects a particular narrative and the privileging of certain world views over others.

In heteroglossia, languages are value-laden, hierarchical and in conflict with one another. There is a dialogic interaction in which those languages which are more dominant seek to maintain their position while others that are less dominant seek to avoid being controlled or subsumed. Bakhtin refers to this struggle as being mediated by centripetal and centrifugal forces. Centripetal forces gravitate towards the dominant language and status quo (Bakhtin et al., 1994). The reasoning that advocates risk assessment, narrowly defined algorithms for clinical decision-making reflects centripetal forces. These seek to diminish difference by gravitating towards the status quo in any given interaction. Centrifugal forces seek difference and challenge the status quo.

The acute care environment of care can thus be described as a multi-voiced affair with competing voices underscored by centrifugal and centripetal forces and underpinning our understanding of the environment. Heteroglossia in the world of acute care thus draws attention to the multi-vocal nature of our everyday speech. The point here is that even as we seek to give voice to different actors and disciplines, our very speech is multi-vocal and imbued with stratifications that reflect competing forces. The issue is not about stakeholder views or involvement but rather the nature of our speech and different voices therein. The idea of plurality of knowing becomes more complex and nuanced in how we privilege different voices on a moment-to-moment basis. Inquiry is thus, an emergent process acknowledging the unfinalizability of heteroglossia. Action research by definition is about unpacking different forces at play in our everyday practice and our interpretations or meanings that we draw from inquiry. In other words, action research might be said to be about revealing and conversing with multiple, unequal and competing voices inherent in our everyday practice.

Through a Bakhtinian lens, we understand inquiry into practice as recognizing the continually shifting meaning-making that occurs when competing discourses are given greater equity with one another. Whether our inquiry intentions are towards first, second or third order change (Coghlan and Rashford, 2006), or single or double loop learning (Argyris, 2006), we are privileging some voices and silencing others. It is our engagement with multiple voices, our privileging some voices over others and our attention to this privileging and silencing that reflect the quality of our action research and our giving voice to the other (Hynes et al., 2012b).

Unit of speech as utterance

The importance of attending to multiple voices might be understood through the idea of utterance in heteroglossia. Bakhtin describes an utterance as a complete thought that may be expressed in one or several sentences. An utterance is always value-laden through social, contextual and historical forces, each determining one's meaning-making. Our meaning-making is 'not only based on the structural features of language or the motivations and predispositions of individuals, but additionally, we grasp language as something a particular other says to us in a specific temporal, spatial and social situation' (Baxter, 2011:29).

As centripetal and centrifugal forces are always forming and reforming in speech, every utterance has its unique matrix of forces or heteroglossia. Recognizing the idea of heteroglossia offers the possibility of entering into a dialogic relationship with different and competing voices within the hospital environment in any given moment. The antithesis of heteroglossia is monoglossia wherein multiple world views are reduced to one, that which is dominant. This may be reflected in the language of care that reduces total pain or suffering to a narrow disease-oriented care approach focusing entirely on biomedical markers.

An action-research project was designed to better understand how practice might be developed to address palliative care in advanced COPD. Participation is a core principle of action research. Giving voice to other and addressing participation as both epistemological and political are manifest in how we consciously unpack the forces that underlie our utterances in a given moment. We see practical knowing as infused with conflicting voices or narratives that may reflect tensions between different notions of what constitutes evidence-based practice. Giving voice or engaging with other becomes less about stakeholders as individuals and more as voices or forces at play.

Developing respiratory nursing practice to address the palliative care needs of patients with advanced COPD

Background

This project was based in an acute general hospital context and sought to develop respiratory nursing practice to address the palliative care needs of patients with advanced COPD. Patients with advanced COPD live with severe breathlessness and experience life-threatening acute exacerbations requiring emergency hospital admissions. Palliative care for this patient group is made complex by a number of factors:

- Difficulties in assessing prognosis
- Complex treatment interventions that may be aggressive to the end
- The acute medical care environment is more geared towards, if not cure, then management of 'an illness episode' and discharge.

These factors can militate against conversations about death and dying, and involvement of the palliative care team. The advanced COPD trajectory reflects that of other advanced chronic illnesses seen in acute hospitals (Lynn and Adamson, 2003; Gott et al., 2007; Health Service Executive and Irish Hospice Foundation, 2008).

The project was designed in collaboration with the respiratory nurse specialists and had two phases. During the design phase, we were interested in attending to the illness experiences of patients and how these might be addressed. However, the respiratory nurses were equally clear that whatever evidence we produced, this would necessarily need to 'speak to' the language of management and medicine by way of disease-oriented measures. Our project design ultimately sought to address the nurses' concerns and the illness focus of palliative care.

Phase 1 aimed to identify palliative care needs through 26 patient interviews. Patients who had had one or more admissions to hospital for treatment of acute exacerbations of COPD were invited to participate. One of the authors (GH) interviewed participants in their homes. Interviews were structured using well-validated disease-specific health status measurement instruments. Interviews were recorded and expanded responses through stories were captured and transcribed.

The findings illustrated high-symptom burden, poor quality of life and the interplay between living with severe breathlessness and suffering. Phase 1 provided a foundation for understanding patients' illness experiences while also demonstrating poor health status through instrument scores.

Phase 2, which is our focus for this chapter, was a cooperative inquiry as a form of action research involving respiratory and palliative care nurses, and a nurse researcher (GH). The intended outcome for this phase was to provide a framework for addressing and embedding palliative care in everyday advanced COPD care.

Cooperative inquiry (CI) is one in which 'all participants work together in an inquiry group as co-researchers and co-subjects' (Reason and Heron, 2008: 366). An inquiry group usually comes together to address a shared concern or interest. The group engages in cycles of action and reflection in a systematic approach to developing understanding and action. The aim of our cooperative inquiry was to make sense of respiratory nursing practice and explore how care needs identified in Phase 1 might be addressed.

The Cooperative Inquiry

The CI group met over a 17-month period and comprised of respiratory and palliative care clinical nurse specialists, ward-based clinical nurse managers and one of the authors (GH) as an action researcher with a respiratory nursing background. Meetings were recorded and transcribed (GH). Each transcript was circulated in advance of the next meeting and then discussed by the group. At 10, 16 and 17 months, GH provided a summary of the inquiry process and emerging themes to date and these were again explored by the group.

Early meetings explored concerns arising from the deaths of patients and how the illness experiences reported in Phase 1 also reflected relationships with patients built up over years. Since these patients were experiencing increasingly frequent admissions as their condition progressed, the nurses built up close relations with them. Patients shared their illness and life experiences with nurses. However, these conversations more typically occurred in the corridors without any formal recognition in documentation or medical rounds.

The group viewed these conversations as separate from formal everyday respiratory care which was underpinned by organizational dictates of what constitutes 'normal' care in terms of bed management, admission and discharge procedures, appropriate time per patient consultation in the outpatients' department and documentation procedures. Criteria for admission and discharge from hospital and assessment in outpatients reflected a focus on a patient's oxygenation levels and related equipment and measurement. Similarly, levels of infection and other patho-physiological markers were a basis for disease-oriented care.

From the CI group meetings, the theme, re/presentation reflected the tensions between formal care delivery and the informal illness-oriented 'corridor' conversations with patients.

Re/presentation of patients

Acknowledging this disease/illness dichotomy drew attention to different ways nurses re/presented patients. Documentation and clinical conversations were disease oriented with a focus on biomedical markers and patients' care needs were described in these terms. This bore little resemblance to the nurses' illness knowledge of individual patients derived from knowledge about their life events and everyday experiences. The conflict between formal description of care needs and knowledge of patients' illness experiences drew attention to not only conflicting philosophies of care but also to the privileging of the more reductionist disease-oriented world view.

In the cooperative inquiry group meetings, the theme, re/presentation, brought to the surface an interest in responding to illness-oriented knowledge of patients' experiences and meaning-making. Conversations with patients and clinical colleagues were revisited during the inquiry group meetings. In these conversations, narratives of suffering, symptomatology, pathology, organization and practice routines, clinical guidelines and efficiency drives were evident. However, the weighting given to different narratives over others on a conversation by conversation basis illustrated disease and illness-oriented care conflicts. In short, re/presentation was central to system-oriented decision-making and control in patient admission and discharge decision-making, and organizational routines and practices. At the same time, the system privileged suffering in other scenarios. Patients dying from cancer were more likely to be under the hospital palliative care team and attending palliative care clinics with 30 minutes for appointments compared with the average 10 minute slots afforded to patients who were dying from COPD and attending the respiratory clinic.

Competing narratives in the acute care environment

No one, least of all patients in Phase 1 of this project, disputed the importance of a dominant biomedical narrative in emergencies. Nevertheless, the conflict between disease and illness narratives brings into sharp relief the reductionist conceptualization of chronic illnesses such as COPD in how acute phases are managed. An action cycle arising from the cooperative inquiry targeted discharge planning for developing an illness-oriented approach to care. However, changing discharge planning practice ultimately failed in the face of increasing pressures to discharge patients quickly with little warning and equally, pressures to process patients quickly in OPD. Thus, in any resistance by the CI group to disease-oriented care there was an implied resistance to the world into which members were socialized.

For Bakhtin, dominant or official narratives seek not to destroy or prevent other narratives but rather to dominate, absorb or monologize them (Bakhtin et al., 1994). Languages are, in this way, central to social conflicts taking 'the form not of a struggle between languages which are developing over time, but of a struggle over the context, narrative or otherwise, which will embody the development of some languages at the expense of others' (Hirschkop, 1999: 266).

Our inquiry process yielded new practical knowledge through greater understanding of how the disease illness dichotomy is mediated through our routine documentation and interactions. However, heteroglossia also brought to the fore the value in looking beyond a view of acute and palliative care as discrete entities. Heteroglossia introduced a way of articulating the hospital environment as a conglomerate of narratives that are continually forming and reforming as privilege is given to particular world views.

Viewed in this way, heteroglossia offers insight into possible reasons why attempts to embed palliative care in general ward settings have largely failed in different health systems (Irish Hospice Foundation,

2010; Gott et al., 2011). Through a heteroglossia lens, any attempt to introduce palliative care as an intervention or alternative approach to care is doomed to being what Bakhtin refers to as monologized by dominant forces supporting acute care. In other words, palliative care itself would be subsumed within a disease-oriented approach to care that is dominant within the acute care environment. Patients deemed to have palliative care needs would be referred to the specialist palliative care teams for symptom management resulting in concerns about reducing palliative care to a series of competencies or technical control of symptoms (Royal College of Physicians of London, 2007). Palliative care then becomes less an approach to care or world view and more an intervention for certain symptoms. Since suffering as a concept is silenced or monologized by disease-oriented care, then it is little wonder that suffering is neither recognized nor reported in official interaction. Thus, the very concept of palliative care as an approach to addressing suffering or total pain is not understood in the context of everyday care of advanced chronic illness. It is, at best, a second language.

Conclusion

Palliative care policy has been in place for over 10 years in Ireland. Yet, we continue to struggle with its implementation in respect of changing practice. The idea of heteroglossia may offer greater understanding of the complexities in addressing policy/practice gaps such as that reported in palliative care (Irish Hospice Foundation, 2010; Gott et al., 2011). The idea of heteroglossia draws attention to competing and hierarchical narratives in everyday speech. How we engage with the values and power underpinning our everyday speech is an integral aspect of participation in action research. This aspect may easily be lost amid concerns for different stakeholder representation in decision-making. In environments such as that of the acute hospital setting, attending to the nature of competing narratives in our everyday moment-to-moment speech may provide a useful framework for exploring any 'how' question in relation to policy implementation.

References

Argyris, Chris. (2006). *Reasons and Rationalizations: The Limits to Organizational Knowledge*. Oxford: Oxford University Press.
Bakhtin, M. M., Holquist, Michael, and Emerson, Caryl. (1981). *The Dialogic Imagination*. Austin (Tex.); London: University of Texas Press.

Bakhtin, M. M., Medvedev, P. N., Voloshinov, V. N., and Morris, Pam. (1994). *The Bakhtin Reader*. London: Arnold.

Baxter, Leslie A. (2011). *Voicing Relationships: A Dialogic Perspective*. London: SAGE.

Bradbury, Hilary and Reason, Peter. (2003). Action research: An opportunity for revitalizing research purpose and practices. *Qualitative Social Work*, 2(2), 155–175. doi: 10.1177/1473325003002002003.

Cassell, Eric J. (1991). *The Nature of Suffering and the Goals of Medicine*. New York; Oxford: Oxford University Press.

Charon, Rita. (2006). *Narrative Medicine: Honoring the Stories of Illness*. New York; Oxford: Oxford University Press.

Coghlan, D., and Rashford, N. S. (2006). *Organizational Change and Strategy: An Interlevel Synamics Approach*. Oxford: Routledge.

Elkington, Helena, White, Patrick, Addington-Hall, Julia, Higgs, Roger, and Pettinari, Catherine. (2004). The last year of life of COPD: A qualitative study of symptoms and services. *Respiratory Medicine*, 98, 439–445. doi:10.1016/j.rmed.2003.11.006.

Fraser, Danielle D., Kee, Carolyn C., and Minick, Ptlene. (2006). Living with chronic obstructive pulmonary disease: Insiders' perspectives. *Journal of Advanced Nursing*, 55(5), 550–558. doi:10.1111/j.1365–2648.2006.03946.x.

Goodridge, D. (2006). People with chronic obstructive pulmonary disease at the end of life: a review of the literature. *International Journal of Palliative Nursing*, 12(8), 390–396.

Goodridge, Donna, Lawson, Josh, Duggleby, Wendy, Marciniuk, Darcy, Rennie, Donna, and Stang, MaryRose. (2008). Health care utilization of patients with chronic obstructive pulmonary disease and lung cancer in the last 12 months of life. *Respiratory Medicine*, 102(6), 885–891.

Gott, Merryn, Barnes, Sarah, Parker, Chris, Payne, Sheila, Seamark, David, Gariballa, Salah, and Small, Neil. (2007). Dying trajectories in heart failure. *Palliative Medicine*, 21(2), 95–99.

Gott, Merryn, Seymour, Jane, Ingleton, Christine, Gardiner, Clare, and Bellamy, Gary. (2011). 'That's part of everybody's job': The perspectives of health care staff in England and New Zealand on the meaning and remit of palliative care. *Palliative Medicine* 26, 232–241. doi: 10.1177/0269216311408993.

Health Service Executive, and Irish Hospice Foundation. (2008). *Palliative Care for All: Integrating Palliative Care into Disease Management Frameworks*. Dublin: Irish Hospice Foundation.

Hirschkop, K. (1999). *Mikhail Bakhtin: An Aesthetic for Democracy*. Oxford: Oxford University Press.

Hynes, G., Coghlan, D., and McCarron, M. (2012a). Developing practice in healthcare: The contribution of bildung to negotiating the tensions among practical, professional and organisational knowing. *International Journal of Action Research*, 8(2), 159–184. doi: 10.1688/1861–9916.

Hynes, G., Coghlan, D., and McCarron, M. (2012b). Participation as a multi-voiced process: Action research in the acute hospital environment. *Action Research*, 10(3), 293–312. doi: 10.1177/1476750312451278.

Irish Hospice Foundation. (2010). *National Audit of End-of-Life Care in Hospitals*. Irish Hospice Foundation.

Kleinman, Arthur. (1988). *The Illness Narratives: Suffering, Healing and the Human Condition*. New York: Basic Books.

Lynn, Joanne, and Adamson, David M. (2003). *Living Well at the End of Life: Adapting Health Care to Serious Chronic Illness in Old Age*. Rand Health, Santa Monica CA.

Martin, Carmel M., and Peterson, Chris (2009). The social construction of chronicity – a key to understanding chronic care transformations. *Journal of Evaluation in Clinical Practice, 15*(3), 578–585. doi: 10.1111/j.1365–2753.2008.01025.

Opie, A. (1997). Teams as author: Narrative and knowledge creation in case discussions in multi-disciplinary health teams. *Sociological Research Online, 2*(3), U63–U76. doi: 10.1111/j.1365-2753.2008.01025.x.

Puustinen, R. (1999). Bakhtin's philosophy and medical practice – toward a semiotic theory of doctor-patient interaction. *Med Health Care Philos, 2*(3), 275–281.

Reason, Peter. (2006). Choice and quality in action research practice. *Journal of Management Inquiry, 15*(2), 187–203. doi: 10.1177/1056492606288074

Reason, Peter, and Heron, John. (2008). Extending epistemology within a co-operative inquiry. In P. Reason and H. Bradbury (Eds.), *The Sage Handbook of Action Research: Participative Inquiry and Practice* (2nd ed., pp. 366–380). London: Sage.

Royal College of Physicians of London. (2007). *Palliative Care Services: Meeting the Needs of Patients* London: Royal College of Physicians of London.

11
Rejections of Treatment Recommendations through Humour

Andrea C. Schöpf, Gillian S. Martin and Mary A. Keating

Introduction

One essential element of patient-centred care is the patients' involvement in their care including treatment decisions (Mead and Bower, 2000). The negotiation and sharing of treatment decisions also comprise patients' rejections of healthcare professionals' recommendations. Recommendations can be interpreted as proposals which require an answer. Acceptance is the preferred reaction, whereas a rejection is less preferred as disagreements are face-threatening (Brown and Levinson, 1987).

The fact that rejections are face-threatening is of particular significance in healthcare professional–patient communication due to the power asymmetry which is assumed to exist between professionals and patients (Pilnick and Dingwall, 2011). The professionals' more powerful position may influence patients' communication style due to face concerns. Face is 'the positive social value a person effectively claims for himself by the line others assume he has taken during a particular contact' (Goffman, 1982, p. 5). Brown and Levinson (1987) have distinguished between positive and negative face. The former refers to people's desire to be liked and to have their wants approved, whilst the latter refers to the wish that others leave them unimpeded. Certain communicative acts threaten the face of the hearer and/or speaker and, thus, they are called face-threatening acts. Normally, a person tries to protect the interlocutor's face, particularly if the other person is more powerful (Brown and Levinson, 1987). As a consequence, patients frequently state their opposition in a less face-threatening way, for example, by limiting their reactions to minimal responses (Aronsson and Sätterlund-Larsson, 1987). Moreover, patients can indirectly resist treatment recommendations by withholding acceptance (passive resistance) and, through this, participate actively in their care (Koenig, 2011).

The aim of this chapter is to explore the use of patient-initiated humour as resistance to treatment recommendations and to shed light on professionals' reactions. Humour is seen as a strategy to mitigate the face-threat of a dispreferred reaction. Hence, these humorous rejections contribute to the accomplishment of an instrumental goal, namely the making of treatment decisions, while simultaneously promoting relational goals. Relational goals concern the relationship between professionals and patients and, according to Grainger (1993), they are 'face-oriented'.

Methods

The research reported here is part of a larger study which analyses humour in diabetes consultations, using an interactional sociolinguistic approach (Gumperz, 1982, 1999). The research project was approved by the ethics committee of the hospital and the hospital administration.

The analysis presented here is based on 50 consultations and 32 interviews. The consultations were recorded over an approximately 9-month period in two locations of the diabetes healthcare setting in an Irish acute city hospital. The sample of 13 Irish patients represents a wide range of characteristics of the diabetes population such as age (between 20 and 81 years), diabetes type (type one vs. type two) and treatment regime (tablets, insulin or only diet and exercise-controlled). Seven doctors, eight nurses and six dietitians consulted with the 13 patients.

All participants were provided with written information and gave written informed consent. The consultations were audio-recorded with the researcher present. Patients were normally interviewed after their last consultation and professionals at the end of the data-collection period or before they left the hospital. Two professionals could not be interviewed. The interviews explored the concept of humour and included the playing back of consultation extracts in order to learn more about the participants' interpretations of humour events.

The first step of the data analysis was to identify humour which is understood as a conscious or subconscious communication strategy used to create amusement or to disguise serious messages under an allegedly amusing surface. The identification of humour was based on verbal, paraverbal and non-verbal cues. Subsequently, humour events were transcribed according to a system based on Jefferson (1978), Jefferson (1985) and Kotthoff (1998) (see Appendix). Interactional Sociolinguistics is a qualitative approach to the analysis of naturally occurring discourse on a micro-level, while also considering the social context of the interaction (Gumperz, 1982, 1999). The analysis of humour also drew on analytical tools and the terminology from Conversation Analysis (e.g. Heritage, 2009) and pragmatics (e.g. Searle, 1985, originally published 1979), while self-reports from the interviews supported the investigation of talk-in-action.

Findings

Humour as face-work

Overall, 295 humour events were identified. Patients used humour 18 times to reject recommendations or suggestions. On first sight, this number may seem small, but its significance becomes clear when considering that patients hardly ever rejected treatment recommendations.

Evidence for the argument that humour can mitigate rejections can be seen in how patients used a humour-disguised rejection after another form of disagreement, that is the face-threatening act has already occurred before humour was used for doing face-work. Extract 1 shows an example of where dietitian HP13 tries to decrease the patient's carbohydrate intake by including foods which do not elevate the blood sugar levels.

Extract 1

```
001   HP13: and then you know, if you wanted to you can uh- just to kind of
002         fill you up a bit, (0.6) I don't mind you having a boiled e:gg every day.
003         [just,   ]
004   P105: [I don't] eat eggs,
005   HP13: you don't eat e[:ggs]
006   P105:              [no. ]
007   HP13: eeh: ok, (0.4) don't do that theHEn HAHA[HAHA  ]HA ('H)
008   P105:                                         [yeaHEh]
009   P105: I'm not. I'm not a [lover.]
010   HP13:                    [I'M   ] NOT GIVING YOU.
011         IF YOU LIKE SOME[THING, YOU LIKE. ok?   ]
012   P105:                 [now I DON'T REALLY NOW] I'll eat a really hard
013         boiled egg. but it'd take me an houHEr to do it in the moHErning. like
014         you know?
015   HP13: ok. ('H) or do you like (0.6) do you eat ↑cheese at all.
```

After an overt rejection to supplement his breakfast with eggs, the dietitian's turn in line 007 indicates her awareness of the delicacy of the situation: she withdraws her suggestion and laughs. The patient weakens his rejection by stating that he is not totally opposed to eggs ('I'm not a <u>lover</u>.'). He mitigates his objection even further by providing another reason which can be classified as humorous due to its exaggeration (lines 013/14). This comment supports his objection, but the humorous surface lessens the face-threat as the rejection is less direct.

Patients also used humour in order to immediately reject a recommendation. Extract 2 illustrates how a patient tries to postpone the next appointment which is part of the treatment plan.

Extract 2

```
001   HP15:   TWO: and TWO: a:nd I'm gonna get you back rea:lly soo:n
002   P126:   .pt °°oh.°°
003   HP15:   in probably about (2.1) a month
004           (1.4)
005   P126:   [°°make six] weeks.°° [HE: ('H) HE            ]
006   HP15:   [wha-    ]            [m: you see the thing is,]
007           it's [so:, it's kind of da:ngerous to go on     ]
008   P126:        [ah no. I'm joking. I'm joking. FORGIVE] ME,
009   HP15:   .pt [↑huh::      ]
010   P126:       [°forgive me°] I'm only joking.
011   HP15:   um (0.4) get you back to see the doctor.
```

The nurse advises an increase in medication and an early return. Her turn in line 003 can be seen as a proposal, and the subsequent delay suggests that a dispreferred response will follow. The patient objects in line 005. This utterance is humorous as he voices his suggestion in a way that is normally used for haggling. Moreover, low voice emphasises the impression of a secretive deal. Through his humorous comment, the patient makes a counterproposal. The nurse does not overtly reject his proposal, but she gives a reason why her suggestion is preferable. As a consequence, the patient reverts to the loophole that the ambiguity of humour leaves open for him: he pretends that the face- threat never occurred, but that it was only a joke.

This section has illustrated that patients use humour to reject treatment recommendations. In addition to engaging in the decision-making process, humour is used to do face-work in two distinct ways: (1) patients use humour to mitigate a face- threat that has already been uttered, while simultaneously insisting on their objection or (2) patients use humour as a second-pair part to a proposed treatment option in order to reduce the face- threat of a rejection.

Healthcare professionals' reactions

The rejection of a recommendation provides an opportunity to discuss the treatment (Stivers, 2005), that is to involve the patient and, thereby, follow a more patient-centred approach. Within the data set, three types of reactions emerged: professionals provided an alternative, professionals defended their recommendation/suggestion or both patient and professionals did not discuss the rejection.

Professionals provide alternatives

Shared decision-making demands that patients are informed about different treatment options (Charles, Gafni, and Whelan, 1999). This requirement is not always fulfilled as alternatives may not always be discussed (Braddock, Edwards, Hasenberg, Laidley, and Levinson, 1999) or information is presented in such a way as to steer patients' decisions (Say and Thomson, 2003). In the context of diabetes care, the discussion of alternatives is particularly desirable as the patient is the main caregiver and has to make most decisions outside the consultation (Bodenheimer, Lorig, Holman, and Grumbach, 2002).

Despite the importance of providing different treatment options, only two professionals gave alternatives after patients rejected recommendations through humour. The best example of providing an alternative is illustrated in Extract 1. After the patient's rejection, the dietitian finishes the discussion about eggs, but she offers an alternative. In contrast to her preceding proposal, she formulates it as a question in order to find out if cheese is a preferable option.

Professionals defend their recommendation/suggestion

More commonly, professionals tried to defend their recommendation/suggestion or attempted to convince the patient of its benefits. In Extract 2, the patient conveys through humour that he would prefer a later appointment. After preparing a dispreferred response (m: you see the thing is,), the nurse gives a reason as to why her suggestion is better. Interestingly, the patient does not accept the suggestion by using an agreement marker but by pretending that the rejection never occurred (ah no. I'm joking.)

No discussion about the rejection

A final type of reaction can also cause the topic to be dropped, that is the rejection is not followed by any discussion, provision of alternatives or persuasion. An example from a dietitian consultation is provided in Extract 3. The diet history revealed several problems with P112's diet. The following excerpt shows a discussion about the possibility that P112's son might accompany her shopping.

Extract 3

001	P112:	my middle guy (0.3) if he comes shopping with me. (0.9) he keeps
002		saying, you don't need that. °why are you buying that.° (0.9) ↑why
003		are you buying- you don't need that. (0.8) ah don't buy that. that's
004		[full of sugar.]
005	HP38:	[↑>then take him] shopping.<
006	P112:	he is so: (0.4) °yeah, but you'll° end up with <u>nothing</u>, (0.8) ↑>you'll be<
007		coming home with ↑nothing,
008	HP38:	perfect. *then the press, there's nothing in the press for you t-* to <u>nibble</u>
009		on then *at three o'clock in the* ↑*morning,*
010	P112:	a gallon drum of protein (0.3) mix HAHAHA
011		HEHEHE[HEHEHE HAHAHAHA]
012	HP38:	[oh y- you say you like the- the] (0.3) the <u>sparkling</u> water.
013	P112:	yeah.
014	HP38:	you can put in, you can get <u>flavoured</u> sparkling water. (0.4) that's swee:t
015		(0.4) as we[:ll]
016	P112:	[oh he's] just gets <u>disgusted</u> now. it's- it's, (1.1) <u>why</u> are you
017		buying that when you <u>know</u> you're not supposed to have it.
018	HP38:	m:
019	P112:	°it's ↓u::::h *don't bring him*° [HAHA]
020	HP38:	[°ok°]
021	HP38:	you know what. I- I'm going to sit- I have your diary here.

In lines 008/009, the dietitian reframes the patient's indirect rejection. This prompts the patient to increase her objection by including an exaggerated humorous statement which is followed by a long laughter sequence (lines 010/011). The dietitian abandons the topic, but the patient continues to talk about the shopping issue. HP38 finishes this discussion again with the closing marker '°ok°', which is interpreted as unmarked acknowledgement, before changing the topic.

This example shows that professionals avoid further discussions not only to assert themselves but also to let the patients get their way. However, this interaction did not lead to a shared decision, nor was a solution found which might help the patient to avoid bad shopping habits.

Negative effects

While humour can be effective when patients get new information or even alternatives, its use can also have negative effects. The professional might misunderstand the conveyed message or the seriousness of the message might be underestimated or ignored.

Misunderstanding

Misunderstood humour can be particularly problematic if the misunderstanding is not revealed during the consultation. In Extract 4, the doctor is informing the patient about necessary improvements in his diet and exercise regime. One suggestion she makes is to join a weight-management group.

Extract 4

```
001   HP32:   and sometimes here they talk about. have you ever °u:h° thought about
002           joining weight watchers.
003           (0.7)
004   P119:   [I was in there for, TWENTY SEVEN weeks I was in it.] yeah,
005   HP32:   [it's supposed to be rea- it is- it's very good.              ]
006   HP32:   WERE YOU,
007   P119:   yeah,
008   HP32:   and?
009   P119:   about two stone, HE
010   HP32:   really you [see:, ] (0.4) and would [you ha-. w- WHY didn't you.]
011   P119:              [yeah]                   [but: I GAVE it up        ] then
012   HP32:   why, cause you've lost the weight?
013   P119:   u:h no. cause it was all a women's class HE °HEHEHE°
014   HP32:   °really?°
015   P119:   yeah.=
016   HP32:   =I think ↑THESE days though it might. when was that,
017   P119:   a couple of year ago,
018   HP32:   ok. [it ↑might] be a bit, ↓>you know< might be, (0.3) I think there is
019   P119:       [yeah    ]
020   HP32:   more MAN going now. I know [what you] mean.
021   P119:                             [yeah    ]
022   HP32:   I hear [a lot of people saying] that. sure get together an HE
024   P119:          [yeah. yeah, yeah,     ]
```

The patient's statement that he had once been a member of such a group prompts the doctor to ask why he did not continue and she adds a likely reason. The patient negates this assumption and adds a comment which is slightly humorous as his reason is quite unexpected (line 013). In this way, he justifies his rejection, thereby softening the face-threatening situation, but simultaneously supports his objection. The doctor does not reject his explanation so as to avoid a face-threat to the patient, rather she mentions that the composition of the groups might have changed.

Critically, the interviews with this patient and professional showed that humour obscured the communication. The patient's interview revealed that the composition of the groups was not the only reason why he would not return. He did not feel motivated enough in the group to lose more weight. By contrast, doctor HP32 thought that his distress was due to the fact that he was the only man in a group of women. She assumed that he was asking for reassurance and that 'maybe [he] wanted to hear that he should go anyway' (Interview HP32). Hence, she did not explore other weight-loss options.

Dismissing rejections

Negative effects can also result when professionals do not take rejections seriously enough or do not explore the patient's reasons for rejection. This is explained with the help of Extract 5 where nurse HP07 recommends the introduction of a cholesterol tablet.

Extract 5

```
001   HP07:   and you (0.3) would you ↑>think of c-< con↑sider (0.3) starting on
002           a: (0.5) a statin something to bring your cholesterol down.
003           (1.5)
004   P105:   ↑>I don't mind (?consider?) whatever it< takes. it basically. I mean
005           I can, I can just go back on the BENEcol uh whatever you know?
006           (0.4) I'm trying that for a couple of months and see what happens.
007           (0.8)
008   HP07:   ↑well no. your benecol is very expensive like and it (1.6) uh °uh°
009   P105:   if I have any more TABlets. I won't need food ↑>befoHAre theA
010           taHAblets HEHEHEHE< ('H)
011           (0.7)
012   HP07:   °alright.°
013   P105:   I've never took a TABLET in me ↑life unless I was diabetes.
014           (1.2)
015           I've never even took a ↑headache tablet.
016           (7.3) +HP07 is writing+
```

In lines 005/006, the patient shows active resistance by proposing an alternative treatment. The false starts are a sign of his awareness that this is the dispreferred answer. HP07 strongly rejects this suggestion. This is followed by the patient's strategic use of humour to support his reluctance (lines 009/010). However, by this time, the nurse has already shifted attention to his notes and only absent-mindedly adds another turn. Two additional comments which show the patient's aversion to tablets also fail to elicit an answer.

Later in the consultation the nurse calls in doctor HP32 to change the prescription. First, HP32 talks about an increase in P105's diabetes tablets. The patient tries to persuade the doctor that he wants to try to lower his sugar levels by an improved diet, but the doctor informs him that changes in medication are also necessary. The patient then repeats the humorous comment he used in Extract 5. Despite the patient's ongoing attempts to postpone the decision, in the end, the doctor prescribes the additional diabetes tablet and the new cholesterol tablet.

The combination of the consultation data with the information from the patient's interview revealed interesting insights. The patient tried to balance relational and instrumental goals by using humour. However, he did not achieve his instrumental goal, namely to postpone the prescription. Moreover, the professionals did not find out that the main problem was the patient's fear of the interaction between tablets. Even more critically, a strong divergence between the patient's interview and the audiotaped consultation emerged. The patient reported in the interview that the nurse HP07 took his opposition voiced through humour seriously as he did not put him on an extra tablet, and the decision to add another tablet was postponed. As a consequence, the patient did not take the new tablet. The consultation data contradicts the patient's statement as it provides evidence that he received a prescription. Furthermore, the fact that HP07 called in doctor HP32 to ask her for the prescription without further discussing the topic with the patient indicates that the nurse disregarded the patient's objections to an additional tablet which was voiced through humour.

Discussion

This chapter has shown that patients reject treatment recommendations and suggestions through humour. The use of humour can show a patient's awareness of the face-threat inherent in the serious underlying message and his/her wish to mitigate it. Due to its ambiguity, humour provides the possibility to ignore or revoke the face-threat. The patient can protect his/her own face by referring to the humorous side of the comment in case that the hearer reacts negatively (Goffman, 1982), and the hearer can pretend to miss the serious underlying message.

Consistent with Stivers' (2005) argumentation, patients do not necessarily need an invitation for participation. However, professionals' reactions strongly determine how successful this participation is. In most cases no alternatives were offered and patients were not asked to provide their own suggestions. Hence, professionals usually missed opportunities to explore patients' perspectives and involve them in decisions. The professional's defence of his/her recommendation can have different impacts. It can be interpreted as persuasion, which confirms the results of Fisher's (1982) study where doctors sometimes presented information in a suggestive or persuasive way in response to patients' objections. Professionals' justifications of treatment decisions can also lead to patients' feeling of ownership of these decisions (Mendick, Young, Holcombe, and Salmon, 2010). Ignoring a rejection is not consistent with patient-centredness, and ending a discussion without a solution can be problematic. While dropping a topic can mean that the patient successfully rejected a treatment recommendation, health outcomes might be negatively affected. However, the professionals might sometimes also abandon the topic or think that the patients' acceptance is unnecessary as they may not perceive the decision to be part of their professional roles. In this study, particularly nurses and dietitians described themselves as educators. Information provision about the best option from a medical perspective might sometimes be seen as sufficient for fulfilling their professional roles. Patients have to decide in their own daily life if they follow this advice.

Conclusion

Sometimes professionals find it challenging to find out if patients want to participate in consultations (Say and Thomson, 2003). A rejection, even when stated in a humorous way, stresses a patient's wish to engage. The fact that these messages are uttered in a humorous way is not necessarily a sign that they are meant less seriously, rather they may indicate patients' perception of being less powerful and/or that they are doing face-work. In the context of patient-centred care, professionals should acknowledge these rejections and discuss them with the patient in order to find a solution that both interlocutors can agree upon. Where they ignore these rejections, patients may find other ways to reject the recommendation, for example by non-adherence. Moreover, a discussion of the rejection can help to prevent misunderstandings. This, in turn, might positively affect compliance and produce better health outcomes.

Appendix: Detailed transcription notation for humour events

HAHAHA	Loud laughter
HEHEHE	Weak laughter
<u>humour</u>	Underline indicates stress, can also be used to mark emphases within a word
HUMOUR	Upper case indicates loud voice
humour	Italics indicate faster speech in contrast to remaining speech
° °	Circles indicate soft voice
°° °°	Double circles indicate very soft voice
:	Colon indicates lengthened syllable
,	Comma indicates continuing or slightly rising intonation
?	Question mark indicates rising intonation
.	Period indicates falling intonation
–	Dash indicates cut-off or self-interruption. Several dashes suggest that the talk has a stammering quality
↑> <	indicates higher-pitched tone of speech in angle brackets
↑	Upward arrow indicates higher pitch of tone within a word
↓	Downward arrow indicates lower pitch of tone within a word
↓> <	indicates a lower pitch of tone in angle brackets
[...] [...]	Speech in brackets placed one below each other is simultaneously
(0.7)	Pause measured in tenth of seconds
(( ))	Various characteristics of non-verbal communication for example ((smiles)), ((points to patient))
++	Various characteristics of conversational setting for example +door bangs+
('H)	Inhalation
(H)	Exhalation
>((rall))<	rallantando, slowdown of speech (comment under speech line)
>((acc))<	accelerando, speech gets increasingly faster (comment under speech line)
>((staccato))<	Word by word (comment under speech line)
>((impression))<	comments about impressions under speech line for example >((weepy))<
(? What's that?)	Uncertain comprehension
(? ?)	Incomprehensible part

References

Aronsson, K. and Sätterlund-Larsson, U. (1987) 'Politeness strategies and doctor-patient communication. On the social choreography of collaborative thinking' *Journal of Language and Social Psychology*, 6(1), 1–27.

Bodenheimer, T., Lorig, K., Holman, H. and Grumbach, K. (2002) 'Patient self-management of chronic disease in primary care' *JAMA: The Journal of the American Medical Association*, 288(19), 2469–2475.

Braddock, C. H., Edwards, K. A., Hasenberg, N. M., Laidley, T. L. and Levinson, W. (1999) 'Informed decision making in outpatient practice' *JAMA: The Journal of the American Medical Association*, 282(24), 2313–2320.

Brown, P. and Levinson, S. C. (1987) *Politeness: Some Universals in Language Usage* (Cambridge: Cambridge University Press).

Charles, C., Gafni, A. and Whelan, T. (1999) 'Decision-making in the physician–patient encounter: Revisiting the shared treatment decision-making model' *Social Science & Medicine*, 49(5), 651–661.

Fisher, S. (1982) 'The decision-making context: How doctors and patients communicate' in R. J. Di Pietro (Ed.) *Linguistics and the Professions: Proceedings of the Second Annual Delaware Symposium on Language Studies* (Norwood, NJ: Ablex Publishing Corporation).

Goffman, E. (1982) *Interaction Ritual: Essays on Face-to-Face Behavior* (New York, NY: Pantheon).

Grainger, K. (1993) ' "That's a lovely bath dear": Reality construction in the discourse of elderly care' *Journal of Aging Studies*, 7(3), 247–262.

Gumperz, J. J. (1982) *Discourse Strategies* (Cambridge: Cambridge University Press).

Gumperz, J. J. (1999) 'On interactional sociolinguistic method' in S. Sarangi and C. Roberts (Eds.) *Talk, Work, and Institutional Order* (Berlin: Mouton de Gruyter).

Heritage, J. (2009) 'Conversation analysis as social theory' in B. S. Turner (Ed.) *The New Blackwell Companion to Social Theory* (Oxford: Blackwell Publishing).

Jefferson, G. (1978) 'Sequential aspects of storytelling in conversation' in J. Schenkein (Ed.) *Studies in the Organization of Conversational Interaction* (New York, NY: Academic Press).

Jefferson, G. (1985) 'An exercise in the transcription and analysis of laughter' in T. A. van Dijk (Ed.) *Handbook of Discourse Analysis*, Vol. 3: Discourse and Dialogue (London: Academic Press).

Koenig, C. J. (2011) 'Patient resistance as agency in treatment decisions' *Social Science & Medicine*, 72(7), 1105–1114.

Kotthoff, H. (1998) *Spaß Verstehen. Zur Pragmatik von Konversationellem Humor* (Tübingen: Niemeyer).

Mead, N. and Bower, P. (2000) 'Patient-centredness: A conceptual framework and review of the empirical literature' *Social Science & Medicine*, 51(7), 1087–1110.

Mendick, N., Young, B., Holcombe, C. and Salmon, P. (2010) 'The ethics of responsibility and ownership in decision-making about treatment for breast cancer: Triangulation of consultation with patient and surgeon perspectives' *Social Science & Medicine*, 70(12), 1904–1911.

Pilnick, A. and Dingwall, R. (2011) 'On the remarkable persistence of asymmetry in doctor/patient interaction: a critical review' *Social Science & Medicine*, 72(8), 1374–1382.

Say, R. E. and Thomson, R. (2003) 'The importance of patient preferences in treatment decisions – challenges for doctors' *British Medical Journal*, *327*(7414), 542–545.

Searle, J. R. (1985) *Expression and Meaning: Studies in the Theory of Speech Acts* (Cambridge: Cambridge University Press).

Stivers, T. (2005). 'Parent resistance to physicians' treatment recommendations: one resource for initiating a negotiation of the treatment decision' *Health Communication*, *18*(1), 41–74.

12
An Expanded Shared Decision-Making Model for Interprofessional Settings

Mirjam Koerner, Anne-Kathrin Steger, Heike Ehrhardt and Juergen Bengel

Introduction

Patient-centredness is often related to patient–healthcare professional interaction and the ensuing relationship, participation, empathy and so on (external patient-centredness). However, the organizational pre-conditions, especially communication, coordination and cooperation in the interprofessional team and organization (internal participation), are often ignored in healthcare practice, although there is general consent that interprofessional teamwork is a key factor for patient-centred care (Norrefalk, 2003; Baldwin et al., 2007; Körner, 2010).

Bruhn (2002), a German researcher on organizational development and customer orientation, divided customer orientation into internal and external factors. Bleses (2005) adapted Bruhn's model on patient orientation. A patient relationship keyed to patient needs and with the primary aim of enabling patient expectations can be described in terms of the aforementioned models as external patient-centredness. We refer to internal patient-centredness when the professionals of a clinic, by focusing on internal clients (internal stakeholders: staff) are able to create in-house conditions that enable them to deliver a continuous strategy aimed at the expectations of external clients (patients). Internal patient-centredness includes all areas of activity related to staff communication processes within the clinic. The model of integrated patient-centredness was developed according to these models and summarizes these two aspects (Körner, 2009; Körner et al., 2013).

The organization of in-house processes (internal patient-centredness) will improve the various elements of patient contact. Through improved team consultations, for example, non-integrated processes with resulting breaks for the patients in the treatment procedure can be avoided, interface activities can be optimized and more personalized aims and treatment plans can be developed and agreed upon. This in turn can lead to enhanced patient loyalty and satisfaction, higher success rates and a competitive edge. Improved interactive behaviour on the side of the healthcare professionals, showing consideration for the different interdisciplinary competences, improves the quality of decision-making and treatment as well as increasing staff motivation and satisfaction (Körner, 2006, 2009).

The concept of shared decision-making (SDM) seems to be the ideal approach to facilitate external patient-centredness. In patient–healthcare professional interaction a common agreement on treatment choices and shared responsibilities is reached (Makoul and Clayman, 2006). According to Charles et al. (1997, 1999a,b), SDM is defined by three factors:

(1) mutual information flow between physician and patient,
(2) the communication of both medical and personal information and
(3) the discussion of everything relevant to the decision.

SDM is usually described in comparison with the paternalistic and information model. The main criteria for the description are flow of information, deliberation and decision-making (Charles et al. 1997, 1999a,b).

The paternalistic model corresponds to the traditional interaction model where the doctor determines the treatment, that means the doctor is autonomous. He knows best what is good for the patient, informs the patient, evaluates the information, deliberates and decides with the patient's welfare in mind. The doctor is therefore responsible for decisions made, while the subjective view and wishes and preferences of the patient are not considered.

The information model is the counterpart to the paternalistic model. Here all information patients would consider important in decision-making flows from the doctor to the patient. The patients weigh up the pros and cons of the options alone, decide themselves and also carry the responsibility for the decision alone. This model requires extremely active, informed and competent patients.

SDM can be located in between these two extremes. This form of interaction involves a reciprocal flow of information, whereby personal as well as medically relevant information flows from the patient to the doctor. Everything relevant to the decision is discussed, thus enabling patients' preferences, expectations and fears to flow into the final decision. Both patient and doctor contribute equally to the deliberating and decision-making process. While the doctor is an 'expert with regard to specialist medical knowledge', the patient is an 'expert with regard to his or her personal wishes and needs' (Makoul and Clayman, 2006; Rockenbauch and Schildmann, 2011).

The expanded (interprofessional) SDM model considers both external participation, which is extended from patient–physician interaction to patient–healthcare professional interaction, and internal participation (interaction within the interprofessional team) (Körner, 2009; Körner et al., 2013). There is a reciprocal flow of information between all parties involved, and treatment options are further discussed and deliberated between the healthcare professionals in the team. Both the information from the conversation between the providers and the results of the coordination process are channelled into the decision-making process in the patient–healthcare professional consultations.

According to Elwyn et al. (2005), the four key principles modified for the interprofessional context are as follows:

1. SDM includes all healthcare professionals participating in the treatment.
2. All healthcare professionals of the treatment team and patients actively participate in the process of decision-making.
3. Basis for SDM in interprofessional context is the exchange of information between the healthcare professionals and the patient (external participation) and among the health care professionals themselves (internal participation), bilaterally or multilaterally in the team.
4. Treatment decisions are made between the healthcare professionals (usually within the provision of the treatment plan: the physician/patient therapist) and the patient, in order that both sides agree with the decision. In addition, internal decisions related to the team and the clinic are made in the team.

In the original SDM model the decisions focus on medical aspects, whereas in the expanded SDM model the field of decision is extended to treatment decisions in general (e.g. treatment planning, goal setting), organizational (e.g. design of treatment concepts, working times schemes, organizational changes) and team decisions (e.g. assignment

Table 12.1 Comparison of the original SDM model with the expanded model for interprofessional settings

	Shared decision-making (original model)	Shared decision-making for interprofessional settings (expanded model)
Focus of decisions	Medical aspects	Treatment (medical, psychological) aspects, organizational and team aspects
Setting	Patient–physician dyad	Patient–physician dyad, interprofessional team
Levels of participation	Micro (patient–healthcare professional interaction)	Micro (patient–healthcare professional interaction) Meso (team) Macro (clinic)
Participation form	External participation	External and internal participation

of tasks, working process). While the setting of the SDM model is patient–physician or healthcare professional-dyad, in the adapted SDM model the interactions are interprofessional. The original SDM model only considers the patient–healthcare professional interaction (micro-level of the healthcare system). Furthermore, the adapted model also concentrates on the meso-level (team) and macro-level (organization) in the healthcare system. Participation in the original model is purely external and in the adaption both external and internal (see Table 12.1).

The aim of this part of the study "Development and evaluation of a shared decision-making training program in medical rehabilitation" was to find the key factors of internal and external participation as a basis for an interprofessional training programme.

Methods

A cross-sectional study with focus groups (six to ten patients, max. two hours) and a survey of experts was conducted in four rehabilitation clinics with different indication fields (Internal Medicine, Oncology, Orthopaedics, Neurology, Cardiology, Angiology, Psychiatry, and Psychosomatic Medicine), to determine the key factors of internal and external participation.

Focus groups are a form of group discussions on a defined issue within a limited time space (Krueger and Casey, 2006; Stewart et al., 2007).

In our study they were implemented to gain insight into the wishes and preferences of patients concerning their treatment in order to determine the key factors of external participation. A contact person in each of the four clinics was responsible for selecting participants for the focus group and ensuring that the group was representative of the usual patient population according to gender, age, education and diagnosis in their clinic. The discussion processes in the groups were led by the university project staff, with two hours reserved for each group interview. The questions discussed within the groups included the patients' role in decision-making, their preferences, needs and wishes concerning patient–healthcare professional interaction, information exchange and communication. Additionally, two questions were asked to determine the wish for and actual degree of involvement in the decision-making process in the clinic (on a scale ranging from $0 =$ the healthcare professional decides alone to $10 =$ the patient decides alone). Data analysis was accomplished through content analysis according to Mayring (2010), and the text analyses using the computer program MAX_{QDA} (http://www.maxqda.de/). The frequency of these categories was calculated in accordance with classification by means of inductive category formation.

The expert survey was conducted by the healthcare professionals in leading positions of different occupational groups (physicians, nurses, physical therapists, psychosocial therapists and others such as dieticians, social workers, sport teachers etc.) within the four rehabilitation clinics. To fulfil the inclusion criteria they had to be healthcare professionals in a functional or disciplinary leading position in these rehabilitation clinics. The experts could choose to complete the survey online or in a paper version. The main question of the self-compiled questionnaire was: How important are the following issues of internal participation for your work? These issues included communication and cooperation in the team (two items), (shared) decision-making in the team (four items), conflict and dialogue management (three items) and leadership (five items). The experts were also asked to rate the importance of the ten key factors of external participation identified in the focus groups. The survey investigated the importance of all these elements on a six-point Likert Scale from $1 =$ not at all important to $6 =$ very important).

The survey data was analysed by means of descriptive statistics using the Statistical Package for Social Science (SPSS Version 19). Before beginning the data analyses, data entry quality was tested by verification of random samples, the items were checked for plausibility and missing data analysis was performed.

Results

Samples of focus groups and expert survey

Overall 36 patients could be recruited for the focus groups in each clinic, with group sizes ranging from six to ten. The average age of the patients was 57 years (min: 19, max: 84) with 23 female and 13 male. Professions and jobs were heterogeneous, for example graduate professions, sales assistant, teacher, facility manager, butcher.

A total 34 of 48 experts participated in the expert survey (rate of return: 71%). Three participants did not match the inclusion criteria (because they do secretarial or other administrative work) and were excluded from the data analysis. The experts came from different occupational groups: ten physicians, four psychologists, six physical or sport therapists, seven nurses and four other occupational groups relevant to the treatment (for example social workers, dieticians, balneotherapists). The sample consisted of 18 women and 13 men; 80% were between 36 and 55 years old, 16% older than 56 and 3% younger than 35. Most of them (80%) had been working longer than five years in their clinics, with three-fourths leading teams of six to 20 members.

Results of focus groups

Most patients in the focus groups (80%) wished more time for medical encounters as well as more respect shown by the healthcare professionals. They felt this should be accompanied by a feeling of being taken seriously, having time to converse with the healthcare professionals and ask questions. Two-thirds wished to participate in treatment decision-making. More than half said that they wanted more individuality, trust and specific treatment. The desired degree of participation averaged higher than the actual opportunities available to them Mean$(M)_{\text{difference}} = 1.95$ (Standard deviation (SD) $= 2.71$), $t_{\text{dependent}} = -4.37(\text{df} = 35, p \leq .001)$). The ten factors most frequently named by patients ($n = 36$) were (frequencies ($= f$) in descending order: time for medical encounter ($f = 29$), respect shown by healthcare professionals ($f = 28$), participation in decision-making (SDM) ($f = 20$), individuality ($f = 20$), trust ($f = 20$), knowledge ($f = 20$), explanation ($f = 19$), cooperation in the team ($f = 19$), responding to individual medical cases ($f = 19$), and acknowledging professional limits ($f = 18$).

Results of expert survey

The healthcare professionals also evaluated the ten most frequently reported patients' needs as very important. The average ratings for the

Table 12.2　Importance of the key issues of internal participation (survey of experts, *n* = 31)

Key issues of internal participation	Items in the survey of experts	Importance	
		M	SD
1. Communication and cooperation			
	• Communication and cooperation in interdisciplinary teams	5.50	.63
	• Moderation of team process	5.14	1.21
2. (Shared) decision-making			
	• Shared decision-making in the team	5.43	.63
	• Designing treatment plans together with the team	5.28	.80
	• Sharing decision-making with different professionals	5.07	1.11
	• The role as executive, especially in team decision-making	5.23	.96
3. Conflict and dialogue management			
	• Moderating conflict discussion	5.38	.90
	• Feedback	5.47	.73
	• Talking with difficult team members	5.48	.64
4. Leadership			
	• Effectiveness of leadership style	5.17	.87
	• Motivating staff	5.48	.62
	• Delegating to staff	5.47	.68
	• Taking responsibility as executive	5.45	.72
	• Goal-setting with staff	5.30	.84

Note: Scale: Importance *(1 = not at all important to 6 = very important)*; M = Mean, SD = Standard deviation.

key elements of external participation were all between 5.2 and 5.8 on a scale from one (not at all important) to six (very important). Similarly, the different aspects of internal participation were evaluated as very important (see Table 12.2).

For internal participation the most important elements were communication and cooperation and SDM in the team, followed by conflict management and leadership.

Figure 12.1 summarizes the results for a participation model in an interprofessional context. The model shows that SDM is a key factor for both participation forms.

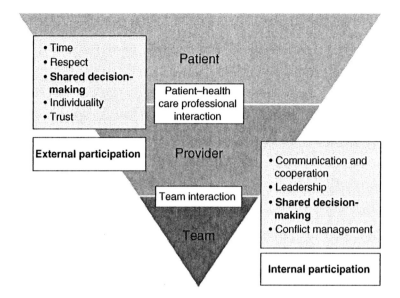

Figure 12.1 Participation model in interprofessional settings

Discussion

The patients and healthcare professionals considered SDM as a key factor of internal and external participation. The patients want to be more involved in interaction. In total, two-thirds of the interviewed patients wish for SDM. This has also been confirmed in other empirical studies (e.g. Coulter and Magee, 2003; Bieber et al., 2007a). The healthcare professionals also evaluated SDM as very important for internal participation ($M = 5.43$, $SD = .63$), with only communication and cooperation rated as slightly more important ($M = 5.50$, $SD = .63$). The results suggest that SDM is a vital success factor for internal and external participation. However, internal participation and organizational conditions are frequently not taken into account in the implementation of SDM in medical facilities. There are only a few approaches which consider organizational conditions and/or the interprofessional context (Montori et al., 2006; Stacey et al., 2010; Körner et al., 2011; Légaré et al., 2011; Lown et al., 2011). There is one model, for example, that acknowledged the healthcare team (Montori et al., 2006), but did not include collaboration in the team (internal participation) and its contribution to decision-making. Lown et al. (2011) defined specific communication skills for providing decision support, such as sharing knowledge salient to the decision and options for particular patients, discussing possible options and approaches to the decision, resolving conflict and reaching agreement among the interprofessional team. These are similar to the resulting key elements – SDM and conflict management – in our model for participation in interprofessional settings (see Figure 12.1). The interprofessional model of SDM from Légaré et al. (2011) considered three levels: the micro-level (individual patient), the meso- (the roles of the individual team members) and macro-level (the system level). Our approach also contains these three levels, but concentrates primarily on the micro- and meso-level.

In addition to participation, the patients wish and the healthcare professionals stated the importance of, more time, individuality, respect and trust in the patient–healthcare professional interaction. A sense of trust among professionals participating in the SDM process is also an essential element in the interprofessional approach of SDM developed by Stacey et al. (2010). Montori et al. (2006) also stated that trust and respect are important for establishing a partnership between patient and healthcare professional and within the team. Barriers to implementing SDM in an interprofessional setting are 'time constraints', 'lack of applicability due to patient characteristics' and 'lack of applicability due to the clinical situation' (Légaré et al., 2008). As barriers, Towle and Godolphin (2009) pointed out inadequate teaching of SDM, lack of time and incentives for staff, tensions between patient autonomy and professional authority, absence of good-role models and non-existent continuing professional development.

Communication and cooperation, leadership, SDM and conflict management are key issues for internal participation. These are all aspects of existing team models and team-development approaches (Baldwin et al., 2007; Nijhuis, 2007; Visser and Wysmans, 2010; Xyrichis and Ream, 2007). SDM in particular is highlighted as a key feature of teamwork (D'Amour et al., 2005; Nijhuis et al., 2007; Xyrichis and Ream, 2007; Visser and Wysmans, 2010). A differentiation in internal and external factors was also made by Baldwin, Royer and Edinberg (2007) when describing team maintenance: 'Both internal and external maintenance require attention for effective teamwork' (Baldwin et al. 2007, p. 39). This also applies to patient-centred care (see Figure 12.1).

Methodical limitations and strengths should be taken into account when interpreting the results. The selection bias (e.g. voluntary participation, non-responder) limits generalizibility, while the strength of the study is its heterogeneous sample, which makes the results more generally applicable and increases external validity.

The synopsis of the study results implies that there is a need for SDM implementation strategies in an interprofessional context. A starting point for facilitating SDM within interprofessional teams is training of the healthcare professionals. Studies provide evidence for the effectiveness of SDM training in physician–patient interaction (Loh et al., 2007; Bieber et al., 2008; Bieber et al., 2009; Towle and Godolphin, 2009). However, none of them consider internal participation and organizational conditions within the establishments. We therefore developed a new interprofessional training programme based on our expanded model of SDM which considers both participation forms, internal and external participation (Körner et al., 2011, Körner et al., 2013). This training programme, 'Fit for SDM', consists of two modules: Module 1, based on the already existing German training programme from Bieber et al. (2007b), teaches SDM in patient–healthcare professional interaction step by step. Based on the results of the study, this training module focuses more than the original SDM training programme on respect, empathy and individuality. Module 2 aims to transfer SDM into the clinic by means of a train-the-trainer approach. For this purpose it concentrates on internal communication and participation, leadership and team decision-making. The main topics are as follows: role as a trainer of the team, communication within the interprofessional team (communication tools and feedback), leadership styles (autocratic, participative, delegative), levels of delegation, basics in conflict management, decision-making tools and transferring these skills to the daily routine.

The current training programme is an essential step towards successful implementation of participation in an interprofessional context and includes the necessary knowledge and skills for implementing interprofessional SDM (Col et al., 2011). The innovative aspect of this approach is the consideration of internal participation, which is a main factor for the patient rehabilitation outcome. Few studies exist which focus on organizational factors in rehabilitation clinics, such as the team and their influence on rehabilitation success (e.g. better functional status of patients, patient satisfaction and treatment acceptance) or economic success. This study contributes to determining the key factors of an interprofessional team which are a precondition to conducting outcome studies in this field.

The interprofessional patient-centred participation model was based on the needs of patients with chronic disease, the preferences of the experts and the complexity of healthcare organizations. Both patients and the healthcare professionals in leading positions were involved in developing the model and subsequent training. The train-the-trainer approach assures the support of the clinic leadership within the implementation process and fosters the establishment of a new learning culture in the clinics (Reeves et al., 2007; Zacher et al., 2008). Implementing internal and external participation via training in rehabilitation clinics is an essential contribution for establishing patient-centred care and maintains a high quality of health care.

References

Baldwin, D., Royer, J. and Edinberg, M.A. (2007) 'Maintenance of health care teams: Internal and external dimensions', *Journal of Interprofessional Care*, 21 (S1), 38–51.

Bieber, C., Ringel, N. and Eich, W. (2007a) 'Partizipative Entscheidungsfindung und ihre Umsetzung im Gesundheitswesen', *Klinikarzt*, 36, 21–25.

Bieber, C., Loh, A., Ringel, N., Eich, W. and Härter, M. (2007b) *Patientenbeteiligung bei medizinischen Entscheidungen. Manual zur partizipativen Entscheidungsfindung (Shared Decision-Making)* (Freiburg: Universitätsklinikum).

Bieber, C., Nicolai, J., Hartmann, M., Blumenstiel, K., Ringel, N., Schneider, A., Härter, M., Eich, W. and Loh, A. (2009) 'Training physicians in shared decision-making – Who can be reached and what is achieved?', *Patient Education and Counseling*, 77, 48–54.

Bieber, C., Müller, K.G., Blumenstiel, K., Hochlehnert, A., Wilke, S., Hartmann, M. and Eich, W. (2008) 'A shared decision-making communication training program for physicians treating fibromyalgia patients: Effects of a randomized controlled trial', *Journal of Psychosomatic Research*, 64, 13–20.

Bleses, H. (2005) *Patientenorientierung als Qualitätsmerkmal* (Berlin: Medizinische Fakultät der Charité, 2005), http://edoc.hu-berlin.de/dissertationen/bleses-helma-2005-01-24/HTML.

Bruhn, M. (2002) *Integrierte Kundenorientierung. Implementierung einer kundenorientierten Unternehmensführung* (Wiesbaden: Gabler).

Campbell, S., Stowe, K. and Ozanne, E.M. (2011) 'Interprofessional practice and decision support: An organisational framework applied to a mental health setting', *Journal of Interprofessional Care*, 56, 423–427.

Charles, C., Gafni, A. and Whelan, T. (1997) 'Shared decision-making in the medical encounter: What does it mean? (or it takes at least two to tango)', *Social Science and Medicine*, 44, 681–692.

Charles, C., Gafni, A. and Whelan, T. (1999a) 'Decision-making in physician-patient encounter: Revisting the shared treatment decision-making model', *Social Science and Medicine*, 49, 651–661.

Charles, C., Whelan, T. and Gafni, A. (1999b) 'What do we mean by partnership in making decisions about treatment?', *British Medical Journal*, 319, 780–782.

Col, N., Bozzuto, L., Kirkegaard, P., Koelewijn-van Loon, M., Majeed, H., Jen Ng, C. and Pacheco-Huergo, V. (2011) 'Interprofessional education about shared decision-making for patients in primary care settings', *Journal of Interprofessional Care*, 25, 209–415.

Coulter, A. and Magee, H. (2003) *The European patient of the future – state of health* (Maidenhead: Open University Press).

D'Amour, D., Ferrada-Videla, M., San Martin Rodriguez, L. and Beaulieu, M.D. (2005) 'The conceptual basis for interprofessional collaboration: Core concepts and theoretical frameworks', *Journal of Interprofessional Care*, 20, Suppl. 1, 116–131.

Elwyn, G., Edwards, A. and Rhydderch, M. (2005) 'Shared Decision Making: das Konzept und seine Anwendung in der klinischen Praxis' in M. Härter, A. Loh, C. Spies (Hrsg) *Gemeinsam entscheiden – erfolgreich behandeln. Neue Wege für Ärzte und Patienten im Gesundheitswesen* (Köln: Deutscher Ärzteverlag), pp. 3–13.

Körner, M. (2006) *Teamanalyse und Teamentwicklung in der medizinischen Rehabilitation* (Regensburg: Roderer).

Körner, M. (2009) Ein Modell der partizipativen Entscheidungsfindung in der medizinischen Rehabilitation', *Die Rehabilitation*, 48, 160–165.

Körner, M. (2010) 'Interprofessional teamwork in medical rehabilitation: A comparison of multidisciplinary and interdisciplinary team models', *Clinical Rehabilitation*, 24, 745–755.

Körner, M., Ehrhardt, H. and Steger, A.-K. (2011) Entwicklung eines interprofessionellen Trainings zur Implementierung der partizipativen Entscheidungsfindung in Rehabilitationskliniken', *Die Rehabilitation*, 50, 331–339.

Körner, M., Ehrhardt, H. and Steger, A.-K. (2013) 'Designing an interprofessional training program for shared decision-making', *Journal of Interprofessional Care*, 27,146–154.

Krueger, R.A. and Casey, M. A. (2006) *Focus groups. A practical guide for applied research*, 3. ed, [Nachdr.] (Thousand Oaks, CA: Sage Publications).

Légaré, F., Ratté, S., Gravel, K. and Graham, I.D. (2008) 'Barriers and facilitators to implementing shared decision-making in clinical practice: Update of a systematic review of health professions' perception', *Patient Education Counseling*, 73, 526–535.

Légaré, F., Stacey, D., Pouliot, S., Gauvin, F.P., Desroches, D., Kryworuchko, J., Dunn, S., Elwyn G., Frosch, D., Gagnon, M.P., Harrison, M.B., Pluye, P. and Graham, I.D. (2011) 'Interprofessionalism and shared decision-making in primary care: A stepwise approach towards a new model', *Journal of Interprofessional Care*, 25, 18–25.

Loh, A., Simon, D., Wills, C.E., Kriston, L., Niebling, W. and Härter, M. (2007) 'The effects of a shared decision-making intervention in primary care of depression; A cluster-randomzied controlled trial', *Patient Education and Counseling*, 67, 324–332.

Lown, B.A., Kryworuchko, J., Bieber, C., Lillie, D.M., Kelly, C., Berger, B. and Loh, A. (2011) 'Continuing professional development for interprofessional teams supporting patients in health care decisions', *Journal of Interprofessional Care*, 25, 401–406.

Makoul, G. and Clayman, M. (2006) 'An integrative model of shared decision making in medical encounters', *Patient Education and Counseling*, 60, 301–12.

Mayring, P. (2010) *Qualitative Inhaltsanalyse: Grundlagen und Techniken* (Weinheim: Beltz).

Montori, V.M., Gafni, A. and Charles, C. (2006) 'A shared treatment decision-making approach beween patients with chronic conditions and their clinicians: The case of diabetes', *Health Expectations*, 9, 25–36.

Nijhuis, B.J.G., Reinders-Messelink, H.A., de Blécourt, A.C.E., Olijve, W.G., Nakken, H. and Postema, K. (2007) 'A review of salient elements defining team collaboration in paediatric rehabilitation', *Clinical Rehabilitation*, 21, 195–211.

Norrefalk, J.R. (2003) 'How do we define multidisciplinary rehabilitation?', *Journal of Rehabilitation Medicine*, 35, 100–102.

Reeves, S., Russel, A., Zwarenstrein, M., Kenaszchuk, C., Conn, L. G., Doran, D. and Strauss, S. (2007) 'Structuring communication relationships for interprofessional teamwork (SCRIPT): A Canadian initiative aimed at improving patient-centred care', *Journal of Interprofessional Care*, 21, 111–114.

Rockenbauch, K. and Schildmann, J. (2011). 'Partizipative Entscheidungsfindung (PEF): eine systematische Übersichtsarbeit zu Begriffsverwendung und Konzeption', *Gesundheitswesen*, *73*, 399–408.

Stacey, D., Légaré, F., Pouliot, S., Kryworuchko, J. and Dunn, S. (2010) 'Shared decision-making models to inform an interprofessional perspective on decision-making: A theory analysis', *Patient Education and Counseling*, 80, 164–72.

Stewart, D.W., Shamdasani, P.N. and Rook, D.W. (2007) *Focus groups. Theory and practice*, 2ed (Thousand Oaks: Sage Publications) (Applied social research methods series, 20).

Towle, A. and Godolphin, W. (2009) 'Education and training of health care professionals' in A. Edwards, G. Elwyn (eds.) *Shared Decision-Making in Health Care. Achieving evidence-based patient choice* (Oxford: University Press), pp. 381–388.

Visser, A. and Wysmans, M. (2010) 'Improving patient education by an in-service communication training for health care providers at a cancer ward: Communication climate, patient satisfaction and the need of lasting implementation', *Patient Education and Counseling*, 78, 402–408.

Xyrichis, A. and Ream, E. (2007) 'Teamwork: a concept analysis', *Journal of Advanced Nursing*, 61, 232–241.

Zacher, H., Felfe, J. and Glander, G. (2008) 'Lernen im Team: Zusammenhänge zwischen Personen- und Teammerkmalen und der Leistung von Multiplikatoren', *Zeitschrift für Arbeits- und Organisationspsychologie*, 52, 81–90.

Part IV

Innovations in Patient-Centred Care

13

Testing Accelerated Experience-Based Co-design: Using a National Archive of Patient Experience Narrative Interviews to Promote Rapid Patient-Centred Service Improvement

Louise Locock, Glenn Robert, Annette Boaz, Caroline Shuldham, Jonathan Fielden and Sue Ziebland

Introduction and background

Measuring, understanding and improving patients' experiences is of central importance to healthcare systems worldwide (Calabrese, 2010). In England, a recent government White Paper on National Health Service (NHS) reform emphasizes 'putting patients and the public first', or 'no decision about without me', as it has been characterized (Secretary of State for Health, 2010). The White Paper notes that:

> The NHS…scores relatively poorly on being responsive to the patients it serves. It lacks a genuinely patient-centred approach in which services are designed around individual needs, lifestyles and aspirations. Too often, patients are expected to fit around services, rather than services around patients.
>
> [section 1.9]

Ethics: This study has been approved by the National Research Ethics Committee North West, reference 11/NW/0653. *Funding*: This project is funded by the National Institute for Health Research Health Services and Delivery Research Programme (project number 10/1009/14). *Department of Health disclaimer*: The views and opinions expressed herein are those of the authors and do not necessarily reflect those of the HS&DR Programme, NIHR, NHS or the Department of Health.

Ensuring that the way care and information are provided reflects what patients themselves think is thus a priority. To do this, healthcare organizations need to draw on the experiences of those who have used services at first hand – but there is debate about the best methods for gathering and understanding patient-experience information and then using it to improve care (Coulter et al., 2009; Foot and Cornwell, 2010; Tsianakas et al., 2012).

Recent research with hospital Board non-executive directors (Dr Foster Intelligence, 2010) has demonstrated that patients' experience of care has become more of an interest and concern at Board level, especially since the publication of the Francis Report into poor quality care and above-average death rates at Mid Staffordshire (House of Commons, 2010). (Recent publication of the Care Quality Commission's findings from its Dignity and Nutrition Inspection (Care Quality Commission, 2011) can only have added to the priority now attached to this issue.) Strikingly however, over 95% of the time, hospital Boards' minuted response to patient-experience reports was to note the report but take no further action. Examples where patient experience data was used to spark debate and action were rare, as were examples of non-executive directors challenging performance. At organizational level, we do not know which national policy levers (incentives, penalties, targets, market competition, publication of information) work best to improve patient experience; this is a relatively 'evidence-light' zone in which to make policy decisions (Robert and Cornwell, 2011). At ward and service level there is anecdotal evidence that clinical teams and middle management make little use of national patient survey data to monitor service quality and drive improvement. It seems that current measures of patient experience are not used meaningfully or systematically at local level for a range of reasons but, not least, because they are not seen as clinically relevant and are captured too infrequently. Thus a significant gap between rhetoric and management action persists. In particular, providers of healthcare struggle to make effective use of qualitative rather than quantitative experiential evidence to improve local services.

In this context, the development, implementation and evaluation of a narrative-based, participatory action research approach known as Experience-Based Co-Design (EBCD) (Bate and Robert, 2007; Robert, 2013) marks a significant contribution to involving patients in quality improvement efforts in health care. Independent evaluations of recent implementations of the approach in both the United Kingdom and Australia (Farr, 2011; Iedema et al., 2008) have found that, as well as making specific changes to particular services, the projects also supported wider improvements across the healthcare system.

The value of narrative

Narrative persuasion is a well-established psychological theory (Green and Brock, 2000). Narratives can engage care providers at a deep emotional level in thinking how services could be improved (Greenhalgh et al., 2005). Narratives are not gathered because they are assumed to be objective, accurate or verifiable but because they are uniquely human and subjective, describing not a fact or a reality but a recalled experience or set of experiences. Patient accounts can nonetheless suggest priorities and solutions that may not occur to people who are immersed in service delivery (Iles and Sutherland, 2001; Locock, 2001). Some NHS organizations are now successfully experimenting with ways of gathering user views and using them to improve services. However, to ensure such work is evidence-based and accurately reflects a full range of different patient perspectives, it is important that it draws on rigorous research with a broad sample of users, rather than relying on a single representative on a committee or the collection of a few anecdotes (Daly et al., 2007). The study reported in this chapter seeks to combine EBCD with another initiative that emphasizes the value of narratives and narrative research.

The Health Experiences Research Group at the University of Oxford collects and analyses video- and audio-recorded interviews with people about their experiences of illness. It now has an innovative national archive of over 2,500 interviews, all collected between 2000 and the present and covering nearly 70 different conditions or topics, which provides a unique source of evidence on patient experiences and priorities. The interviews combine an unstructured narrative ('tell me your story') followed by semi-structured prompting. For each condition approximately 40 interviews are collected and coded and analysed thematically using the constant comparative method.

The interviews are approved for use in research, teaching, publication, broadcasting and dissemination on an award-winning patient information website www.healthtalkonline.org, one of the first health information sources to meet the Department of Health's new Information Standard. The interviews are increasingly used in teaching health professionals and to inform health policy – for example, National Institute for Health and Care Excellence (NICE) guideline development now frequently incorporates evidence from Healthtalkonline, and it is the only source of patient experience evidence recommended by NHS Evidence. Recent General Medical Council guidance on end-of-life care drew on a specially commissioned analysis of interviews from the archive. This analysis has recently been compared with a local set of interviews on end-of-life care. This showed that very few themes were identified locally that could not have been anticipated from the national data set (Calabrese, 2010). The archive thus has enormous potential as an evidence base of patients' experiences to support service change.

As outlined above, EBCD has been implemented in collaboration with patients, families and staff in service improvement efforts in various settings, care pathways and countries. A follow-up evaluation in Australia (Piper and Iedema, 2010) specifically explored the sustainability of the impact of EBCD two years after implementation and reported,

> Co-design has been shown to strengthen service provider-service user relationships ... co-design harbours a collaborative principle that should be woven into how health services and health departments conceptualise and structure their communication with patients, families and the public.

Previous implementations of EBCD – including the examples above – have therefore resulted in tangible improvements that have been felt by patients and staff, with many leaving a significant legacy in terms of patient-centred working, support groups and information for patients, as well as cultural change and a recognition by staff and patients that its collaborative approach is radically different to other change initiatives (Tsianakas et al., 2012). EBCD is now also being adapted for use by commissioning organizations in England ('Experience-led commissioning') and has recently been piloted in the context of end-of-life-care services in the West Midlands, where evaluation has shown similar positive impact (Cheshire and Ridge, 2012).

Integral to the approach is that patient, carer and staff experiences are used systematically to co-design and improve services. To date, this has involved an intensive local diagnostic phase, using rigorous qualitative research, including video- or audio-recorded narrative interviews in which participants are invited to recount their experiences using a story-telling approach, highlighting concerns and priorities and identifying 'touchpoints' (key interaction points) along their journey. The methods used to collect these interviews are very similar to those used by the national archive described above. Trigger films based on these experiences are then used, firstly to enable patients and carers to share and discuss their experiences with each other and then to stimulate discussion between local staff and patients, who can then jointly identify actions to bring about systematic, sustainable improvements.

The challenge

As noted above, independent evaluations have shown EBCD to be effective in improving the quality of healthcare services. However, the diagnostic phase before service improvement can begin is undoubtedly lengthy and costly and has been noted in evaluation as a barrier to uptake. Replicating 5–6 months of qualitative interviewing on each pathway in each hospital is impractical. We are therefore developing and testing a new accelerated form of EBCD by using the national interview archive to provide the majority of the evidence on patients' experiences and thereby scaling up EBCD more efficiently across different settings.

Methods

A traditional EBCD cycle typically takes around 12 months' work in each hospital to complete one pathway. In the accelerated version, we are halving the cycle to 6 months per pathway. We are thus:

> Identifying common themes arising from the national patient narrative archive in each of two exemplar care pathways (lung cancer and intensive care) Using this analysis to create 'trigger films' illustrating these themes which can in future be accessed and used by all NHS acute hospitals Testing these films alongside techniques that are part of the existing EBCD approach to stimulate service improvement work led by staff, patients and carers in two provider organisations in each of the two pathways.
>
> (Royal Berkshire NHS Foundation Trust and Royal Brompton and Harefield NHS Foundation trust)

Because we do not know how far using national rather than local narratives will affect local credibility and engagement, we are also conducting a process evaluation. From this we plan to make recommendations for quality improvement practice in the NHS.

Further detail on the methods for the intervention and the evaluation are provided in turn below, though in practice they are proceeding side-by-side.

THE INTERVENTION – accelerated EBCD

Steps in the process

For each of our four pathways (two in each hospital), the accelerated form of EBCD involves seven stages, adapted from traditional EBCD, as follows:

Secondary analysis of relevant narratives from the national patient experience interview archive to identify 'touchpoints' in our exemplar pathways, intensive care and lung cancer. Touchpoints are key moments of interaction between patients/carers and the service that shaped their overall experiences. Secondary analysis involves reusing data collected for another prior purpose to answer a new or different question (Heaton, 2004). The interviews in the archive have all been collected to understand people's experience of particular illnesses or health topics, ranging widely across social, physical and emotional issues, as well as experiences of services. The archive contains 40 interviews with people who have been in intensive care, 38 with relatives and friends of people who have been in intensive care, and 46 interviews with people with lung cancer.

Creation of trigger films drawing on the key themes and issues we identify as relevant for service improvement in the secondary analysis, and illustrating the touchpoints. Each film lasts around half an hour and uses extracts from a range of different individual interviews.

Discovery work with staff – whilst the trigger films were being developed, local service improvement facilitators were identified in each hospital and trained in co-design techniques. The facilitators used a combination of observation and one-to-one discovery interviews with staff from a range of disciplines (including medicine, nursing, allied health professions) to learn about their experiences of the two exemplar pathways and their views and expectations about what local patients experience. Findings were then presented and discussed at a staff feedback meeting where staff priorities for improvement were agreed.

Focus group workshops with local patients and carers were held in each hospital around each pathway, facilitated by local service improvement facilitators. The aim was to show patients and carers the trigger films and then use EBCD techniques such as emotional mapping to discuss their own experiences and priorities for improvement and raise specific local issues which may not have been captured in the film.

Co-design workshops with local staff, patients and carers – The facilitators brought together a multi-disciplinary group of local staff, patients and carers to exchange their experiences of giving and receiving services, again using the trigger films to focus on key 'touchpoints' where systematic and sustainable improvements might be made in each pathway. Participants shared their respective priorities for improvement and agreed which they would work on together in the co-design subgroups (see below). Building a coalition for change between staff and patients is central at this stage.

Co-design subgroups of staff, patients and carers were set up in each hospital to respond to the agreed priorities for improvement. A key feature of the approach is that the interventions should be designed collaboratively by patients and staff, with continued support from local facilitators.

Event – participants from each pathway and each hospital come together to review and celebrate their achievements, and plan further joint work.

Table 13.1 A comparison of a traditional EBCD pathway against an accelerated EBCD pathway

Experience-Based Co-Design (EBCD)		Accelerated EBCD
Months 1 and 2: Setting up		Months 1 and 2: Trigger film development and facilitator training
Months 3–5: Gathering staff experiences	Months: 4–6: Gathering patient experiences	Month 3: Staff engagement and patient workshop
		Month 4: Staff and patient co-design meeting
		Months 5–7: Co-design work
Month 7: Staff and patient co-design meeting		
Months 8–11: Co-design work		Month 8: Celebration event
Month 12: Celebration event		

A comparison of a traditional EBCD pathway against an accelerated EBCD pathway is shown above. The two months initial secondary analysis and development of the trigger film is of course a one-off investment; once a trigger film has been produced on a particular condition it can be reused in any hospital.

The evaluation

The evaluation is a process evaluation and cost analysis, building on existing evidence about the effectiveness of patient-led service improvement approaches. Whilst we are documenting improvement activities that take place as a result of the intervention in each hospital, our aim is not to evaluate EBCD in itself. Our starting-point is that it has already been shown to be an effective approach, and our aim with the evaluation is rather to demonstrate whether an accelerated version of it is a workable, affordable and acceptable alternative.

The evaluation is led by an organizational ethnographer, using a longitudinal comparative case study design and observational methods well suited to the study of complex change (Pettigrew et al., 1992; Dopson et al., 2001). In effect we have four 'cases': two different pathways in each of two hospitals. All the key research team participants are being interviewed and observed at several points during the life of the project.

All staff and patient workshops and meetings associated with the co-design process have been observed, as well as the training events held for the service improvement facilitators. We are also using a brief post-event survey used in previous EBCD initiatives to gauge participant reactions to the style and content of the workshops. Patient and staff participants have also been interviewed about their experience.

The analysis of observational and interview data includes both comparative case study analysis (Fitzgerald and Dopson, 2009) and framework analysis (Ritchie and Spencer, 2004).

An administrative system is in place to capture costing data, under the supervision of a health economist. The ethnographer is collating costing data from previous EBCD studies. The analysis will focus on the accounting cost differences between EBCD and Accelerated experience based co-design (AEBCD).

At all stages of the evaluation, the ethnographer has collected data to address our research questions:

Is the accelerated approach acceptable to staff and patients?

How does using films of national rather than local narratives affect the level and quality of engagement with service improvement by local NHS staff? Does this have implications for the overall impact of the approach?

From local patients' perspective, how well do they feel national narratives capture and represent themes important to their own experience?

Does any additional work need to be done to supplement the national narratives at the local level? If so, what form might this take?

What improvement activities does the approach, stimulate and how do these activities impact on the quality of healthcare services?

What are the costs of this approach compared to traditional EBCD?

Can accelerated EBCD be recommended as a rigorous and effective patient-centred service improvement approach which could use common 'trigger' films to be rolled out nationally?

Discussion and emerging findings

At the outset, we recognized that the accelerated approach might not work as well as a traditional approach, if local engagement were less forthcoming. We hypothesized that staff might feel unconvinced that issues raised by patients in the film applied to them locally; that it might be easier to say 'that never happens here' and feel less moved by the narratives to think differently about the care they offer. On the other hand, we speculated that seeing a different sample of patients could diffuse critical comments and make staff feel less defensive. The very fact that it is not local could enable a more collaborative approach.

As far as patients and families were concerned, we debated whether they would feel the issues raised in the film did not resonate sufficiently with their own experiences or with specific local concerns – or whether it might in fact be easier for them to raise difficult issues with staff indirectly by appealing to what others in the trigger film have said rather than in potential direct confrontation.

In our evaluation, patients have reported a reasonable agreement with the issues raised in the national archive. If anything, patients reported that their experiences were more positive and the films were 'too negative'. However, as group discussions have continued in the co-design workshops, more negative experiences have been disclosed. We have noted that in previous EBCD evaluations some participants have also said the films do not resonate well with their own experiences, even though extracts from their own interviews were included. It is possible that participants find it more difficult to voice or endorse more negative views in the setting of a hospital-based workshop with staff than in an interview off-site, especially if they feel a sense of gratitude for potentially life-saving care. It may also be that people who volunteer to take part in service improvement initiatives are more likely to be those who have had an overall positive experience and are motivated to 'give something back'.

Staff, on the other hand, have fully identified with the experiences shown in the films and have even been observed to take issue with patients who say that such things 'do not happen in this hospital' and assure them that they do. The service improvement facilitators have argued that the fact that staff are not listening to their own patients in the films has indeed made it easier for them to discuss openly how care sometimes falls short without defensiveness. Although not a central focus of our comparison between EBCD and AEBCD, another emerging finding is that – just as with EBCD – the capacities and capabilities of the internal facilitators in our case studies are key in shaping the nature of the change process and its outcomes.

As the intervention has progressed, we have started to feel that the extent of agreement or identification with the content of the films is not really the central issue. It is important to remember that the purpose of the films is to 'trigger' discussion. In traditional EBCD, too, they are only the start of a process of sharing ideas and worries, and working together to redesign care. If the national trigger films do enough to get this conversation underway, local specifics can then be brought into discussion along the way, and even disagreement with the content can generate fruitful discussion. Our evaluation so far suggests that the themes identified through national research and represented in the films have sufficient resonance with both staff and patients to start a conversation in a very similar way to traditional EBCD. Following this initial phase, we are observing considerable similarity between traditional and accelerated EBCD in the type of priorities selected for co-design, the relationships and working patterns of the co-design groups, the nature of the celebration events, the radical altering of perspectives amongst staff and the enthusiasm of staff and patients alike for the process. The key difference is that by using the national archive the accelerated form costs significantly less and the co-design (improvement) phase of the overall change process can begin much sooner. Ethnographic methods are helping us to identify and explore organizational cultural variation and power dynamics as they shape the change process, as well as fine tune our interview schedules and questionnaire design (and help map the costs of the approach); they also provide a longitudinal perspective on local implementation processes and are helping to capture differences in how participants feel about the approach in 'real-time'.

Conclusion

This research will add to our collective knowledge about how best to ensure patient perspectives are at the heart of service change and to ensure this is done as quickly and cost-effectively as possible. Accelerated EBCD has the potential to be a less costly, more efficient and therefore more feasible way of implementing EBCD locally, but one that still draws on rigorously conducted and analysed qualitative research, which has been one of the hallmarks of EBCD. The need for the NHS to seek ways to improve patient experience is a political and ethical 'given', so if this project can demonstrate a faster and less costly way to do it, there could be substantial gains for both clinical staff and patients.

The evaluation findings presented here are still being analysed at the time of writing and should be treated as emerging. However, a full peer-reviewed report of the study will be published in 2013–2014 in the new NIHR Health Services and Delivery Research (HS&DR) journal, within the NIHR Journals Library.

References

Bate SP and Robert G. (2007) *Bringing user experience to healthcare improvement: The concepts, methods and practices of experience-based design* (Oxford: Radcliffe Publishing).

Calabrese J. (2010) *A comparison of data on patient experiences of end of life care* (Oxford: Green Templeton College).

Care Quality Commission (2011) *Dignity and nutrition inspection programme: National overview* (London: Care Quality Commission).

Cheshire A and Ridge D. (2012) *Evaluation of the experience-led commissioning in end of life care project* (London: University of Westminster).

Coulter A, Fitzpatrick R and Cornwell J. (2009) *The point of care. Measures of patients' experience in hospital: Purpose, methods and uses* (London: The King's Fund).

Daly K, Willis K, Small R, Green J, Welch N, Kealy M and Hughes E. (2007) 'A hierarchy of evidence for assessing qualitative health research', *Journal of Clinical Epidemiology* 60(1): 43–9.

Dopson S, Locock L, Chambers D and Gabbay J. (2001) 'Implementation of evidence-based medicine: Evaluation of the Promoting Action on Clinical

Effectiveness programme (PACE)', *Journal of Health Services Research and Policy* 6(1): 23–31.

Dr Foster Intelligence (2010) *Intelligent Board 2010 – Patient experience* (London: Dr Foster Intelligence).

Farr M. (2011) *Evaluation report of the patient centred care project* (London: King's Fund).

Fitzgerald L and Dopson S. (2009) 'Comparative case study design: Their utility and development in organizational research' in D Buchanan, A Bryman (eds.) *Handbook of organizational research methods* (London: Sage).

Foot C and Cornwell J. (2010) *Improving patients' experiences: An analysis of the evidence to inform future policy development. Internal report to the Department of Health* (London: The King's Fund).

Garratt AM, Solheim E and Danielsen K. (2008) *National and cross-national surveys of patient experience: A structured review* (Oslo: Norwegian Knowledge Centre for the Health Services (Kunnskapssenteret)), http://www.oecd.org/dataoecd/43/58/39493930.pdf.

Green MC and Brock TC. (2000) 'The role of transportation in the persuasiveness of public narratives', *Journal of Personality and Social Psychology* 79(5): 701–21.

Greenhalgh T, Russell J and Swinglehurst D. (2005) 'Narrative methods in quality improvement research'. *Quality & Safety in Health Care*, 14:443–49.

Heaton, J. (2004) *Reworking qualitative data: The possibility of secondary analysis* (London: Sage).

House of Commons (2010) *The Mid Staffordshire NHS Foundation Trust Inquiry (The Francis report)* (London: The Stationery Office).

Iedema R, Merrick E, Piper D and Walsh J. (2008) *Emergency department co-design stage 1 evaluation – report to health services performance improvement branch, NSW health* (Sydney: Centre for Health Communication, University of Technology, Sydney).

Iles V and Sutherland K. (2001) *Organisational change: A review for healthcare managers, professionals and researchers* (London: SDO).

Locock L. (2001) *Maps and journeys: Redesign in the NHS* (Birmingham: University of Birmingham).

Pettigrew AM, Ferlie E and McKee L. (1992) *Shaping strategic change; Making change in large organizations; The case of the National Health Service* (London: Sage).

Piper D and Iedema R. (2010) *Emergency department co-design program 1 Stage 2 evaluation report* (Sydney: Centre for Health Communication (UTS) and NSW Health).

Ritchie J and Spencer L. (2004) 'Qualitative data analysis for applied policy research' in A Bryman, RG Burgess (eds.) *Analyzing qualitative data* (London: Routledge).

Robert G and Cornwell J. (2011) *What matters to patients? Policy Recommendations – A report for the Department of Health and NHS Institute for innovation & improvement* (Warwick: NHS Institute for Innovation & Improvement).

Robert G. (2013) 'Participatory action research: using experience-based co-design (EBCD) to improve health care services' in S Ziebland, A Coulter, J Calabrese and L Locock (eds.) *Understanding and using health experiences: improving patient care* (Oxford: Oxford University Press).

Secretary of State for Health (2010) *Equity and excellence: Liberating the NHS* (London: HMSO).

Tsianakas V, Maben J, Wiseman T, Robert G, Richardson A, Madden P and Davies E. (2012) 'Using patients' experiences' to identify priorities for quality improvement in breast cancer care: patient narratives, surveys or both?', *BMC Health Services Research*, 12:271.

Tsianakas V, Robert G, Maben J, Richardson A, Dale C and Wiseman T. (2012) 'Implementing patient centred cancer care: using experience-based co-design to improve patient experience in breast and lung cancer services', *Journal of Supportive Care in Cancer*, 20(11):2639–47.

14
Shared Decision-Making and Decision Aid Implementation: Stakeholder Views

Anne D. Renz, Carolyn A. Watts and Douglas A. Conrad

Introduction

Patient-centred care has captured the attention of healthcare providers, payers (public and private) and patients in many North American and European health systems. 'One of the ethical imperatives of patient-centered care is the balanced, evidence-based presentation of risks and benefits by providers to patients' (Weinstein et al. 2007). This ethical imperative may be put into practice through the use of shared decision-making (SDM). SDM is defined as 'a collaborative process that allows patients and their providers to make health care decisions together, taking into account the best scientific evidence available, as well as the patient's values and preferences' (American Medical Association 2010).

The concept of SDM as a component of patient-centred care has been circulating in the United States and other countries for years. The American Medical Association states, 'Formal shared decision-making processes and patient decision aids are potentially useful tools to help the US move toward more patient-centered care, which has the potential to improve the overall quality and efficiency of the health care system' (American Medical Association 2010). The National Institutes of Health (NIH) notes that SDM aligns with NIH's priorities on 'promoting effective communication and coordination of care'. NIH's Agency-Specific Quality Plan states: 'Shared decisionmaking [sic] has been widely advocated as an effective means for reaching agreement on the best strategy for treatment' (National Institutes of Health 2012).

In 2007, the Washington State Legislature mandated a demonstration pilot on the implementation of SDM (Keiser et al. 2007). This chapter reports on a two-year SDM implementation pilot project that arose in response to the legislation. We focus on the perspectives of five stakeholder groups who have been key to the implementation and sustainability of SDM in Washington and elsewhere.

Background

Shared decision-making and patient decision aids

According to the Informed Medical Decisions Foundation, SDM 'honors both the provider's expert knowledge and the patient's right to be fully informed of all care options and the potential harms and benefits' (Informed Medical Decision Foundation 2012). Patient decision aids (DAs) are often used to facilitate such patient-centred communication with the provider about treatment options. DAs are electronic or printed materials that present evidence-based, balanced medical information in a patient-friendly format (Informed Medical Decision Foundation 2012). In conjunction with DAs, 'shared decision-making tools and processes [are] known to improve knowledge, adjust unrealistic expectations, and elicit values about benefits desired and the degree of acceptable risks for individual patients' (Weinstein et al. 2007).

The importance of stakeholders

This demonstration project was mandated by state legislation. However, because the mandate was not accompanied by funding, the pilot had to rely on the interest, cooperation and commitment of several key stakeholder groups. Our team of researchers, with private funding from the Informed Medical Decisions Foundation and in-kind support from Health Dialog, worked with state agency personnel to secure the commitment of three western Washington health systems. The systems included a large multi-specialty clinic with 300-plus physicians and 16 practice sites, a 2-physician rural clinic that was part of a non-profit comprehensive healthcare system, and a large urban non-profit integrated system with a 300-bed hospital and more than 400 physicians.

With the support of the senior leadership in each of the health systems, we worked with designated project managers to develop processes to identify appropriate patients, distribute DAs and encourage the continued commitment of the clinical providers whose buy-in was critical to successful implementation. At the end of the two-year pilot, nearly 200 DAs for six preference-sensitive conditions and four chronic conditions had been distributed.

Over the two years of the demonstration, state and national conversations about how best to achieve patient-centred health care intensified. The role of SDM in patient-centred care, while not always a centrepiece, was often a component of the discussion. In particular, health plans and providers were interested in whether and how reimbursement might be offered to providers for their SDM activities. In Washington State, the conversation also included discussion of medical malpractice liability because of a provision unique to the Washington legislation. The provision offered increased liability protection for providers who engaged in SDM using nationally certified DAs (there was no certification process in place as of this writing in autumn 2012).

As the demonstration progressed, it became clear to the research team that the success of the pilot depended very heavily on the behaviour and investment of three key stakeholder groups: health system leaders, practicing providers and SDM implementation project managers. The practice penetration of SDM beyond the pilot period will also be influenced by the behaviour of two additional stakeholder groups: health plan leaders and medical malpractice liability insurers. Thus, we designed a qualitative analysis of the perspectives of these five stakeholder groups. Our analysis, based on grounded theory, used a sample of individuals in each of these groups.

Methods

Data collection

We conducted 15 interviews, including the senior medical officer, a provider engaged in SDM and an implementation project manager from all three demonstration sites. Our interviews focused on 'politically important stakeholders': individuals with the decisional authority to invest in an SDM demonstration project (three health system leaders), those who would be involved in implementation (three providers and three project managers), and those with a particular interest in the demonstration's outcomes (four health plan leaders and two medical malpractice insurers).

The University of Washington's Human Subjects Division approved the study protocol, and interviewees provided informed consent. Two study team members (an interviewer and a note taker) conducted the semi-structured interviews using similar questions across stakeholder groups where possible.

Data analysis

The interview transcripts served as the source of data for qualitative analysis. We performed open coding and used inductive reasoning to determine the thematic constructs. After pilot testing and revising the codebook, one person coded the transcripts. Intra-rater reliability was verified through a quality assurance process of re-coding 10% of the transcripts.

Results

Eight themes arose from qualitative analysis of the interview transcripts, many of which related to how SDM fits within patient-centred care. The thematic constructs were patient engagement, facilitators, barriers, benefits, financial/reimbursement structures, medical malpractice liability, perceptions of the value of SDM and general observations. A more detailed presentation of our findings can be found in the *International Journal of Healthcare Management* [in press, 2013].

Patient engagement

Though most stakeholders touched on almost all of the eight thematic constructs, the construct that emerged most often was patient engagement. Aspects of patient engagement included the following: the benefits of patient activation, involvement in treatment and self-determination; identification of patient goals and how those goals are connected with behaviour; providers' management of risk. Some interviewees emphasized the engagement of patients in medical treatment while others focused on increasing patients' awareness of the financial implications. While many interviewees spoke of patient engagement in terms of patient–provider interactions, some mentioned alternative and electronic means such as patient care coordinators, health coaches and online resources. There was also limited discussion of lack of metrics to define and measure patient engagement.

Facilitators

Stakeholders listed numerous facilitators, either factors that facilitated their own SDM implementation or that they predicted would have been helpful. The factors may be categorized into four areas:

- *Staff*: leadership and provider interest; availability of a patient care coordinator

- *Electronic health record system*: identification of appropriate candidates for SDM; 'prescription' of DAs; electronic reminders to providers to engage in SDM
- *DAs*: a convenient space to store and access DAs; self-explanatory introductory materials to minimize burden on providers
- *External organizations*: existence of competitors for motivation; presence of consultants or collaborative organizations for learning; supportive actions by government (e.g. encouraging the use of SDM and DAs through mandates or public purchasing)

Barriers

In addition to facilitators, interviewees listed a number of barriers that may be grouped into several types. In some cases, the barriers reflect the absence of facilitators.

- *Staff*: insufficient interest/investment among leaders and/or implementation staff
- *Electronic health record system*: limited ability to identify appropriate candidates for SDM; difficulty in 'prescribing' DAs
- *Organization*: structure that is not conducive to SDM and DAs; competing priorities within the organization
- *Cost*: DA materials; start-up time for implementation; ongoing staff time for SDM process
- *Reimbursement*: current system typically pays for volume of services

Benefits

Stakeholders identified several benefits of SDM and DAs. The benefits accrued to a range of parties:

- *Patients* would have more timely access to specialty care because the number of unnecessary referrals would decrease. Patients would also receive more evidence-based information about their treatment options.
- *Providers* might save time during the office visit with the use of DAs because the patient would be more informed. Even if no time was saved, provider–patient communication may improve: because the basic information about medical treatment options would have been covered, they could use the time to discuss the patient's values and preferences or to delve into treatment options in more detail. Providers also expressed that SDM and DAs can motivate patients

with chronic conditions to engage in goal-setting and to increase self-determination.

- *Health plans and patients* would benefit long term from improvements in the rate of appropriate utilization, both in the reduction of unnecessary services and in the increase of under-utilized appropriate services.

Reimbursement incentives

All 15 interviewees referenced reimbursement's effects on SDM implementation at least once. The comments may be grouped into the following areas:

- *Current reimbursement system*: fee-for-service, the predominant system, results in pressure to increase volume; both office visits and elective services declined with the recession; SDM may result in less invasive treatment choices, thereby lowering revenue
- *Predictions for the next 3–5 years*: increase in capitated or bundled payment; increase in payment for value; increase in accountable care organizations
- *Preferences with regard to reimbursement*: payment for value over volume; salaried healthcare providers; quality-based bonuses

Medical malpractice liability and shared decision-making legislation

The Washington State Legislature passed a law in 2007 that would raise the burden of proof needed for medical malpractice claims if healthcare providers used a certified DA with the patient. Though the providers we interviewed believed in the importance of documenting the patient's informed consent, few were aware of the legislation. The health system leaders, health plan leaders and implementation project managers had few comments on this topic.

By contrast, the malpractice liability insurers spent most of the interview discussing the basis of lawsuits, the state legislation and its potential effects. They noted that the law was unlikely to have much direct impact because few lawsuits are specifically based on a claim of lack of informed consent. More often, lawsuits are based on adverse events, which are a possibility with any procedure and might occur either by chance or by negligence. Thus, the legislation may indirectly reduce lawsuits because it encourages providers to ensure that patients understand their treatment options and the risks and benefits of each. The informed patient may be less likely to file suit for an adverse event that occurs by chance.

Perceptions of the value of shared decision-making and decision aids

Each stakeholder group perceived the value of SDM and DAs differently and thought they would be useful for different reasons.

- *Healthcare providers*: The DAs were viewed as educational materials that would be most helpful for patients with new conditions, particularly conditions with several treatment options (e.g. acute back pain). Patients with long-term chronic conditions, such as Type II diabetes, were already aware of their options for treatment and disease management. For patients in the latter category, providers thought the DAs might serve as motivational reminders to continue self-management.
- *Medical malpractice insurers*: Though they thought the use of SDM and DAs would be unlikely to affect the number of lawsuits filed, the malpractice insurers felt that their use could impact patient–provider communication positively.
- *Health system leaders*: The leaders of the demonstration sites were interested in the potential for SDM and DAs to improve patient satisfaction and quality measures/outcomes while possibly reducing costs. Although some of the interviewees planned to make the SDM/DA demonstration project a permanent and expanded part of their operations, they also noted that their organizations had several competing initiatives.
- *Health plan leaders*: The leaders of health plans were specifically interested in the (financial) engagement of enrollees in decision-making. To the extent that SDM and DAs were the vehicles to do so, health plans were interested. However, unless SDM/DAs resulted in changes from usual care, plans had little interest in paying for them, preferring to design global incentives and move away from individual service payments.

General observations

The medical malpractice insurers and health system leaders observed that their level of interest in SDM and DAs was based on how well they fit their respective organizations' needs. The malpractice insurers had limited interest in DAs because the DAs assist in informed consent, which does not tend to be the basis of lawsuits. The health system leaders' interest in (and emphasis on) SDM and DAs was correlated with how well they aligned with organizational priorities.

Interviewees' opinions of SDM and DAs were influenced by which party first introduced them and for what purpose. Interviewees tended to view SDM and DAs positively when they were introduced by medical professionals they held in high regard. Malpractice insurers, however, were uninterested in SDM and DAs because they were introduced by a state agency. The insurers stated that they favour using actuarial projections in determining rates, which would require credible data on cost savings or other clear value improvements attributable to the use of DAs.

Thematic constructs by stakeholder group

The eight thematic constructs contained a number of sub-themes. Each set of stakeholders focused on different thematic constructs and even different sub-themes when the constructs overlapped. The stakeholders viewed SDM and DAs through differing lenses, for different purposes, with differing facilitators, barriers, benefits and perceived values.

Healthcare providers focused on facilitators and benefits of SDM and DAs. In particular, they noted two facilitators: having organizational support and having a patient care coordinator to distribute DAs and answer questions. The predominant barrier mentioned was time. Additional sub-themes included patient engagement and how to identify which patients and conditions would be appropriate for SDM and DAs. The two thematic constructs that received the least discussion were medical malpractice and reimbursement.

Medical malpractice insurers, unlike the other stakeholder groups, focused on malpractice liability and the implications of the state legislation. The interviewees noted that their company had produced tools that were similar to DAs. The malpractice insurers framed the benefits of SDM and DAs in somewhat different terms than other groups, stating that they could reduce risk to healthcare providers; if patients have a better understanding of the outcomes and expectations for their chosen treatment decision, they will be less likely to file suit. The drawbacks of implementing SDM and DAs were primarily framed in terms of staff time and cost. The least-mentioned thematic constructs were patient engagement, facilitators and perceived value.

Health system leaders spoke at length of the potential for SDM and DAs to lower costs, improve quality and enhance patient engagement. These system leaders discussed the responses of three groups with whom the leaders were connected: they themselves thought SDM was valuable although their organizations have a number of competing priorities; their healthcare providers tended to support the concept of

SDM while recognizing its potential to decrease revenue in the current system and purchasers were open to discussing SDM while negotiating contracts. While health system leaders mentioned reimbursement and organizational structure as barriers, they made few remarks about facilitators, patient engagement or liability.

Health plan leaders introduced a financial aspect to the discussion of patient engagement, namely, that patients should be more aware of quality as well as financial implications. Plans were supportive of any means to encourage patient engagement and education, whether through SDM and DAs or through alternate approaches. They were not inclined towards paying for SDM and DAs unless it could be shown that their use resulted in treatment patterns that improve upon usual care. Rather than adding another discrete service for payment, plans preferred to create global incentives for healthcare providers and to offer tiered benefits to enrollees. Benefits, facilitators, barriers and the state legislation were mentioned much less frequently.

Project managers spoke at length about implementation facilitators and barriers. The top two factors that they saw as facilitators (or barriers) were leadership's support of SDM and DAs (or lack thereof) and the ability (or inability) of the electronic health record system to identify appropriate patients and issue DAs. Project managers specified three parts to leadership support: having SDM and DAs as a top priority, including relevant metrics in annual evaluations and fitting them within the existing priorities and workflow. Interviewees further identified as facilitators the buy-in of clinicians and staff and the help provided by other organizations in sharing lessons learned. The barriers they listed were time, cost and some cases of insufficient staff commitment.

Limitations of the demonstration

Patients are one significant stakeholder group that was not interviewed because of the project's scope. Given the potential for SDM to be a tenet of 'patient-centred care', patient perspectives would be valuable in informing the implementation and use of SDM and DA. Also, this demonstration project was implemented in multispecialty healthcare systems with primarily fee-for-service reimbursement, so our findings may hold less relevance in other contexts. Because the field of SDM is still relatively young, the relevant factors may evolve as it develops and spreads to other types of organizations. In particular, the spread of patient-centred care and the shift towards value-based payment align well with SDM, which may present opportunities and efficiencies that were not prevalent during this demonstration project.

Discussion

The five key stakeholder groups that were the focus of this study have a generally positive view of SDM. However, the positive view is tempered by the costs of implementing SDM, the ongoing time commitment and the urgency of competing organizational priorities. Thus, SDM must demonstrate sufficient benefit to make the value proposition worthwhile to policy makers and payers who must decide to pay for SDM, to health system leaders who must decide to implement SDM and to providers and patients who must decide to engage in SDM.

The experience of Group Health Cooperative (headquartered in Seattle, Washington) offers an illustrative example of how a robust, carefully phased implementation of SDM and use of DAs can affect treatment decisions and healthcare costs. Arterburn and colleagues (Arterburn et al. 2012) found that hip and knee replacement surgery rates were 26% and 38% lower at six months post-intervention, and costs were 12–21% lower. Based on Group Health's example, one promising combination for successful roll-out is capitation payment to the organization, salaried physician compensation and system-wide commitment to implementation and maintenance of the use of SDM and DAs.

The current reimbursement barrier in the United States, where provider reimbursement is based on volume, may be reduced somewhat as payers move towards bundled and/or capitated payments and healthcare systems move towards patient-centred medical homes and accountable care organizations. In addition, employers and health plans may provide other portals for patient access to the information and DAs that are a key part of the SDM process.

Ultimately, SDM is about the conversation between an informed and engaged patient and an informed and engaged provider. Trends in the United States and elsewhere point to increased access to information and increased accountability for patients, and more outcome-based rewards and accountability for physicians and other members of the expanding provider teams. This is a future conducive to the growth of patient-centred care, in which some form of SDM is likely to play a central role.

Acknowledgements

The authors thank research assistant Judy Chang for providing assistance with key informant interviews. The study was funded by grants from the Informed Medical Decisions Foundation (FIMDM Site Grants 0137–1 and 0137–2), Boston, Massachusetts, United States. The sponsor was not involved in the study design, data collection and analysis, or the writing of the manuscript.

Conflict of interest notification

The authors declare that they have no conflicts of interest.

References

American Medical Association. (2010) 'Shared decision-making,' *CMS Report* 7-A-10:1–6.

Arterburn, D., Wellman, R., Westbrook, E., Rutter, C., Ross, T., McCulloch, D., et al. (2012) 'Introducing decision aids at Group Health was linked to sharply lower hip and knee surgery rates and costs.' *Health Affairs* 31(9): 2094–2104.

Informed Medical Decisions Foundation. (2012) 'What is Shared Decision Making?' http://informedmedicaldecisions.org/what-is-shared-decision-making/. Accessed 11/18/12.

Keiser, K., Kohl-Welles, J., Shin, P., Rasmussen, M. (2007) 'Providing high quality, affordable health care to Washingtonians based on the recommendations of the blue ribbon commission on health care costs and access.' SB 5930 (60th Legislature, Washington State Senate).

National Institutes of Health. (2012) 'National Institutes of Health (NIH) Agency-Specific Quality Strategic Plan.' *National Strategy for Quality Improvement in Health Care* http://www.ahrq.gov/workingforquality/nqs/nqsplans5.htm. Accessed 11/18/12.

Weinstein, JN., Clay, K., Morgan, TS. (2007) 'Informed patient choice: Patient-centered valuing of surgical risks and benefits.' *Health Affairs* 26(3): 726–730.

15
Coordination of Care in Emergency Departments: A Comparative International Ethnography

Peter Nugus, Anne Schoenmakers and Jeffrey Braithwaite

Introduction

This chapter examines the role of ethnography in organizational behaviour in healthcare (OBHC) research through an analysis of comparative international ethnographic data. Ethnography is prolonged and immersed observation in a setting, to understand the patterns of behaviour of individuals in interacting with other people and elements of their environment (Spradley, 1980). Despite the increased profile of qualitative research, research in OB is, in the main, dominated by quantitative approaches (e.g. Miner, 2006; Hackman, 2009). Such research has been focused largely on prediction, based on controlling variables related to organizational inputs and outputs (Guzzo and Dickson, 1996).

Qualitative research, in the form of interviews and focus groups, has taken on a higher profile in OBHC over the years. For example, interviews and focus groups have shown the processes by which actors – including clinical staff policy makers and consumers – negotiate meanings, performance, quality and policy in health care (e.g. Currie and Suhomlinova, 2006; Miller, 2009; Hyde et al., 2012). The field's qualitative and mixed method repertoire has been expanded through the deployment of case study methods and analysis (e.g. Ferlie et al., 2005; McDermott and Keating, 2012).

Ethnography remains relatively marginal in OB and OBHC research. This is surprising, given its emphasis on enacted behaviour (Hammersley and Atkinson, 1995). However, ethnography is labour-intensive. It involves spending considerable time in one or more settings. Ethnography is a composite approach because it encompasses various methods to understand behaviour in context – including observing, shadowing, document analysis, interviewing, sense-making, making field notes to reflect what has been uncovered and even counting the frequency of particular events (Becker and Greer, 1960). Ethnography has sometimes been used interchangeably with qualitative methods, but we believe it must involve in-depth observation to retain its distinctive flavour. Situated observation helps build a picture of how individuals work as members of organizational cultures (Braithwaite, 2006a, 2006b). Ethnography is valuable for understanding the processes through which contexts or systems produce particular organizational or health outcomes. Rather than controlling for variables, ethnographers focus on the way those variables operate together interactionally. Even acts and interactions with objects, in everyday contexts, are documented. In terms of organizational behaviour, then, ethnography is valuable for exploring how interdependent individuals, groups and organizations function, or fail to function. Policy makers and practitioners can benefit from the information about factors that support or impede high-quality care, such as unanticipated negative consequences of well-intentioned actions or policies (Murphy and Dingwall, 2007).

Some theoretical underpinnings of ethnographic approaches

Ethnography is a methodology that focuses on behaviour-in-context. Yet, it presupposes a more abstract theoretical perspective that human beings and their contexts are interdependent. To this extent, various theories can underpin ethnography. For instance, healthcare settings are complex adaptive systems (CAS). They are dynamic, adaptive and self-organizing rather than static, and the key character of relationships among elements in a system is that the behaviours they create are emergent (Nugus et al., 2010a; Braithwaite et al., 2013a). Actor-network theory (ANT) represents action and change, not as stemming from a single or central cause, but the relations of effect that flow from the interaction of human and non-human elements (Mol, 2002; Law, 2008). Activity theory emphasizes the relationship between people and objects, in context, that influences how people internalize the external world (Engeström et al., 1999). Symbolic interactionism holds that people communicate on the basis of unspoken meanings, or symbols, about the purpose of their communication and respective roles in it (Blumer, 1969). Interaction represents the negotiation over shared meanings from the various communities to which the participants in interaction belong (Nugus, 2008). These conceptual exemplars of social action theories share the perspective of influence among human beings or among human and non-human elements. Such elements are linked in a chain of influence to broader social structures which guide what is perceived to be acceptable and unacceptable human behaviour.

By contrast, an assumption is made by many OB researchers that findings have to be statistically generalizable to be transferable to other settings (Hackman, 2009). Even in sociology, a conceptually comfortable home of social action theories, ethnography has often been marginalized on the assumption that its emphasis on local sites of interaction renders it 'astructural' – that is, incapable of accounting for broader 'structural' influences on the free 'agency' evident in individual behaviour (Prendergast and Knotterus, 1993; Dennis and Martin, 2005). Yet, the emphasis of social action theories on chains of influence – rather than disconnection between local and global activity – suggests the possibility of social structures being apparent in local interaction.

The emergency department as a setting for ethnography

The international context of emergency department (ED) care is a fertile setting to examine the potential influence and negotiation by individual clinicians of influences on their behaviour that originate beyond their interactive environments. Work in the ED has been shown to be complex and cognitively taxing (Laxisman et al., 2007; Patel et al., 2008; Nugus et al., 2010a, 2010b). There is a pattern of difference in the development of emergency medicine (EM) in developed nations that allow for comparison. In the United States, where EM was developed in the 1970s as a separate medical specialty, EM doctors practice an interventional model of EM. This means that they seek to provide assessment, diagnosis and full treatment, sometimes in consultation with doctors from other in-patient medical and surgical specialties, with the aim of discharging the patient directly from the ED, if possible (Zink, 2006). Australia and Canada subsequently pursued a North American model, developing independent organizations to credential emergency specialist physicians through structured training programmes and examinations in the 1980s (Cameron, 2003; Holroyd et al., 2004).

In continental European countries, EM is not an independently certified medical specialty and is typically practiced more conservatively,
where treatment stops at stabilization of urgent patient conditions,
rather than full treatment (Araujo et al., 2002). Although broadly
conforming to this model, The Netherlands has, in the last 10 years,
embarked on a process of professionalization of EM including formal
specialization training of three years, with the hope of developing a
programme to credential emergency specialist physicians, independent
of other medical and surgical specialties (Gaakeer et al., 2012; Thijssen
et al., 2012). Emergency doctors in The Netherlands are fully salaried
by the hospital and, unlike doctors from some other medical and surgical specialties, are not allowed to invoice the hospital for patient
treatment. Certification as an emergency specialist physician in The
Netherlands is provided by the national professional association of
EM, but under the auspice of the College of Physicians and Surgeons.
The relatively minimalist model of EM practiced in the Netherlands
is mirrored in a relatively strong primary care sector, where a referral by a primary care doctor (or general practitioner) is the common
route to access in-patient specialist hospital treatment (Kulu-Glassgow
et al., 1998). These differences in system-wide and organizational contexts provide an opportunity to examine the degree to which local
practices reflect and show the negotiation of system-wide influences.
We use findings from an ethnographic study to explore the potential for the unique contextual and systemic insights it can deliver into
organizational behaviour.

Methods

To examine influences on frontline ED clinical practice, we purposively
sampled five EDs in three countries at different stages in the development of the professional discipline of EM: two in Sydney, Australia, one
in a major urban region of The Netherlands and two in the United States
(Los Angeles and New York City), as suggested above. The EDs were
purposively sampled to feature EDs of large, well-known metropolitan
teaching hospitals.

We undertook observations and semi-structured interviews in all five
EDs over a total of approximately 10 months. Within the Australian
part of the study we drew on data from non-participant observation
of three doctors and three nurses at different levels of seniority from
each of two hospitals, over two shifts each. This meant that 12 clinicians were accompanied for 24 shifts. We replicated this method in one

Dutch ED and two US EDs, producing a sample of 60 shifts and 30 focal observational participants through whom we observed the meaning systems in each ED multiple times.

The Australian and US observations were conducted by the first author. The Dutch observations were conducted by the first and second authors. Field notes were recorded by hand. Semi-structured interviews were conducted with 50 participants, including five emergency nurses and five emergency doctors from each site. Interviews were conducted either by hand-written field notes or were audio-recorded and were subsequently transcribed. Interviews for the Australian study were a randomly selected subset of a larger set of interviews. Human research ethics approvals were secured for all sites, either from a university or hospital human research ethics committee or institutional review board.

The anonymized transcripts featured data from a number of individuals repeatedly over a number of sites, and both via observations and interviews, providing multiple points of comparison and contrast (Nugus, 2008). The transcripts were analysed using conventional thematic analysis, which involved the systematic search for variation in the data (Silverman, 2010). Particular attention was paid to the work of emergency clinicians in organizing patient care focusing mainly on relations with clinicians and organizations outside the ED. The themes were refined in a series of cycles, involving all authors, to derive an ever smaller and more abstract set of themes.

Findings

Pace of work, role and flow: What does it mean to be an emergency clinician?

In all settings, the function of particular roles and ranks was to learn how to be emergency clinician (doctor or nurse). In the case of Australia and the United States, where two departments were sampled in each country, the broad patterns of findings were similar across departments. Broad patterns were also evident in spite of individual behavioural differences, such as differing degrees of assertiveness in response to the high pace of work.

> *'We have to decide whether they should come into hospital or whether they can go to the outpatient department, or back to their GP'.*
> *(Interview, Senior Emergency Nurse, The Netherlands)*

It's about organising ourselves to get them in and out. That's really the basis of it.... You just don't know what's coming through the door.... Obviously, you have to make sure, if you're going to discharge them they have the proper support and they're safe to go.
                    (*Observation, Emergency Resident, Shift A,*
                                      Australian Hospital A)

There's so much demand on us and it's just relentless. We have to get them through as fast as possible.... We try and limit getting people in (as in-patients) unless they really need it. But we have to set it up so that they don't need to come back and back and back.... It seems to be getting worse.
          (*Observation, Emergency Specialist Physician,*
                                      Shift A, US Hospital B)

The function of the ED in all three national settings, then, was to assess and treat the conditions of ED patients as quickly and as safely as possible. In general, the Dutch ED was perceived by clinicians to be less 'busy' than elsewhere.

It's a different situation here ... I think it's partly because we have a really good primary care system. That's how people come here generally. And it's not that busy.... We don't have that much trauma . . . . . In fact I find it a bit boring ... I worked in the UK and it was totally different.
          (*Interview, Emergency Specialist Physician, The Netherlands*)

This was supported by observations. For example, an overhead intercom system frequently relayed messages, in a similar way as is used in airports and supermarkets. One such message, in an US ED, heard several times but no more than once per day, requested the family and friends of patients to leave the department for an hour given the work pressure on clinicians and staff. This did not happen in the Dutch and Australian EDs.

In all settings, doctors had primary responsibility for the medical management of patients. This involved 'work-up' – assessment in the form of history-taking and physical examination and review of previous medical records, stabilization, commencement of the treatment plan and disposition usually to an in-patient hospital unit or to their home or community facility. Such management occurred in discussion with doctors of various medical and surgical specialties. Emergency nurses cared for a particular subset of patients and generally remained in their vicinity, sometimes moving to and from the central nursing station to communicate with the charge nurse (also called the nursing team leader or nurse unit manager). The charge nurse (who was rostered on for each shift) moved around the department, liaising with the triage nurse (who gave an initial category of urgency to each presenting patient) and with other emergency nurses and emergency doctors to supervise the overall flow of the department (Nugus et al., 2012).

Inter-departmental relations: Who 'owns' the ED?

In all settings, interactions inter-professionally (across clinicians from different occupations) and between emergency clinicians and clinicians from other in-patient hospital departments were generally cordial, relatively informal and efficient. Patterns of difference were evident in relations between emergency clinicians and clinicians from in-patient departments. These differences manifested in the degree of 'ownership' emergency clinicians had over the ED and ED patients. Most doctors in the US and Australian EDs were more junior doctors (called residents or registrars) who were either in residency training to qualify as specialist EM physicians (called attending physicians in the United States), or were on rotation to the ED while in a specialty training programme of another medical or surgical discipline. Both groups were under the supervision of emergency specialist physicians. In The Netherlands, ED medical staff consisted mainly of residents from in-patient medical and surgical departments, especially neurology, cardiology, internal medicine and general surgery, who were supervised by specialist physicians in their respective departments elsewhere in the hospital. While in-patient residents who were rostered in the ED had allocated desks in The Netherlands, where they spent about half their day, in-patient residents in the United States and Australia attended only at the invitation of emergency doctors. They sat down in the ED only to write or type in the patient medical record.

The ED in The Netherlands was a sub-department of the Department of Surgery, whereas the EDs in Australia and the United States were independent organizational units. In The Netherlands, in-patient doctors admitted patients who needed to remain in the hospital for more than 24 hours, and, in doing so, rarely consulted emergency doctors. This situation was reversed in the United States, where emergency doctors generally made admission decisions without consultation with in-patient doctors. They entered the admission into an online system. The Bed Management Unit would allocate the bed, in consultation with a specific in-patient medical or surgical department. Emergency doctors in the United States would telephone or page in-patient doctors either as a courtesy, or if they believed the admission might be controversial. Even though most interactions in person were, and on the telephone appeared, courteous, Australian emergency doctors needed to persuade in-patient doctors to agree to review ED patients or accept ED patients for in-patient admission. This is evident in the following call by an emergency resident to a gastroenterology resident:

> Hi 'Paul'... We've got a very nice 81 years old gentleman called [names patient] on ... [medication] ... which is not bad ... His aspirin was stopped today but he's still on [medication]... A gastro patient? I think it's pretty easy ... (Pause)... Two weeks ago (Pause). Exactly. He's on [medication]. I suspect he has from what you're saying. (Pause). Yep ...Absolutely. [He's in resuscitation bay] 2 ... (Pause). Better today... Cheers mate. Bye.
>
> (*Observation, Shadowing Emergency Resident,*
> *Shift B, Hospital B, Australia*)

Following a similar pattern, the charge nurse, triage nurse and other emergency nurses in The Netherlands were much more likely than in Australia and the United States to liaise directly with in-patient doctors in the ED.

> **[Nurse] talks to [patient] in hallway. He is not allowed to eat. [Patient rudely asks the nurse to check with the surgical resident] to check to be sure [he] is not allowed to eat before his scan.**
> **[Nurse]** '*Does he need to be fasting?*'
> [Surgical resident]: '*Yes definitely – might be appendicitis.*'
> [Nurse]: '*He doesn't get it.*'
> [Surgical resident]: '*Oh. Well, I'm very busy.*'
> [Nurse]: '*I'll call Radiology.*'
> [Surgical resident]: '*Always a good thing.*' (*Smiling, possibly mildly sarcastic. [They need to be chased]*).
>
> (*Observation, Shadowing Junior Emergency Nurse,*
> *Shift B, The Netherlands*)

Such liaison only happened in the United States and Australia with patients who had been admitted to the hospital as in-patients and were only in the ED because no in-patient beds were yet available. A further difference was that in the US and Australian EDs, unlike The Netherlands, physical and occupational therapists, social workers and care coordination, geriatric and psychiatric liaison nurses were, at least part-time, based in the EDs.

Inter-organizational relations: The function EDs in broader health systems

In The Netherlands, compared with the United States and Australia, the ED functioned merely as a gateway for patients to enter the hospital via direct referral from a primary care doctor. This was the case for two-thirds of the patients who presented at the ED. This meant that the role of in-patient residents based in the ED was to receive primary-care referred patients on behalf of their respective departments.

> [Internal Medicine (IM) Resident] *gets a phone call about a nephrology patient from [a nearby town]. The patient's GP phoned the nephrology department. The nephrologists told the GP to [to contact] the ED [and come to the ED].*
>
> [IM Resident 1] *(on phone): '... and labs and an x-ray. Yes. No. Not any-more. No, that is unlikely. We will do that. Shall I discuss that with you*
>
> *or-. Okay. How should I call? [patient identification number and name]. I'll do that. Thank you. Bye.'*
>
> ....
>
> Male Receptionist*: 'Did you get an announcement about [patient's name] from Haematology?'*
>
> ....
>
> [IM Resident 2]*: 'Is something finally going to happen?'*
> [IM Resident 1]*: 'Yes, we've got an announcement.'*
> When [the patient] is announced by phone, [IM Resident 1] starts filling in an announcement form. This needs to go to the reception, so the secretary can put the [patient's] details into the computer and page [IM Resident 1] when [the patient] arrives. [IM Resident 1] also needs to find the nurse coordinator to update them about the announcement.
>
> *(Observation, Shadowing Internal Medicine*
> *Resident, The Netherlands)*

In-patient residents, in consultation with a supervising physician from their specialty, determined whether the patient warranted hospitalization for more than 24 hours, and, if so, whether admission would be most appropriate under theirs or another department. The role of attending emergency physicians in The Netherlands was relegated to caring for a smaller number of unplanned admissions. However, this was limited to patients with relatively minor conditions. In all departments, trauma calls were attended by an on-duty trauma team consisting, for example, of a general surgeon, an anaesthetist, a neurologist or neurosurgeon and emergency doctors and nurses. We never witnessed emergency doctors leading a trauma in The Netherlands. They were led only by residents or attending physicians of in-patient teams, most typically, from general surgery. However, in the United States, only emergency residents led inter-departmental trauma calls.

The EDs in all systems functioned to attend to unexpected illness or as a potential gateway to the hospital. The centrality of external relations manifested differently in each system. In The Netherlands, clinicians generally perceived that the ED ought to have a 'minimalist' role, characterized by receipt only of patients who had 'real emergencies'. Nurses, in particular, complained that the ED was being used as a place for the Outpatient Department (OPD) care, to send patients to have tests, such as blood tests, performed more quickly than in the OPD.

> Nurse: *[Patient's name]*
> *[IM Resident 1 to*
> *IM Resident 2] 'Do you know anything about that?'*
> Nurse: *'It's announced by ['Dr van Dijk']. With a SCI. Already did a CT. He wanted to come over earlier but couldn't arrange it.'*
> [IM Resident 1]: *'Just ask what we need to do. We just wanted to go for lunch. Sounds a bit OPD [outpatient department]-like.'*
> Nurse: *'Yeah, but they're coming here. We are the overflow OPD (sarcastic). The ED is called OPD-1 for a reason.'*
> [IM Resident 2]: *'Really?'*
> Nurse: *'Well, we are seeing quite a lot of OPD patients over here ....'*
> Nurse: *'['Dr van Dijk'] will page you with more info.' S' pager goes off. [IM Resident 2] to*
> [IM Resident 2]: *'Can you give this announcement to the nurse coordinator?'*
>
> (*Observation, Shadowing Internal Medicine Resident, The Netherlands*)

While, in general, Dutch emergency clinicians perceived communication, information technology and electronic record-keeping across sectors, and ambulance services, to be well organized, United States and Australia emergency clinicians were more likely to express concerns about lack of coordination in the broader health system beyond the ED and the hospital. Accordingly, the EDs in the United States and Australia saw their roles as more expansive – or 'maximalist' than in The Netherlands. This involved assessment, categorization and treatment of all patients with undifferentiated conditions, even if their conditions did not seem to be 'urgent'.

> [Senior resident to junior resident after junior resident complained about patient not being urgent]: 'Patients aren't psychic and they're not doctors. That's why they're here.... (later)... He needs IV steroids and magnesium. He'll be here for a while.... I'm gonna put him in'. Senior Resident confirmed that admitted patient electronically.
>
> > (*Observation, Shadowing Senior Emergency Resident, Shift A, Hospital B, US*)

> [During sign out of emergency specialist physicians]
> [*Male emergency physician*]: 'He's definitely tender... Tachy [tachycardic] to 120 which is why I brought him back to resus'.
> [*Female emergency physician*]: 'He refused a chest x-ray'.
> [*Male emergency physician*]: 'We'll see what the basic labs show. He assisted us
> taking labs'.
> [*Female emergency physician*]: '[I admitted him] but you guys [next shift of physicians] still should know'.
>
> > (*Observation, Shadowing Emergency Specialist Physician, Shift A, Hospital B, US*)

In Australia, emergency doctors spent more time than their Dutch counterparts in negotiating coordination of care with General Practitioners (GPs). The Dutch internal hospital-based doctors generally received calls from GPs, announcing the impending arrival of one of their patients. Without the ability to assume patients would be cared for by a GP, Australian emergency doctors valued effective communication with GPs.

> GP patients are not always known to us. Some ring. Some send a letter. Some don't. It makes such a difference if they ring on the mobile. We advise them or know to expect [the patient].... Sometimes they don't need to come in.... (Later)... See, the GP sends this guy in. No communication... no ultrasound... He'll wait for two hours and get

angry. The GP looks bad.... If they'd just phone we could talk and advise.

(*Observation, Shadowing Emergency Specialist Physician, Shift B, Hospital A, Australia*)

US EDs are more likely to be used as primary care facilities than in either The Netherlands or Australia.

There's a lot more primary care...because patients have no insurance or even illegal [immigrants]. Like, today, someone had abdominal pain for three years and came in today because they got a lift to the hospital. They've got no primary care. It's not their fault. They've got nowhere else to go.

(*Interview, Junior Emergency Resident, Hospital A, US*)

Although US EDs are required by law to treat all patients regardless of their financial status, emergency doctors sometimes sought the coordinate care for poorer patients in ways other than in-patient admission.

[Junior Resident to Researcher]: [I'll arrange an outpatient consultation]. He really should come in.... But there's no point. He won't get in. He's not insured.

(*Observation, Shadowing Emergency Junior Resident, Shift A, Hospital B, US*)

Accordingly, US emergency doctors spent more time and placed greater emphasis on coordination of care, especially for older, psychiatric and indigent patients, than in The Netherlands or Australia. In the Netherlands, for instance, doctors and nurses believed that patients attended their GPs first. Emergency clinicians in the United States were much more likely to know particular patients than in The Netherlands and Australia. Unlike in The Netherlands and Australia, the two US EDs had specific committees to attempt to plan coordination of care for patients who frequently attended the ED. Such patients were colloquially and, according to some emergency clinicians, inappropriately, called 'frequent flyers'. US emergency doctors were more likely to exercise 'positive discrimination'. This included several instances where a patient was kept in the ED for more than one day if they had a follow-up appointment at a hospital clinic, and the doctor feared that would not otherwise keep the appointment.

Discussion

Overall, we found three distinguishable features of ED work across countries: the pace of work, clinical roles and workflow in terms of determining what it means to be an ED service and clinician; differences in 'ownership' levels of the ED and the function of the ED vis-à-vis the broader health system. Despite emergency care being a superficially similar cross-country activity and having an analogous look and feel in differing health systems, the ethnography drew out differences across international settings that would not have been exposed readily or even at all by other research methods such as statistical comparisons or questionnaire surveys.

This chapter thereby showed distinctive meaning systems made available in ethnographic research. But an ethnographic approach alone is insufficient to maximize the comprehension of such meaning systems. The perspective of interdependence derived from social action theories makes connections between the micro and the macro, or the local and the global, possible (Blumer, 1969). Broad historical and national patterns were evident in the micro social world of interaction. The study showed a shared understanding of the role of the ED and emergency clinicians as members of worldwide professional communities of practice. The sphere of local interaction also bore witness to the influence of, and need to negotiate, unique political, economic, social and legal features of national contexts. The interconnectedness of the participants that produced the findings provides a conceptual rationale for comparative international ethnographic research.

Social action theories have been considered astructural in their focus on situated activity (Prendergast and Knotterus, 1993; Dennis and Martin, 2005). This study showed the influence of and negotiation about structural influences in everyday work. Far from being astructural, only in moment-to-moment activity is the influence of social structures evident (Mills, 1940). Large-scale structures, such as policies, systemic inequalities and professional regulation manifest in interaction. They are also upheld and challenged in interaction, showing the interconnected web of social relations. Indeed if there was not predominant agreement over meaning systems in relation to a groups' function and the roles of individuals in that function, cooperative work, such as that in EDs or any health service organization, would not be possible at all (McCall, 2003). The capacity of ethnography to account for behaviours and to show what and how broader political, social, historical, legal and economic structures manifest justifies greater deployment of ethnography in OB research.

A broad sweep of three national ED systems inevitably has limitations. Despite the evident patterns in the data, such a limited number of EDs across nations will inevitably produce a partial account of ED work in those countries. Purposive sampling served to provide relatively comparable sites of large-scale and prominent EDs. There is always variation within particular sites and even inconsistency of the views of particular individuals. Caution is needed in assumptions of generalizability of these findings. Nevertheless, the study shows patterns of influence about the universal need to engage external resources to build internal capacity to process a continuing flow of patients, and the universal presence and negotiation of broad-scale influences in local interaction. Transferability and credibility are the desirable features of ethnographic work rather than generalizability.

Conclusion

The capacity to reveal patterns of similarity and difference across national borders underlines the lessons comparative international ethnography can provide. Such a multinational perspective can yield insights not otherwise derivable about specific health settings.

Further comparative international research could be useful in illuminating cross-national characteristics of cursorily similar phenomenon. For example, work is needed on the role of distinguishable financial incentives in different countries and how they affect local settings. Comparative research on differing levels of quality and efficiency of care in rural and regional areas, and especially in relation to the growing population of older people whose complex conditions provide challenges in all health systems, would be of value. A new international ethnographic agenda might compare coalface settings in the private system of the United States versus public systems in Europe, and another might provide a comparison between mixed public–private systems such as Australia, the United Kingdom and Canada, and how these play out locally. Such future research can be framed around what we have designated 'comparative international ethnography'. In its various forms, ethnography can be deployed to expose the nature of healthcare complexity (Braithwaite et al., 2012); as an interventional tool (Nugus et al., 2012; Braithwaite et al., 2013b); and, as video ethnography (Carroll et al., 2008), to optimize understanding of the world of practice.

References

Araujo, R., Corte, F.D., Dick, W., Driscoll, P., Girbes, R. and Lorenzo, A.E., et al. (2002). European comprehensive training course on prehospital advanced trauma life support in adults. *European Journal of Emergency Medicine*, 9(3): 280–282.

Becker, H.S. and Greer, B. (1960). Participant observation: The analysis of qualitative field data and field research techniques. In R.M. Adamds and J.J. Preiss (Eds). *Human Organisation Research: Field Relations & Techniques* (pp.267–289). Hoewood, Il: Dorsey Press.

Blumer, H. (1969). *Symbolic Interactionism: Perspective & Method*. Englewood Cliffs, NJ: Prentice Hall.

Braithwaite, J. (2006a). Analysing structural and cultural change in acute settings using a Giddens-Weick paradigmatic approach. *Health Care Analysis*, 14(2): 91–102.

Braithwaite, J. (2006b). An empirical assessment of social structural and cultural change in clinical directorates. *Health Care Analysis*, 14(4): 185–193.

Braithwaite, J., Westbrook, M., Nugus, P., Greenfield, D., Travaglia, J., Runciman, W. et al. (2012). A four-year, systems-wide intervention promoting interprofessional collaboration. *BMC Health Services Research*, 12: 99.

Braithwaite, J., Clay-Williams, R., Nugus, P. and Plumb, J. (2013a). Health care as a complex adaptive system. In E. Hollnagel, J. Braithwaite and R.L. Wears (Eds). *Resilient Health Care*. Surrey, UK: Ashgate Publishing Limited.

Braithwaite, J., Westbrook, M., Nugus, P., Greenfield, D., Travaglia, J., Runciman, W., Foxwell, R.A., Boyce, R.A., Devinney, T. and Westbrook, J. (2013b). Continuing differences between health professions' attitudes: The saga of accomplishing systems-wide interprofessionalism. *International Journal for Quality in Health Care*, 25(1): 8–15.

Cameron, P. (2003). Emergency medicine: Are we the systems specialists? *Emergency Medicine Australasia*, 15(1): 1–3.

Carroll, K., Iedema, R. and Kerridge, R. (2008). Reshaping ICU ward round practices using video-reflexive ethnography. *Qualitative Health Research*, 18(3): 380–390.

Currie, G. and Suhomlinova, O. (2006). The impact of institutional forces upon knowledge sharing in the UK NHS: The triumph of professional power and the inconsistency of policy. *Public Administration*, 84(1): 1–30.

Dennis, A. and Martin, P.J. (2005). Symbolic interactionism and the concept of power. *British Journal of Sociology*, 56(2): 191–213.

Engeström, Yrjö, Miettinen, Reijo and Punamäki, Raija-Leena (1999). *Perspectives on Activity Theory*. Cambridge University Press.

Ferlie, E., Fitzgerald, L., Wood, M. and Hawkins, C. (2005). The (non)spread of innovations: The mediating role of professionals. *Academy of Management Journal*, 48(1): 117–134.

Gaakeer, M.I, van den Brand, C.L. and Patka, P. (2012). Emergency medicine in the Netherlands: A short history provides a solid basis for future challenges. *European Journal of Emergency Medicine*, 19(3): 131–135.

Guzzo, R.A. and Dickson, M.W. (1996). Teams in organizations: Recent research on performance and effectiveness. *Annual Review of Psychology*, 47: 307–338.

Hackman, J.R. (2009). The perils of positivity. *Journal of Organizational Behavior*, 30: 309–319.

Hammersley, M. and Atkinson, P. (1995). *Ethnography: Practices & Principles*. (2nd ed.). New York: Routledge.

Holroyd, B.R., Rowe, B.H. and Sinclair, D. (2004). Current political issues facing emergency medicine in Canada. *Emergency Medicine Australasia*, 16(3): 190–194.

Hyde, P., Granter, E., McCann, L. and Hassard, J. (2012). The lost health service tribe: In search of middle managers (pp. 7–20). In H. Dickinson and R.Mannion (Eds). *The Reform of Health Care: Shaping, Adapting & Resisting Policy Developments*. Basingstoke, UKL Palgrave Macmillan.

Kulu-Glasgow, I., Delnoii, D. and de Bakker, D. (1998). Self-referral in a gatekeeping system: Patients' reasons for skipping the general-practitioner. *Health Policy*, 45(3): 221–238.

Laxisman, A., Hakimzada, F., Sayan, O.R., Green, R.A., Zhang, J. and Patel, V.L. (2007). The multitasking clinician: Decision-making and cognitive demand during and after team handoffs in emergency care. *International Journal of Medical Informatics*, 76: 801–811.

Law, J. (2008). Actor-Network theory and material semiotics (pp. 141–158). In Bryan S. Turner (Ed.) *The New Blackwell Companion to Social Theory* (3rd Edition), Oxford: Wiley-Blackwell.

McCall, G.J. (2003). Interaction. In H.T. Reynolds and N.J. Herman-Kinney (Eds). *Handbook of Symbolic Interactionism* (pp. 327–348). Walnut Creek, CA: AltaMira Press.

McDermott, A.M. and Keating, M.A. (2012) Making service improvement happen the importance of social context. *Journal of Applied Behavioral Science*, 48(1): 62–92.

Miller, K. (2009). Gendered nature of managerialism? Case of the National Health Service. *International Journal of Public Sector Management*, 22(2): 104–113.

Mills, C.W. (1940). 'Situated action and vocabularies of motive.' *American Sociological Review* 5: 904–13.

Miner, J.B. (Ed.) (2006). *Organizational Behavior: Historical Origins, Theoretical Foundations & the Future*. Armonk, NY: M.E. Sharpe, Inc.

Mol, A. (2002). *The Body Multiple: Ontology in Medical Practice*, Durham, NC: Duke University Press.

Murphy, E. and Dingwall, R. (2007). Informed consent, anticipatory regulation and ethnographic practice. *Social Science & Medicine*, 65(11): 2223–2234.

Nugus, P. (2008). The interactionist self and grounded research: Reflexivity in a study of emergency department clinicians. *Qualitative Sociology Review*, 4(1): 189–204.

Nugus, P. and Braithwaite, J. (2010). The dynamic interaction of quality and efficiency in the emergency department: Squaring the circle? *Social Science & Medicine*, 70(4): 511–517.

Nugus, P., Carroll, K., Hewett, D.G., Short, A., Forero, R. and Braithwaite, J. (2010). Integrated care in the emergency department: A complex adaptive systems perspective. *Social Science & Medicine*, 71(11): 1997–2004.

Nugus, P., Greenfield, D., Travaglia, J. and Braithwaite, J. (2012). The politics of action research: 'If you don't like the way things are going, get off the bus'. *Social Science & Medicine*, 75(11): 1946–1953.

Patel, V.L., Zhang, J., Yoskowitz, N.A., Green, R. and Sayan, O.R. (2008). Translational cognition for decision support in critical care environments: A review. *Journal of Biomedical Informatics*, 41(3): 413–431.

Prendergast, C. and Knotterus, J.D. (1993). 'The New studies in social organization: Overcoming the Astructural Bias', pp. 158–185, in L.T. Reynolds (Ed.) *Interactionism: Exposition and Critique.* Dix Hills, NY: General Hall, Inc.

Silverman, D. (2010). *Doing Qualitative Research* (3rd ed.). London, UK: Sage.

Spradley, J.P. (1980). *Participant Observation.* New York, NY: Holt, Rinehart and Winston.

Thijssen, W.A.M.H., Giesen, P.H.J. and Wensing, (2012). M. Emergency medicine in the Netherlands, *Emergency Medicine Journal*, 29(6–9).

Zink, B.J. (2006). *Anyone, Anything, Anytime: A History of Emergency Medicine.* Philadelphia, PA: Mosby-Elsevier, Inc.

16
Models of User Involvement in Mental Health

Marianne Storm and Adrian Edwards

Introduction

In the literature, patient-centred care, shared decision-making, patient participation and the recovery model incorporate user involvement and patients' perspectives on their treatment and care. User involvement has been introduced in response to advocacy from some patients' associations and features in political documents of some specific national healthcare systems (Department of Health, 1999; DHHS, 2003). User involvement is intended to increase the 'real' influence of patients on decisions about their treatment to ensure that services meet patients' needs and to enhance patients' control over their health care. User involvement challenges paternalistic care models and assumptions that healthcare providers know what is in the best interest of their patients (Coulter, 1999).

In the mental health field, developments in user involvement for people with long-lasting mental health disorders have paralleled the shift from institutionalized care to community mental health care (Petrea and Muijen, 2008). While service user involvement is applauded in the mental health field, there are concerns regarding implementation, especially in relation to in-patient care (Bee et al., 2008; Oeye et al., 2009). We aim to examine patient-centred care, shared decision-making, patient participation and the recovery model, their association with user involvement in the mental health context and to discuss their implementation challenges for the in-patient mental health setting.

The mental health context

Mental health policies

A core aim in both European and US mental health policies is to reduce institutional forms of care, developing community-based mental health services and integrating people with mental health disorders in the community (DHHS, 2003; WHO, 2005; Petrea and Muijen, 2008). Involvement of users, families and carers is an important strategy to support this (WHO, 2009). Health legislation complements and reinforces mental health policies especially for user involvement (WHO, 2009). Some European countries[1] have established separate bills on patients' rights, ensuring patients have rights to make informed decisions, rights to comprehensible information and that decisions are made in partnership between clinician and patient. Other countries use multiple pieces of legislation to protect patients' rights (Härter, 2011). Patients' rights are complemented by mental health legislation addressing users', family members' or carers' rights, competence and capacity issues for people with mental disorders and voluntary and involuntary treatment (Petrea and Muijen, 2008).

Organization of mental health services

The movement towards community-based mental health services has been followed by a growing complexity of in-patient and out-patient mental health service provision (Petrea and Muijen, 2008). Several system tools are implemented to support user involvement. People in need of long-term and coordinated services are entitled to an individualized care plan. The plan should provide information about the person's treatment goals and outline responsibilities of those involved in treatment and follow-up to ensure continuity and person-centred care (Department of Health, 2009; DHHS, 2003). Case management involves coordination of services for people with mental disorders. The underlying tasks of case management include the following: organizing meetings, assessment of the person's needs, care planning, implementation and regular review (Dieterich et al., 2011). Assertive outreach teams (also called assertive community treatment (ACT)) are multidisciplinary and work intensively with people with complex mental health needs to support recovery (Shean, 2009). ACT teams provide all necessary care in the person's home, persistently try to engage uncooperative clients and provide 24-hour emergency cover (Dieterich et al., 2011). Dieterich et al. (2011) showed that both ACT teams and intensive case management provide good alternatives to hospitalization; they are associated with reduced hospitalizations, better integration of the person in the community and reduced costs. These approaches to care reflect care models such as patient-centredness, shared decision-making, patient participation and the recovery model. These models will now be examined.

User-involvement models

Patient-centred care

Patient-centred care is acknowledged in psychiatric nursing, psychotherapy and in medicine. Mead and Bower (2000) reviewed patient-centredness in medical care and the doctor–patient relationship. They identified five key dimensions: (1) acknowledging a bio-psychosocial perspective and including psychological and social aspects in the understanding of disease and illness; (2) considering 'the patient as person' attending to the patient's stories of their illness, their feelings and fears; (3) 'Sharing power and responsibility' with the patient encouraging greater patient involvement in care and decision-making; (4) 'Therapeutic alliance', that is development of a professional relationship based on care, sensitivity and empathy; (5) Providers' self-awareness and attention to emotional aspects in the relationship with the patient. Although patient-centredness is advocated and integrated in training for healthcare providers in general, there has been little understanding of how to promote and measure its core components (Lewin et al., 2009). Lewin et al. (2009) conclude that training of providers in patient-centredness may improve communication with patients, but it remains unclear if training affects healthcare use or outcomes for patients.

Patient-centredness has received much attention in the psychiatric nursing literature. Many definitions of the concept exist, and frequently cited components include mutuality or collaboration and truthfulness (O'Donovan, 2007). According to Wills (2010) psychiatric nursing practice is patient-centred because effective working alliances and nursing care have to incorporate an understanding of the patient's perspective. Nurses attempt to 'see the situation through the client's eyes' but at the same time acknowledge that they can never fully grasp the patient's experience (McCann and Baker, 2001). An effective working relationship between nurse and patient involves truthfulness and mutuality where both parties share information and collaborate to make decisions on jointly agreed goals (Wills, 2010).

Few studies have explored how patient-centredness is implemented in psychiatric nursing practice. The Tidal Model is one example of a model where respect, collaboration and gaining understanding of the person's perspective are considered as the basis for nursing practice (Barker and Buchanan-Barker, 2010). Whilst the Tidal Model is used in practice, only a few evaluations of the model have taken place (O'Donovan, 2007). These suggest improved staff and user satisfaction and more user involvement following implementation of the model (Taylor et al., 2009).

Shared decision-making

Shared decision-making is a means to placing the person at the centre of care, focusing primarily on the process of treatment decisions (Duncan et al., 2010). Shared decision-making aims to increase patients' knowledge and control over treatment decisions (Charles et al., 1997). For a decision to be 'shared' it must involve at least two persons: the patient and the provider. With serious or long-term mental health conditions, it is often necessary to involve several members of the clinical team, family members or caregivers in the 'distributed' shared decision-making process (Rapley, 2008; Duncan et al., 2010). Shared decision-making can refer to both process and outcome (Edwards and Elwyn, 2006). The process relates to the role the patient and provider play in the encounter, while outcome refers to agreement versus non-agreement over a treatment decision (Charles et al., 1997). It also involves opportunities to review and revise decisions after they are made (Curtis et al., 2010).

Sharing information is fundamental to shared decision-making. Based on available evidence the provider offers information, explains options, their potential consequences and explores the patient's potential worries and expectations. Patients bring their experiences, values and opinions to the encounter and various types of decision aids (e.g. information brochures, films, web pages) are often used as an adjunct to the providers' counseling (O'Connor et al., 2009).

In the context of mental health there is growing attention to shared decision-making, emphasizing its important role in the person's recovery process (Deegan and Drake, 2006). It is suggested as an approach to medication management, and also to support decision-making in psychosocial matters such as work, housing, psychotherapy and other service provision (Deegan and Drake, 2006; Curtis et al., 2010). In relation to medication, there are usually several options available, each with risks, benefits and potential unpleasant side-effects. Decisions about medications are both professionally influenced and personal for the patient, and the outcome (the decision to take prescribed medication) may reflect the individual's active involvement in the decision-making process (Curtis et al., 2010). Despite these arguments, there is limited empirical knowledge about the associations between shared decision-making and clinical outcomes for patients with mental disorders. Duncan et al.'s systematic review (2010) concludes that shared decision-making interventions may not improve patients' health outcomes but do increase patient participation in decision-making and satisfaction with care, without increasing the need for resources (e.g. consultation time).

Patient participation

Patient participation concerns the patient's involvement and role in decision-making in matters relating to their own treatment and care. A common way of conceptualizing participation has been by refer-ring to different categories of patient participation and involvement in healthcare decision-making (Thompson, 2007). Hickey and Kipping (1998) use a participation continuum in a mental health context with four positions (information/explanation, consultation, partnership and user control). Thompson (2007) argues that the four categories of partic-ipation are reflected in the most discussed models of treatment decision-making: paternalism (patient involvement is limited to being given information or giving consent), 'professional as agent' (providers hold the expertise, but patients' preferences are incorporated in decision-making), 'shared decision-making' (providers and patients share the process and outcome of a decision) and 'informed decision-making' where patients are regarded as fully autonomous and expected to make their own decisions (Charles et al., 1997).

Participation as described by Hickey and Kipping (1998) and Thompson (2007) illustrates participation as a process in an in-patient mental health context, where patients can be passive (no participation) or active participants in their treatment and care, depending on mental health symptoms, motivation and interests for participation. However, the model has not been subject to extensive empirical research and is criticized as based on providers' professional judgements and not derived from users themselves (Thompson, 2007).

Patient participation also addresses involvement at service level, including patients or users in quality-development initiatives such as advisory boards, in training of providers and employment of service users in mental health organizations. These issues have received theoret-ical, practical and research-based attention in mental health (Crawford et al., 2003; Rutter et al., 2004). Some potential benefits from this level of user involvement are clarification of the patients' perspectives on service delivery, more responsive and accessible services, changes in the attitudes of providers and organizations to involving patients and positive feedback from involved patients (Crawford et al., 2002).

Recovery model

The recovery model goes beyond patient participation, patient-centredness and shared decision-making. Patient-centredness and shared decision-making in treatment decisions are important models that support people's recovery (Wills, 2010). Recovery ideas have largely been formulated by the consumer movements and persons experiencing mental illnesses. The recovery model of mental health emphasizes control being placed in the hands of individuals, not professionals, and emphasizes collaborative care between providers, individuals and families (Duncan et al., 2010). Service user participation is fundamental to recovery. Consumers and their families are considered as active participants in designing and implementing care systems in which they are involved, as well as being part of developing recovery-oriented mental health services (DHHS, 2003).

Recovery has been associated with two different meanings: 'recovery from mental health disorders and recovery in mental health disorders' (Davidson and Roe, 2007). Recovery means that the person takes part in the same personal and social activities as before they became ill, and some also show no further signs or symptoms of mental illness (Wilken, 2007). Recovery is also a social mental health model, emphasizing inclusion and continuous participation within the community for people suffering from mental illnesses. Recovery does not require remission of symptoms and return to normal function or cure, but rather implies overcoming the effects of becoming a mentally ill person (Davidson et al., 2005).

Recovery-oriented care focuses on the roles and responsibilities of service providers to provide services that promote and facilitate the person's recovery (Davidson et al., 2006). Services are to be person-centred, attending to the person's own goals, strengths, hopes and needs, employing everyday language attending to personal relationships and promoting community integration (Borg, et al., 2009; Storm and Davidson, 2010).

Shean (2009) summarized the following evidence-based psychosocial treatment approaches involved in a person's recovery: supported employment, family interventions, ACT, skill training and cognitive behavioural therapy, most often used in combination with access to pharmacotherapy. When a person needs in-patient care, restraints and seclusion should be kept to a minimum, given that the person has a right to self-determination and to support his or her recovery (Taylor et al., 2009).

Synthesis

Patient-oriented care models are advocated in the literature and in mental health care; they incorporate user involvement but have only to varying degrees been subject to empirical research. The four models have common features and overlaps, and we represent these in Figure 16.1. In the figure patient-centredness is a context for applying patient participation, and shared decision-making is a tool within this approach. Shared decision-making enhances patient participation, by setting the person at the centre of care and the process of treatment decisions. Patient-centredness involves tailoring general care to the individual's needs and preferences, recognizing the value of patient participation, and shared decision-making as an important tool to achieve this (Duncan et al., 2010). Recovery-oriented care goes beyond

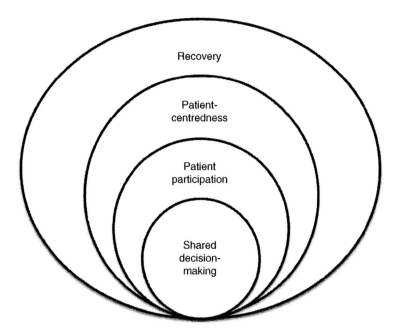

Recovery

Patient-
centredness

Patient
participation

Shared
decision-
making

Figure 16.1 Illustration of the Recovery Model as an over-arching model and philosophy within which the other models are applied (Storm and Edwards, 2012)

patient-centredness as it involves supporting people through their mental health concerns in order to live a meaningful life in the community (Borg et al., 2009).

In mental health care the recovery model can be considered as an overarching frame, in which the other models are applied (Figure 16.1). Service user participation is fundamental to recovery and recovery-oriented mental health systems. Shared decision-making is further recognized as a promising tool in the process of transforming mental health services to a recovery orientation where user involvement is a core value (Shepherd et al., 2008).

Patient-oriented care models should be implemented at different levels of the healthcare system: at the 'macro' level where service users influence policy making and legislation, at the 'meso' level where institutions involve service users in planning and delivery of health services, and at the 'micro' level of the interaction between the person and their family and service providers (Härter et al., 2011). Whether these aspirations to adopt the models of care with mental health service users are realized will now be examined.

Examining the user involvement care models in in-patient mental health

Although sharing information, patient participation and user involvement are applauded, there are concerns regarding implementation of patient-oriented care models in in-patient mental health care. Bee et al. (2008) conducted a systematic review of users' views and expectations of UK-registered mental health nurses. They found little evidence of user collaboration in mental health services. Users reported inadequate information provision, poor inter-professional communication and a lack of opportunities for collaborative care. In-patient mental health nurses were perceived as particularly inaccessible. When relevant information was not provided, patients were more likely to perceive providers as impersonal or paternalistic. Storm et al. (2011) used cross-sectional data from in-patient mental health service providers to investigate user involvement. Involving users in planning and delivery of services was infrequent though with differences between mental health institutions. Providers more often reported user involvement at the individual ('micro') level, in terms of collaboration about treatment and follow-up.

Oeye et al. (2009) point to tensions in implementing user participation in the hierarchical psychiatric hospital structure such as: (1) difficulties with individual user participation whilst also upholding collective house rules, (2) difficulties when patients' views are different and challenge staff judgements, (3) challenges in establishing equal relationships between staff and patients within the hospital structure. Storm and Davidson (2010) found that in-patients reported few opportunities to have meaningful input in decision-making about their care, and they often felt they were not being seen and heard as unique individuals. From the providers' perspectives, patients were perceived as poorly motivated for user involvement, and providers experienced difficulties in making treatment goal-directed, in involving in-patients in developing individual care plans or in engaging them in meetings about treatment. In the United Kingdom, the National Health Service (NHS, 2010) recognizes that although there is considerable support for involving patients and their carers in decision-making, implementation will require a significant culture shift and strong leadership to achieve shared decision-making in the clinical encounter.

'Putting patients and the public first' is a UK government vision to develop a patient-centred NHS. Patients and their carers are to be in charge of decision-making about their health (NHS, 2010). There are several issues that affect the person's capacity for participation in decision-making. Common experiences following living with a long-standing mental disorder such as schizophrenia are as follows: deficits in social skills and judgements, thought disorder, attention, concentration, communication difficulties, interpersonal conflict and loss of self (Davidson et al., 2001). Patients may be incapable of participation in decision-making in certain instances and instead need safety and stabilization of their disorder (Davidson et al., 2006). Preferred level of involvement in decision-making can also vary across individuals and at different points in time. When patients' symptoms improve, patients tend to show increased participation (Simon et al., 2007).

Issues of risk are an area of concern to users and providers and are related to community integration and patient participation in decision-making. In the United States, the New Freedom Commission (DHHS, 2003) strongly endorsed the importance of protecting and enhancing the civil rights of people with severe mental disorders with particular attention to limiting seclusion and restraint and supporting community integration. Davidson et al. (2006) emphasize that the majority of people with mental health disorders do not pose a significant risk, either to the community or to the person themselves. Restrictions on people's decision-making must only be imposed, if the person represents a sufficient degree of risk, to avoid harm to itself or others. In such circumstances, the person will need to have others (service providers or family members) make decisions for them. Such situations pose important challenges to collaborative care models.

Effective self-advocacy and involvement in decision-making require efforts from the person to claim their own rights, for example being prepared for treatment meetings and engaging in formulation of treatment goals (Storm and Davidson, 2010). Age, educational status, severity of the disorder and ethnic or cultural difference can affect people's preferences for involvement (Curtis et al., 2010). Loh et al. (2007) reported research showing that depressed patients were interested in more information and engagement in shared decision-making than previously had been assumed, even when experiencing moderate and severe major depression. Hamann et al. (2006) reported that several patients with schizophrenia were considered 'permanently too ill' by doctors and nurses to take part in shared decision-making. The authors questioned whether the lack of opportunity for user involvement reflected incapacity from patients or prejudice from staff. Bee et al. (2008) reported that few opportunities for nursing contact, lack of staff enthusiasm, high staff workloads and high staff turnover or sick leave all affect opportunities for user involvement and collaborative care.

Recommendations for policy and practice

To overcome some of the challenges in translating user-oriented care models into practice in mental health, competence development and training of providers is essential. 'Competencies' cover both attitudinal and cultural disposition and specific behaviors and skills (Boyatzis, 1982). Communication skills training is a key means of promoting competence development for all four care models, especially shared decision-making, patient-centredness and the recovery model.

User-oriented care models have implications for the roles of patients and service users. Training in skills to enhance communication may encourage a more active patient role and enable users to claim their rights more effectively in clinical encounters in in-patient mental health care (Storm and Davidson, 2010). To achieve service transformation, we need to ensure that providers gain experience of working with people with mental health disorder in different roles and positions than solely as patients. Some key areas include involving people with mental health disorders in the running of health organizations, in the training of providers and in the recruitment of peer or consumer providers. Such initiatives require supportive organizational leaders and staff and are fundamental in developing organizational cultures that promote user involvement at all levels of services.

Acknowledgement

We thank Professor Karina Aase for her comments during the manuscript preparation.

Note

1. Norwegian Patient Rights Act, 2001, The Finnish Act on the Status and Rights of Patients No. 785/1992 and the Public Health Code. Law of March 4th 2002 in France pertaining to patients' rights and the quality of the healthcare system.

References

Barker, P., and Buchanan-Barker, P. 2010. The tidal model of mental health recovery and reclamation: application in acute care settings. *Issues in Mental Health Nursing*, 31(3), 171–180.

Bee, P., Playle, J., Lovell, K., Barnes, P., Gray, R., and Keeley, P. 2008. Service user views and expectations of UK-registered mental health nurses: A systematic review of empirical research. *International Journal of Nursing Studies*, 45(3), 442–457.

Borg, M., Karlsson, B., and Kim, H.S. 2009. User involvement in community mental health services – principles and practices. *Journal of Psychiatric and Mental Health Nursing*, 16(3), 285–292.

Borg, M., Karlsson, B., Tondora, J., and Davidson, L. 2009. Implementing person-centered care in psychiatric rehabilitation: what does this involve? *The Israel Journal of Psychiatry and Related Sciences*, 46(2), 84–93.

Boyatzis, R.E. 1982. *The competent manager. A model for effective performance.* New York: John Wiley and Sons.

Charles, C., Gafni, A., and Whelan, T. 1997. Shared decision-making in the medical encounter: what does it mean? (or it takes at least two to tango). *Social Science & Medicine (1982)*, 44(5), 681–692.

Coulter, A. 1999. Paternalism or partnership? *British Medical Journal*, 319(7212), 719–720.

Crawford, M.J., Aldridge, T., Bhui, K., Rutter, D., Manley, C., Weaver, T., … Fulop, N. 2003. User involvement in the planning and delivery of mental health services: a cross-sectional survey of service users and providers. *Acta Psychiatrica Scandinavica*, 107(6), 410–414.

Crawford, M.J., Rutter, D., Manley, C., Weaver, T., Bhui, K., Fulop, N., and Tyrer, P. 2002. Systematic review of involving patients in the planning and development of health care. *British Medical Journal*, 325(7375), 1263–1265.

Curtis, L.C., Wells, S.M., Penney, D.J., Ghose, S.S., Mistler, L.A., Mahone, I.H., Lesko, S. 2010. Pushing the envelope: shared decision making in mental health. *Psychiatric Rehabilitation Journal*, 34(1), 14–22.

Davidson, L., Haglund, K., Stayner, D.A., Rakfeldt, J., Chinman, M.J., and Kraemer, T.J. 2001. 'It was just realizing . . . that life isn't one big horror': A qualitative study of supported socialization. *Psychiatric Rehabilitation Journal*, 24(3), 275–292.

Davidson, L., O'Connell, M.J., Tondora, J., Lawless, M., and Evans, A.C. 2005. Recovery in serious mental illness: A new wine or just a new bottle? *Professional Psychology-Research and Practice*, 36(5), 480–487.

Davidson, L., O'Connell, M., Tondora, J., Styron, T., and Kangas, K. 2006. The top ten concerns about recovery encountered in mental health system transformation. *Psychiatric Services*, 57(5), 640–645.

Davidson, L., and Roe, D. 2007. Recovery from versus recovery in serious mental illness: One strategy for lessening confusion plaguing recovery. *Journal of Mental Health*, 16(4), 459–470.

Deegan, P.E., and Drake, R.E. 2006. Shared decision making and medication management in the recovery process. *Psychiatric Services*, 57(11), 1636–1639.

Department of Health 1999. *Patient and Public Involvement in the new NHS*. London: Statitionary Office.

Department of Health/Long Term Conditions 2009. *Supporting People with Long Term Conditions. Commissioning Personalised Care Planning: A Guide for Commissioners*. London: COI.

DHHS 2003 *New Freedom Commission on Mental Health, Achieving the Promise: Transforming Mental Health Care in America*. (Final Report). Rockville, MD: Author.

Dieterich, M., Irving, C.B., Park, B., and Marshall, M. 2011. Intensive case management for severe mental illness (Review). *Cochrane Database Of Systematic Reviews (Online)*(2).

Duncan, E., Best, C., and Hagen, S. 2010. Shared decision making interventions for people with mental health conditions (Review). *Cochrane Database Of Systematic Reviews (Online)*,(1).

Edwards A, and Elwyn, G. 2006. Inside the black box of shared decision-making distinguishing between the process of involvement and who makes the decision. *Health Expectations*, (9), 307–20.

Hamann, J., Langer, B., Winkler, V., Busch, R., Cohen, R., Leucht, S., and Kissling, W. 2006. Shared decision making for in-patients with schizophrenia. *Acta Psychiatrica Scandinavica*, 114(4), 265–273.

Hickey, G., and Kipping, C. 1998. Exploring the concept of user involvement in mental health through a participation continuum. *Journal of Clinical Nursing*, 7(1), 83–88.

Härter, M., Müller, H., Dirmaier, J., Donner-Banzhoff, N., Bieber, C., and Eich, W. 2011. Patient participation and shared decision making in Germany – history, agents and current transfer to practice. *Zeitschrift Für Evidenz, Fortbildung Und Qualität Im Gesundheitswesen*, 105(4), 263–270.

Härter, M., van der Weijden, T., and Elwyn, G. 2011. Policy and practice developments in the implementation of shared decision making: an international perspective. *Zeitschrift Für Evidenz, Fortbildung Und Qualität Im Gesundheitswesen*, 105(4), 229–233.

Lewin, S., Skea, Z., Entwistle, V., Zwarenstein, M., and Dick, J. 2009. Intervention for providers to promote a patient-centered approach in clinical consultations (Review). *Cochrane Database of Systematic Reviews (Online)* (1).

Loh, A., Simon, D., Wills, C.E., Kriston, L., Niebling, W., and Härter, M. 2007. The effects of a shared decision-making intervention in primary care of depression: a cluster-randomized controlled trial. *Patient Education and Counseling*, 67(3), 324–332.

McCann, T.V., and Baker, H. 2001. Mutual relating: developing interpersonal relationships in the community. *Journal of Advanced Nursing*, 34(4), 530–537.

Mead, N., and Bower, P. 2000. Patient-centredness: a conceptual framework and review of the empirical literature. *Social Science & Medicine*, 51(7), 1087–1110.

NHS Department of Health 2010. *Liberating the NHS: Legislative framework and next steps – Executive Summary*. Whitehall: Department of Health.

O'Connor, A., Bennett, C., Stacey, D., Barry, M., Col, N., Eden, K., Rovner, D. 2009. Decision aids for pople facing health treatment or screening decisions (Review). *Cochrane Database of Systematic Reviews (Online)* (3).

O'Donovan, A. 2007. Patient-centred care in acute psychiatric admission units: reality or rhetoric? *Journal of Psychiatric & Mental Health Nursing*, 14(6), 542–548.

Oeye, C., Bjelland, A.K., Skorpen, A., and Anderssen, N. 2009. User participation when using milieu therapy in a psychiatric hospital in Norway: a mission impossible? *Nursing Inquiry*, 16(4), 287–296.

Petrea, I., and Muijen, M. 2008. *Policies and practices for mental health in Europe – meeting the challenges*. Copenhagen, Denmark: WHO Regional office for Europe.

Rapley, T. 2008. Distributed decision making: the anatomy of decisions-in-action. *Sociology of Health & Illness*, 30(3), 429–444.

Rutter, D., Manley, C., Weaver, T., Crawford, M.J., and Fulop, N. 2004. Patients or partners? Case studies of user involvement in the planning and delivery of adult mental health services in London. *Social Science & Medicine*, 58(10), 1973–1984.

Shean, G.D. 2009. Evidence-based psychosocial practices and recovery from schizophrenia. *Psychiatry*, 72(4), 307–320.

Shepherd, G., Boardman, J., and Slade, M. 2008. *Making recovery a reality*. London: Sainsbury Centre for Mental Health,.

Simon, D., Loh, A., Wills, C.E., and Härter, M. 2007. Depressed patients' perceptions of depression treatment decision-making. *Health Expectations: An International Journal Of Public Participation In Health Care And Health Policy*, 10(1), 62–74.

Storm, M., and Davidson, L. 2010. Inpatients' and providers' experiences with user involvement in inpatient care. *The Psychiatric Quarterly*, 81(2), 111–125.

Storm, M., Hausken, K.; and Knudsen, K. 2011. Inpatient service providers' perspectives on service user involvement in Norwegian community mental health centres. *International Journal of Social Psychiatry*, 57(6), 551–563.

Storm, M., and Edwards, E. 2012. Models of User Involvement in the Mental Health Context: Intentions and Implementation Challenges. *The Psychiatric Quarterly*, 84(3):313–317. 10.1007/s11126–012–9247–x.

Taylor, T.L., Killaspy, H., Wright, C., Turton, P., White, S., Kallert, T.W., *ldots* King, M.B. 2009. A systematic review of the international published literature relating to quality of institutional care for people with longer term mental health problems. (Review). *BMC Psychiatry*, (9), 30.

Thompson, A.G.H. 2007. The meaning of patient involvement and participation in health care consultations: A taxonomy. *Social Science & Medicine,* 64(6), 1297–1310.

WHO 2005. *Mental health: Facing the challenges, building solutions.* Copenhagen: World Health Organization Regional office for Europe.

WHO 2009. *Improving health systems and services for mental health.* Geneva: WHO.

Wilken, J.P. 2007. Understanding recovery from psychosis. A growing body of knowledge. *Tidsskrift for Norsk Psykologforening,* 44(5), 658–666.

Wills, C.E. 2010. Sharing decisions with patients: Moving beyond patient-centered care. *Journal of Psychosocial Nursing and Mental Health Services,* 48(3), 4–5.

Concluding Comments

Patient-centred care: Concept, contest and challenge

In these brief concluding comments, we draw together the range of contributions made in this book. Despite major differences across academic disciplines, geographic locations, methodology and healthcare settings, we can identify commonalities in the themes of the 16 chapters presented. These have questioned and informed conceptualizations of patient-centred care, provided suggestions for enhancing coordination and communication processes and presented innovations in how patient-centred care can be delivered. Here, we aggregate the emergent themes evident and consider where they might lead us in the future.

Clarifying or contesting the concept of patient-centred care

Our contributors emphasize the need to identify the role of patients in patient-centred care – and potential limits to patient-centredness arising from personal or medical considerations. Patients may lack capacity (Storm and Edwards) or interest in engaging in their care, challenging notions of informed choice and consent. Such situations raise questions regarding how patients can be supported to engage in decision-making regarding their personal care (Renz et al.) and the role and status of non-engagement as a legitimate patient choice. Alternatively, limits to patient-centredness may arise for medical reasons – with practical and ethical implications (Montgomery). Thus, our contributions draw attention to the need for clarification of some of the more complex and contested aspects of patient-centredness that have as yet to be fully explored – let alone reconciled.

Mind the gap: Rising to the implementation challenge

A large number of chapters draw our attention to the practical challenges of achieving patient-centredness. These relate to common day-to-day life issues, such as managing meals and toileting in a range of care settings (Burns et al.; Castle and Ferguson-Rome), as well broader medical issues and end of life care (Hynes et al.). Lipworth et al. and Bridges et al. both note strong professional commitment to patient-centredness. However, in practice Schopf et al. illustrate that many opportunities for engagements with patients are missed. In consequence, authors emphasize the need to afford attention to institutional structures (Nugus et al.), professional training (Koerner et al.), inter-organizational (Kislov), organizational, inter-professional (Greenfield et al.) and team/unit-level (Sorensen et al.) structures to facilitate the enactment of patient-centredness. Strategies for patient engagement may enhance any such service redesign (Locock et al.).

Looking beyond patients to achieve patient-centredness: The role of the organization behaviour in healthcare community

Patient-centredness is fundamentally concerned with enhancing the patient experience. However, our contributors evidence that focusing on patients is not alone sufficient. Patients, their families, carers and health service staff all have a role to play (Nolan), as do the contexts in which they work. Attention needs to be afforded to the design of health systems, professional training and education, organizational management, team and individual behaviour to enhance patient-centredness. This is where we, the organizational behaviour in healthcare community, have a strong role to play.

In Ireland, where we hosted our last OBHC conference, it is often said that 'Tús maith, leath na hoibre' (a good start is half the work). We have made more than a good start – with coherent international themes and strong practical suggestions for improvement. It is our hope that the contributions in this volume may act as a springboard not alone to future studies, but to tangible enhancements in our understandings of patient-centred care and renewed energy in our endeavours to achieve it.

Index